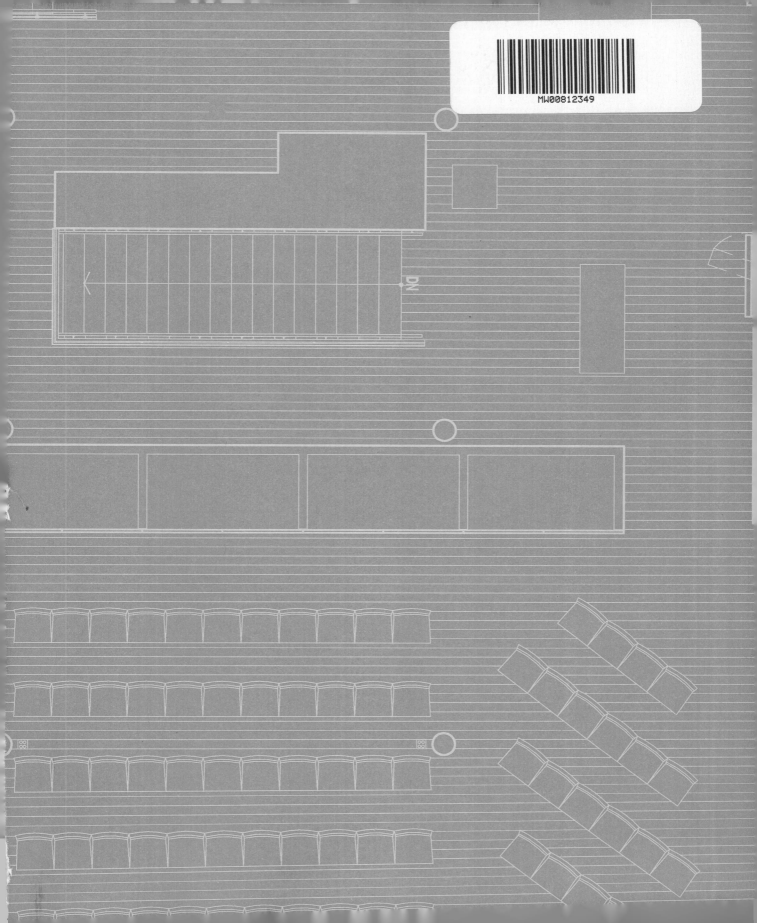

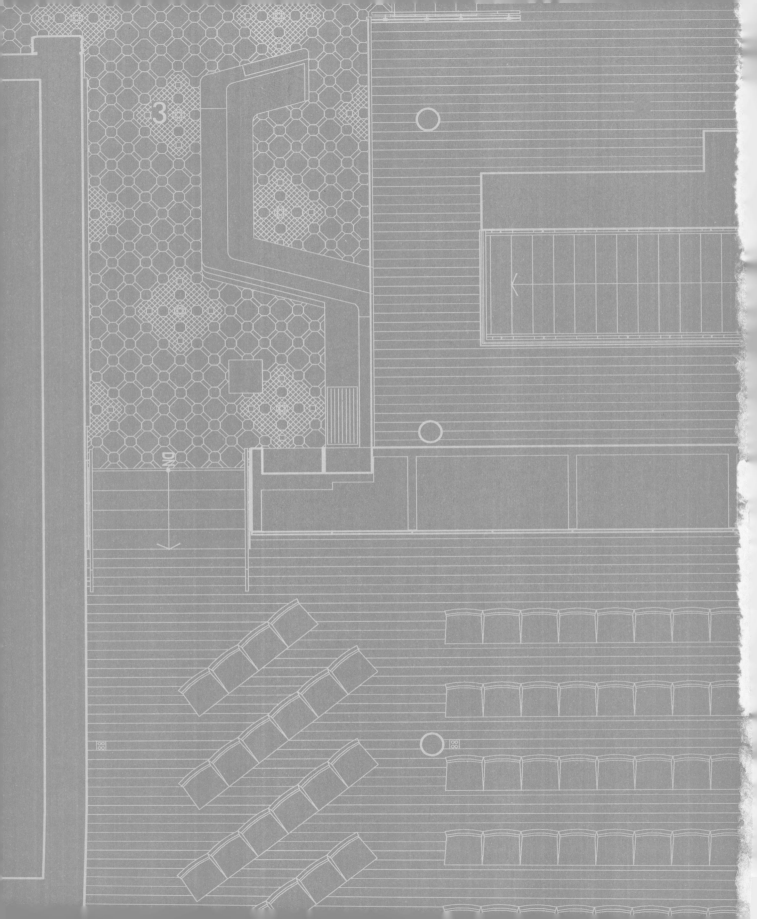

WE BUILD THE CITY

NYC'S DESIGN + CONSTRUCTION EXCELLENCE PROGRAM

FOREWORD BY
MAYOR MICHAEL R. BLOOMBERG

ORO
EDITIONS

NEW YORK CITY DEPARTMENT OF
DESIGN + CONSTRUCTION

CONTENTS

Our Administration has worked hard to ensure that New York City remains a world capital of design. We took an important step in these efforts in 2004, when the Department of Design and Construction launched the Design + Construction Excellence Program.

Over the past decade, the very best architects and designers have worked on City projects. They have helped us set a new standard for how public art and architecture can enhance not only an urban center's visual aesthetic, but also our quality of life. This book highlights many of New York's most important projects – and provides a look at what a safe, resilient, and still-growing 21st-century global city can look like.

Facing the challenges of climate change and population growth alike, we are re-imagining our built environment. We are committed to making our waterfront communities, especially, more resistant to the effects of climate change. That is why we have strengthened our building codes and expanded coastal wetlands to help capture stormwater. In the Bronx, we are restoring the city's oldest bridge, and building a sustainable service center for families in need. On Staten Island, we are opening a new police precinct station house, designed by one of the world's foremost architects. Citywide, we are creating pedestrian plazas to open up more of our public spaces – both for our millions of residents and daily commuters, and for the millions more who come to New York every year to visit the world's finest arts and culture venues.

New York's success in attracting talent, capital, and new development is not something we take for granted. Building on our success will take bold ideas and the expertise to turn them into reality – and we can expect the Department of Design and Construction and its partners to lead the way in realizing our vision for a stronger, more sustainable city.

MICHAEL R. BLOOMBERG
Mayor

INTRODUCTION » » » » » » »

I have been especially privileged to work under Mayor Michael Bloomberg during one of the most innovative periods in New York City's history.

Mayor Bloomberg launched PlaNYC 2030 on Earth Day, April 2007. Right from the start, it established New York City as a global leader in sustainability planning. PlaNYC, with its many initiatives, was largely a response to the question: What do we want our City to look like in 2030? A growing population, aging infrastructure, climate change, and a changing economy pose challenges to our city's success and quality of life. PlaNYC considers the fact that all cities depend crucially upon infrastructure, and that construction and maintenance of infrastructure is an important determinant of a livable city. We see urban infrastructure in terms of hard infrastructure (systems for water, energy, waste and transportation, and networks of buildings, parks, and open spaces) and soft infrastructure (institutions and programs that promote education, culture, recreation, health, and safety).

Transportation, water and power systems, adaptation to rising seas or persistent drought, access to housing, and services for rapidly rising populations—all these require such intensive and sustained capital investment and affect the lives of so many people, that they cannot be left only to the volatile forces of the free market. Equally, cities must invest in their educational, cultural and recreational infrastructure if they are to maintain the quality of life that defines a successful city.

The New York City Department of Design and Construction has played an important role in PlaNYC's implementation. DDC has worked with more than 20 different City departments including Transportation, Environmental Protection, Sanitation, and Parks and Recreation to repair, remodel, and expand the city's existing hard infrastructure, and with the departments of Cultural Affairs, Homeless Services, Health and Mental Hygiene, and the three public library systems—New York, Brooklyn, and Queens—to provide social and cultural resources, and the Police and Fire departments to provide the public safety facilities required in this great city.

New York is fortunate to have relatively reliable hard infrastructure. There is an extensive system of roads and mass transit, including the subway and bus networks. The freshwater catchment areas north and west of the city—including the mid-19th century Croton Reservoir—provide an abundant and stable water supply, although this system is now under threat from land development and, possibly, from natural gas exploration (fracking) near the watersheds.

For New York City, the challenge is to maintain and improve these infrastructures and, in the process, to create a more sustainable city. The original PlaNYC document comprised 127 policy initiatives designed to shape the future of the city by 2030 and to allow for the population to increase from 8 to 9 million. The 2011 update added more initiatives. The goals are big and most are also long-range, and you can track the progress in some detail on the PlaNYC website.

Much of the essential work to maintain this infrastructure is not visible to the general public. For instance, to ensure the long-term viability of our water supply, the NYC Department of Environmental Protection has spent several decades building a new water tunnel—the City's third, and the first to be built since the 1930s—that will bring water from the Croton Reservoir and allow one of the two existing tunnels to be repaired. "Tunnel No. 3," some 600 feet below street level, and stretches 60 miles, was put into service this year. DDC designed and built the distribution water mains that delivered water from the new tunnel through the city streets.

Measures are under way to reduce the amount of solid waste sent to landfills and to remove solid waste by barge, reducing the amount of truck traffic through the city streets, saving energy and improving air quality.

To better manage stormwater and prevent it from overloading the waste treatment facilities, PlaNYC envisions a more "upstream" approach: preventing rainwater from entering the drainage system in the first place by requiring buildings to have rainwater-retention systems, constructing bioswales and tree-pits that absorb rainwater, retrofitting parking lots with permeable pavement, and increasing the city's "bluebelt" network of coastal wetlands.

The implementation requires coordination of the policies and actions of the Department of Environmental Protection (which manages the waste and water systems), the Department of Transportation (which manages the roads and sidewalks), the Department of Parks and Recreation (which maintain the trees and bioswales), and the Department of Buildings (which ensures new construction complies with water retention requirements). DDC's role is to design and build these systems, reconcile the budgets of collaborating agencies to fund and obtain approvals for construction plans, and coordinate the agencies' involvement throughout the design and construction process.

One important achievement of the Bloomberg administration has been the steady transformation of public space. For a long time, New York has been associated with the skyscraper, and with the sheer density of its population. Yet public space was something of an afterthought (usually just the space left over between buildings) and the street grid was dominated by the car. Most of the space on city streets—89 percent—was devoted to the car. There was not much left for pedestrians, and cyclists were hardly in the picture. So during the past decade, the Department of Transportation, under Commissioner Janette Sa-dik-Khan, has implemented a "Complete Streets" policy, to give pedestrians and cyclists equal rights with motor vehicles. By expanding the width of sidewalks, creating new plazas, and adding a network of bike lanes, the streets are more walkable and bikeable; the city is now a more enjoyable experience. You can see this in Times Square, where closing Broadway to automobile traffic from 42nd Street to 47th Street produced five new public plazas, which immediately filled with people. The traffic closure was initially temporary; this year it will be made permanent, with a new design by the integrated landscape and architectural design firm Snøhetta.

But a city with only hard infrastructure would be an empty city. Soft infrastructures are fundamental to quality of life—from low crime rates and safe streets, to accessible health care, to high-performing schools, to cultural and recreational opportunities like museums, libraries, symphonies, and professional sports.

You will also see in the pages of this book the enormous investment the City has made over the past 12 years in its cultural and recreational infrastructure. New and expanded libraries in all five Boroughs; museums and centers for art and music; firehouse and ambulance stations; police precincts and health centers; park comfort stations and recreation centers. Designed by some of the best established and emerging architects in the City, these projects bring the benefits of design and construction excellence to every neighborhood and every community. We hope that they have made a contribution to the quality of life in New York as we envision our city for 2030 and beyond.

DAVID J. BURNEY, FAIA
Commissioner
Department of Design + Construction

NEW YORK CITY'S GROUNDBREAKING DESIGN + CONSTRUCTION EXCELLENCE PROGRAM

New York City is known for its skyline—its five boroughs stretch over an archipelago with 578 miles of shoreline and more than 40 separate islands. Manhattan and Staten Island occupy islands of their own. Brooklyn and Queens form the western edge of Long Island, and only the Bronx is on the mainland. With its population of 8.3 million, New York is the most populous city in the United States and, having been settled by the Dutch in 1625, it is also one of the oldest, predating Williamsburg, Boston, and Philadelphia.

New York is the capital of capitalism, but it is also an international center for the arts, education, publishing, fashion, and trade, as well as the home of the United Nations. More major architectural practices are located in New York than in any other city, and during the last decade, many of them have been designing buildings for the public in the poorest neighborhoods as well as in the city center, under the auspices of

Mayor Michael Bloomberg's Design and Construction Excellence (D+CE) program, led by the New York City Department of Design and Construction (DDC).

In 2004, Mayor Bloomberg appointed architect David Burney as DDC Commissioner. This agency was created in 1996 to build more efficiently and cost effectively than in the past by centralizing the management and coordination of the City's design and construction projects under one roof. Today, DDC manages capital projects on behalf of more than 20 City agencies, with a diverse working portfolio valued at $8 billion. At DDC, with the support of Mayor Bloomberg and Deputy Mayor Patricia Harris, Burney developed a D+CE program modeled on the one that the federal General Services Administration (GSA) had initiated in 1992.

Although, in the early years of the Republic, the most admired architects were hired and the finest

materials were used in buildings like the United States Capitol (1793-1811), New York City Hall (1811), and the University of Virginia (1818-26), after World War II, things changed. Faced with a burgeoning population, chastened by the War and the Great Depression, and influenced by the modern movement in architecture which valued "function" (factory-like practicality) above all else, governments started building the cheapest, plainest, and most mundane facilities possible.

Instead of seeking the most talented architects and able contractors, governments instituted business practices that, while intended to be open and competitive, created an environment where, more often than not, the designs produced were uninspiring, not ideally suited to their site, and poorly suited to their function. Additionally, the bid process became increasingly dysfunctional, as a limited number of contractors who had learned how to "game the system" underbid each other in their efforts to get the job and then tried to make up their lost profit through contract change orders and claims, ultimately compromising the finished quality of the buildings and driving up costs for the City.

As this downward trajectory in the quality of public works played out, in 1962, President Kennedy, concerned about the decline, created an Ad Hoc Committee on Federal Office Space to develop new principles to guide the design of public buildings. YoungDaniel Patrick Moynihan, who later became a United States Senator from New York, developed what became known as the "Guiding Principles for Federal Architecture." These said, "Federal office buildings...must provide efficient and economical facilities" and "reflect the dignity, enterprise, vigor, and stability of the American National Government."

These "Guiding Principles..." called for "designs that embody the finest contemporary American architectural thought. Specific attention should be paid to the possibilities of incorporating...qualities which reflect the regional architectural traditions of that part of the Nation in which buildings are located. Where appropriate, fine art should be incorporated in the designs, with emphasis on the work of living American artists. Designs shall adhere to sound construction practice and utilize materials, methods and equipment of proven dependability. Buildings shall be economical to build, operate, and maintain, and should be accessible to the handicapped. The development of an official style must be avoided. Design must flow from the architectural profession to the Government and not vice versa..."

Following these guidelines, a few ambitious federal buildings were constructed, such as Marcel Breuer's swooping headquarters for the United States Department of Housing and Urban Development and Mies van der Rohe's dignified Federal Center in Chicago.

For the most part, however, the goals of economy, efficiency, and standardization remained the

norm in federal construction until 1992 when the GSA instituted a Design Excellence Program to finally put these "Guiding Principles for Federal Architecture" into practice, insuring that at least some federal buildings would embody the ambition and values of the federal government and "provide high quality, cost-effective, and lasting public buildings for the enjoyment of future generations."

Inspired by the GSA, under David Burney, working with the City Public Design Commission, the Mayor's office and with other City agencies, DDC developed its own D+CE program to improve the quality of the buildings and street infrastructure projects in New York City. DDC manages the design and construction of buildings that provide the full range of municipal services. Some are buildings that people use directly, like public libraries, theaters, and museums. Others serve the public, like police precincts, firehouses, and emergency medical services facilities. Still others provide a welcoming place where people can access social services at critical junctures in their lives.

DESIGN MATTERS

By ensuring that the design of every project is considered to be as important as the timeliness and cost of its delivery, the D+CE program has brought a new sense of vitality to the day-to-day experience of those who live and work in New York—as well as to the millions who visit the city for business or pleasure every year, making it a global center of commerce and culture.

What is meant by design in this context is not just how the building looks, but extends to how well it is detailed, to the durability of its materials and construction systems, to how the building supports its function, and perhaps the most elusive yet important goal of all,

how it elevates the lives of those who use and enjoy the services the building provides. It is a holistic understanding of the word design that encompasses the three attributes espoused by Vitruvius: *Firmitas*, *Utilitas*, *Venustas* (*translated as Firmness, Commodity and Delight*).

QUALITY-BASED SELECTION

To implement the D+CE program, DDC needed to change several business practices that were perceived as obstacles to realizing good design in public works. The first challenge was to tap more fully into the enormous pool of design talent available in New York City (and beyond), to encourage a wider range of good design firms to take on City work. With a history of fee competition in procurement of designers and a stifling bureaucracy, many talented firms did not even want to work on City projects. Working with government partners, DDC was able to adopt Quality-Based Selection (QBS) for design services. Under this new methodology, the selection of a firm for a City project is based on the quality of their past work and the qualifications of their team. Once the best team is selected, fair and reasonable fees are negotiated for their services.

PUBLIC BUILDINGS

>> >> >> >> >> >> >> >> >> >> >> >> >> >>

$2.02 BILLION
WORK COMPLETED FOR CULTURAL ORGANIZATIONS

>> Weeksville Heritage Center, Brooklyn.

$680 MILLION
WORK COMPLETED FOR NEW YORK'S THREE LIBRARY SYSTEMS

>> Cambria Heights Library, Queens.

323
NUMBER OF PROJECTS COMPLETED FOR THE FDNY

>> EC277, Brooklyn.

110
RENOVATIONS AND UPGRADES FOR THE NYPD

>> Central Park Precinct, Manhattan.

One of DDC's most important roles is that of match-maker. DDC is diligent at "matching" the right design team to each project, and then ensuring that the design process runs smoothly. Since projects are created by teams, DDC staffers work closely with City agencies and professionals in the private sector's architectural, engineering, and construction communities. DDC has been particularly effective in finding and mentoring emerging design talent in New York, enabling New Yorkers to benefit from their innovations and creativity.

DESIGN LIAISONS

The D+CE program also implemented several innovations created to ensure that the designs produced by our teams survive the City review process and budget constraints. Every project has a dedicated project manager whose main responsibility is to deliver the project on time and on budget. The challenge was to see to it that, by accomplishing this, the project did not suffer in design quality, thereby subverting the very goal we set out to achieve. To this end, under the D+CE program, each project also has a Design Liaison who has sole responsibility for being certain that the quality of the design is not lost in the rush to meet budgets and schedules.

PEER REVIEW

DDC recognizes the importance of engaging outside experts throughout the commissioning and development of City projects and, as part of that commitment, has implemented a peer review program which has several components. Professional peers from the private sector participate in consultant selection and also provide independent reviews during the design process. Peers are selected from a register maintained by the Mayor's office based on professional experience

DDC worked with the American Institute of Architects to advertise this change and encourage the top design firms to compete for City work. Many small and emerging firms were hesitant because they found it very difficult to compete with the larger, more established firms even under the QBS selection process. DDC wanted to attract these firms as they are often best suited to deliver the City's smaller projects, which represent a significant portion of DDC's portfolio. To do so, DDC set aside all of its projects under $10 million (now $15 million) in construction value and only allowed small firms (those with 10 or fewer professional staff members) to compete for them. In this book, you will see the results—many high quality public buildings designed by emerging firms that would otherwise may not have been able to secure these commissions.

and demonstrated excellence in architectural and engineering design. These outside peers volunteer their time to review and critique new designs in the schematic or conceptual stage, ensuring that the best possible design solution goes forward. The City's Public Design Commission (formerly the Art Commission) provides a final review, further ensuring that only quality design work goes into the construction process.

CONSTRUCTABILITY REVIEW

To help ensure a smooth construction process and decrease the likelihood of problems due to incomplete or flawed documents, the D+CE program incorporates a comprehensive review of construction documents before they are put out to bid to contractors.

DESIGN METRIC

To counter the perception that design quality is subjective and too difficult to define and measure, the D+CE program utilizes a tool for assessing and measuring the design quality. The Design Metric tool establishes a consensus on design priorities at the outset of a project and tracks that the project continues to meet those priorities as the design proceeds.

EDUCATION

In addition to DDC's role managing the design and construction of City projects, the agency acts as the City's engine of research on best practices in the built environment. A number of important city-wide programs and initiatives have sprung from the research done at DDC. Perhaps foremost among these is the *Design and Construction Excellence* report that describes in detail the business practices that form the foundation of the program.

DDC has also released a number of technical reports that give guidance to design professionals who are, or might become engaged in City design

STREET INFRASTRUCTURE

863 MILES
SIDEWALKS AND STREETS PAVED

797 MILES
NEW WATER MAINS INSTALLED

588 MILES
STORM AND SANITARY SEWERS INSTALLED

15,140
HYDRANTS REPLACED

39,180
PEDESTRIAN RAMPS INSTALLED

10,790
HOMES CONNECTED TO THE MUNICIPAL SYSTEM FOR THE FIRST TIME

projects. These include *High Performance Building* and *High Performance Infrastructure Guidelines*; the *Geothermal Heat Pump Manual*; *Water Matters* (a guide on water management) and *BIM Guidelines*, in which DDC presents its methodology for the emerging use of Building Information Modeling in its projects. These publications are available for free download on DDC's website.

PROGRAMS

One of DDC's most innovative publications is the *Active Design Guidelines*. As part of Mayor Bloomberg administration's fight against the growing obesity epidemic (the most serious public health issue in the United States today), DDC worked with the Department of Health and several other City agencies to research ways in which changes to the built environment could encourage greater physical activity. The Guidelines were published in 2010 and covered "best practices" to encourage mobility in building design and urban design. Several supplements have been issued as more guidance has emerged in this growing field. In 2013, Mayor Bloomberg created the Center for Active Design (www.centerforactivedesign.org) to continue this work in the future. The Mayor also issued an Executive Order requiring all City projects to incorporate Active Design principles wherever feasible.

Another important initiative is the "Town+Gown" program developed by DDC. To bring the intellectual resources of academia to solve long-standing problems or research on City issues, Town+Gown marshals academic resources to create applied research projects in the built environment. The annual *Research Agenda* is the primary resource for participating members to use in collaborating on research projects. Completed research projects are abstracted annually in *Building Ideas*. Completed projects also serve as the foundation for symposium events within the Town+Gown community.

The projects in this book represent the body of work that has been produced under the D+CE program, and highlights the full range of public buildings, streetscape, and infrastructure projects built for a variety of City agencies in all five boroughs. These are not only some of the most visible projects of the last decade, but they have brought design quality to the many quotidian public works that serve every neighborhood and community in the City.

PUBLIC BUILDING PROJECTS IN THE 5 BOROUGHS

>> **CORRECTION**
>> **COURTS**
>> **FIRE**
>> **POLICE**
>> **CULTURAL FACILITIES**
>> **LIBRARIES**
>> **HEALTH**
>> **HUMAN SERVICES**

STREETSCAPES +
PLAZAS +
PARKS +
RECREATIONAL
FACILITIES

» **STREETSCAPES + PLAZAS**

» **PARKS + RECREATIONAL FACILITIES**

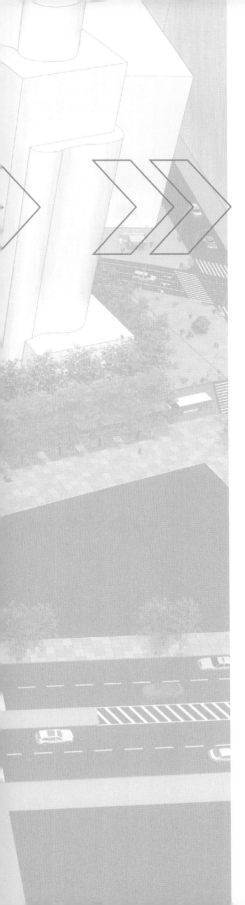

Among the exciting new public projects in New York City, perhaps the most public of all are the re-envisioned, revitalized, and pedestrian-friendly streets, plazas, and parks. Stretches of some of the most famous streets in the city, like Broadway, have effectively become parks. New parks are also emerging in unexpected places, such as on top of the Croton Water Treatment Plant in the Bronx. Times Square has been transformed into a lively plaza with tables and chairs where traffic used to clog the street. Farther south, in Greenwich Village, where Broadway runs into Astor Place, another new public plaza is being created in a dynamic triangular space.

New places for people to gather are also underway in the other boroughs— in Brooklyn's DUMBO area, on Queens' Myrtle Plaza, at the busy Bronx transportation hub and shopping area at Roberto Clemente Plaza. In all of these areas, award-winning architects are creating places with distinctive local character within neighborhood hubs.

Since Hurricane Sandy devastated New York City waterfronts, DDC and the Department of Parks and Recreation have instituted several programs to creatively restore popular beaches, including a series of elevated boardwalk islands that connect the beach with nearby streets, and modular lifeguard stations for Coney Island, Rockaway Beach, and Wolfe's Pond Park on Staten Island. Each of these designs considers rising sea levels and increasingly frequent and severe storms.

Access to water has been the stimulus of new parks throughout the five boroughs. On the banks of the Hudson River in Harlem and near Yankee Stadium, in densely settled areas where recreational space was badly needed, engineers and landscape architects are designing vital, usable places, many of which are described on the upcoming pages.

STREETSCAPES
+
PLAZAS

» ASTOR PLACE AND COOPER SQUARE

> MANHATTAN, between East 9th and East 6th streets
> WXY ARCHITECTURE, with Quennell Rothschild and Partners
> Department of Transportation and Department of Parks and Recreation, 2015

BELOW » Circular rendering.

At the crossroads of Greenwich Village and the East Village, where a seam appears when Bowery opens into Third Avenue, Cooper Square and Fourth Avenue, an opportunity to re-design much-needed public arose as the result of a Department of Transportation pedestrian improvement plan and a Department of Environmental Protection water main replacement plan. The neighborhood has recently experienced a construction boom that includes a new boutique hotel and a major new university building for Cooper Union. But, despite a mix of residents, students, and professionals in this neighborhood, places for enjoying the urban scene or simply having lunch outdoors are scarce.

Sensitive to day and night-time needs, WXY Architecture teamed up with Quennell Rothschild and Partners landscape designers and Tillett Lighting Design to create four linked plazas along Fourth Avenue. Each has its own distinct lighting, resulting in a rich pedestrian environment made out of pieces of

ABOVE » Aerial view of Astor Place and Cooper Square, Manhattan.

reclaimed streets. Elliptical shapes of different scales and materials provide a flexible geometry for each plaza, while a consistent paving strategy connects them. Tinted concrete and staggered scoring patterns take cues from the existing sidewalk around the Cooper Union Foundation building.

Surrounded by historically significant buildings and monuments, the newly coherent progression of civic spaces will reinvent the quality and variety of local experience while implementing sustainability strategies. Throughout, new trees and plantings on former streets and sidewalks will reduce stormwater runoff and provide shade. Planting will complement the new seating and bicycle racks near the Astor Place subway canopy, improve access around Tony Rosenthal's famous Cube sculpture, and increase the sense of enjoyable space near the Village Voice building. With a number of high performance materials, such as high fly-ash concrete and structural soil, as well as

TOP LEFT » Astor Place Subway
Plaza. TOP RIGHT » Pavement
detail. RIGHT » Cooper Park Walk.
OPPOSITE » Proposed plan.

permeable paving that will allow stormwater to percolate into the water table
and bio-filtration strips to help cleanse runoff, the project will implement many
of the goals of the PlaNYC 2030.

The plan also includes a new design for Cooper Park, linking it with the
other spaces and solving various problems inherent in its design. This redesign
expands the planting areas, improves pedestrian circulation through the park
with the addition of several entrances, and enhances security.

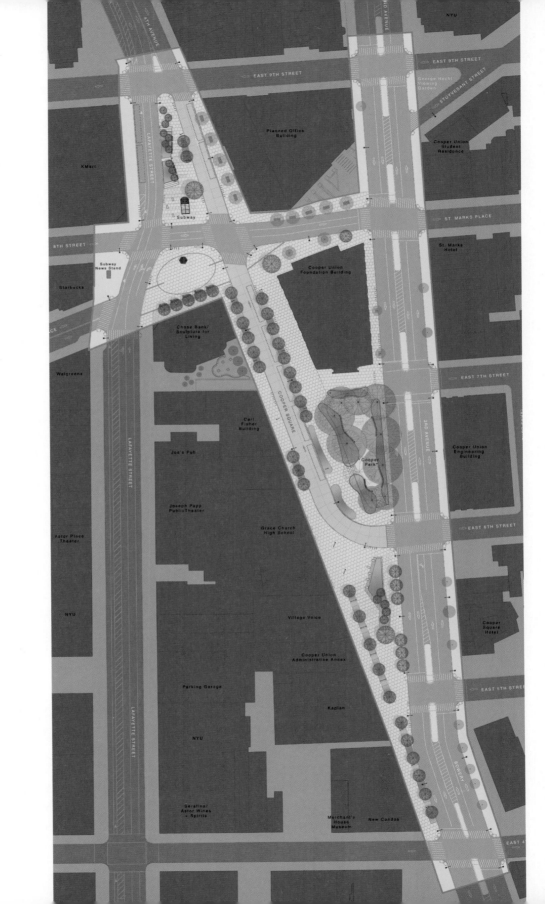

» CITY LIGHTS

> ALL FIVE BOROUGHS
> THOMAS PHIFER AND PARTNERS, Office for Visual Interaction
> with Structural Engineer Werner Sobek
> Department of Transportation, 2013

DDC with the Department of Transportation, launched an international design competition to create a new standard streetlight for the City of New York. Thomas Phifer and Partners teamed up with the Office for Visual Interaction (lighting designers) and Werner Sobek (structural engineers) and created the winning design for the City Lights competition, out of more than 200 anonymous submissions from 23 countries. This "Streelight for the Future" was designed as a one-to-one replacement for the ubiquitous 250-watt high-pressure sodium Cobra Head, introduced more than 50 years ago. The LED streetlight will be added to the Department of Transportation's street lighting catalogue, making it the new citywide standard for installations within the five boroughs.

The development of high output, "small package" LEDs has allowed re-fine- ment of the shape and proportions of the streetlight, though the apparent simplicity of the design belies its mechanical complexity. Even the support pole has multiple design features and requirements: slight tapering over its 30-foot height slims its appearance while maintaining an indiscernible conical shape that provides increased structural stability. The curving arc of the luminaire is a direct expression of the linear arrays of LEDs it contains, resulting in a luminaire that is at once technically superior and aesthetically timeless. The sculptural base, along with the fluid contours of the pole top and luminaire head, work together to create an elegant composition that integrates just as well with New York City's modern skyscrapers as it does with its most classic monuments.

A great deal of coordination and development led to the realization of an LED streetlight, which, compared to a standard streetlight with a single point source, has a more even distribution of light, better contrast ratios, greater accuracy of color rendering, and minimized glare. All of these aspects contribute to better safety and security along city streets and sidewalks, as well as making for a more refined and visually imaginative design.

During the evolution of the design, a variety of LED clustering options were explored to define and optimize the LED configuration. The LEDs were eventually staggered, then streamlined into a linear array and paired with micro-sized, lensed optics, significantly reducing luminaire size and fabrica-

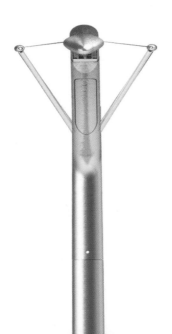

OPPOSITE » City Lights front elevation, City Lights side elevation. ABOVE » City lights street pole rendering. BELOW » City Lights front elevation.

tion cost. Custom optics allow for a controlled overlap between light beams, accounting for the possibility of an LED failure and ensuring uniformity and safety on the roadway.

The streetlight uses 84 low-wattage LEDs, achieving a significant energy savings of more than 40 percent from the 250-watt high-pressure sodium lamp. As the technology improves, even further savings will be achieved. The flexibility of the system ensures that lighting modules can be swapped out with new modules, which may use fewer LEDs to generate the same amount of light. The streetlight thus has the ability to advance with time, becoming less costly and more sustainable as technology develops.

Distinguished from other LED streetlights that have appeared on the market since the groundbreaking design, the City Lights streetlight has undergone rigorous testing and prototyping to meet the stringent technical and aesthetic requirements of DDC, Department of Transportation, and Public Design Commission. The result is a lighting design for the future, a new icon for the New York City urban landscape.

⟫ DUMBO AND VINEGAR HILL PLAZA

> ⟩ BROOKLYN, East River waterfront
> ⟩ AECOM TECHNOLOGY CORPORATION
> ⟩ Department of Transportation, 2015

OPPOSITE ⟫ Aerial view of Pearl Street Plaza. ABOVE ⟫ Plaza at night.

This project, in the formerly industrial neighborhood of DUMBO, involves the transformation of a parking lot into a plaza with adjacent street closures integrating the Manhattan Bridge Archway. The project restores the historic cobblestone to the main streets and creates bike lanes connected to the neighborhood of Vinegar Hill. The unique space under the Manhattan Bridge will be linked with the plaza to create a dynamic new destination for the community and the greater city of New York.

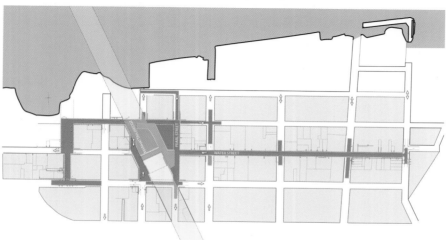

ABOVE » Plaza view from Archway.
LEFT » Area of work.

The plaza paving echoes the language of the cobbled streets with a contemporary approach. Permanent seating will be located in the primary plaza area, which provides a large gathering space for projections, performance, and events, as well as planted areas that create a more private environment for small groups.

To make the space flexible, movable tables, planters, and chairs are also proposed for the plaza, designed to be rearranged depending on the group or event occupying the space.

TOP RIGHT » Plaza.
RIGHT » Anchorage Place.

>> FORDHAM PLAZA

> THE BRONX, Third Avenue and Park Avenue, East Fordham Road and East 189th Street
> GRIMSHAW
> Department of Transportation, 2015

Fordham Plaza, a 1.7-acre public plaza in the Bronx, sits on top of commuter rail tracks, adjacent to a number of busy streets. Grimshaw's design aims to enhance pedestrian safety, offer clear and easy access to transit options, and create a vibrant public space capable of holding a wide variety of gatherings and events.

At its core, the reinvigorated plaza is designed to guide pedestrians safely and intuitively to and from various transit modes while offering passersby and the resident community opportunities to engage with other amenities within the plaza. New entry structures and wayfinding systems, with real time transit information, will guide rail passengers to and from the platforms beneath the plaza to a reconfigured bus drop-off. The plaza is framed by two canopy structures above a central, flexible area available for different uses throughout the year.

Beneath the northern canopy are waiting areas, additional access to the commuter rail platforms, and a new enclosed café. The southern canopy provides space for a farmer's market and other vendors to increase foot traffic and retail opportunities. Modular kiosks can be deployed to provide additional venues for retail and dining. Thoughtful paving design and landscaping reinforce the circulation patterns through the plaza and provides a buffer to adjacent traffic.

OPPOSITE, BOTTOM >> Kiosks will provide further venues for retail and dining options. ABOVE >> The Metro North canopy provides shelter and can be used as a waiting area for passengers. RIGHT >> The view from Fordham Road illustrates the new circulation patterns which will guide passengers intuitively to their transit modes.

>> FREDERICK DOUGLASS CIRCLE

> MANHATTAN, Central Park West and 110th Street
> URS CORPORATION, with Quennell Rothschild and Partners
> Percent for Art: Algernon Miller (Artist), Gabriel Koren (Sculptor)
> Department of Transportation, 2010

ABOVE >> Frederick Douglass statue, Manhattan.
OPPOSITE >> Water fountain.

For the reconstruction of Frederick Douglass Circle, the northwest corner of Central Park was converted from a conventional intersection to a traffic circle that enclosed public space and a memorial commemorating Frederick Douglass.

The quarter-acre central memorial includes a figurative sculpture and a series of elements that illuminate Frederick Douglass' life and the plight of escaping slaves, which was the focus of much of Douglass' writing and oratory. Varying hues of granite pavement and sculptural benches describe patterns from the quilts associated with the flight from slavery. Other interpretive elements include a metal railing patterned after wagon wheels and

FREDERICK DOUGLASS
1818–1895

BORN INTO SLAVERY IN MARYLAND, FREDERICK
BAILEY FOUND THE WAY TO FREEDOM ALONG THE
UNDERGROUND RAILROAD IN 1838. DISGUISED AS A
SAILOR, HE TRAVELED TO MANHATTAN BY SHIP, AND
FOUND SHELTER AT THE HOUSE OF ABOLITIONIST
DAVID RUGGLES ON LISPENARD STREET. THERE, HE
AWAITED THE ARRIVAL OF HIS FIANCÉE, ANNA
MURRAY, A FREE BLACK WOMAN FROM MARYLAND.
THEY MARRIED, AND TOGETHER CONTINUED
BAILEY'S FREEDOM JOURNEY TO MASSACHUSETTS,
WHERE HE CHANGED HIS NAME TO DOUGLASS.
LAUDED FOR HIS ORATION, HE BECAME A PROMINENT
ABOLITIONIST AND PURCHASED HIS LEGAL FREEDOM
FROM SLAVERY. PUBLISHER OF THE ABOLITIONIST
JOURNAL THE NORTH STAR, HE CHAMPIONED
FREEDOM FOR ALL AMERICANS AND ENDORSED
WOMEN'S SUFFRAGE. DOUGLASS LATER HELD POSTS
AS ASSISTANT SECRETARY OF THE SANTO DOMINGO
COMMISSION (1871), MARSHALL OF THE DISTRICT OF
COLUMBIA (1877–1881) AND U.S. MINISTER TO HAITI
(1889–1891). FOLLOWING THE DEATH OF HIS WIFE
IN 1882, DOUGLASS MARRIED HELEN PITTS. HE DIED
IN WASHINGTON, D.C. ON FEBRUARY 20, 1895.

ABOVE ≫ Wagon wheel railing detail. OPPOSITE, TOP ≫ Sculptural triangular benches in quilt paving pattern. OPPOSITE, BOTTOM ≫ Sculptural "puzzle" benches in quilt paving pattern.

a linear fountain studded with illuminated stars, which suggest the celestial constellations that guided slaves escaping by night.

The project team also included landscape architect Quennell Rothschild and Partners, LLP, and the Harlem-based architectural firm J-P Design Group, Inc. The project received an Engineering Excellence Silver Award from the American Council of Engineering Companies in 2011.

⟩⟩ LONG ISLAND CITY WAYFINDING PROJECT

⟩ QUEENS, throughout Long Island City
⟩ RICE+LIPKA ARCHITECTS
⟩ Department of Transportation, no date

OPPOSITE AND BELOW » Wayfinding
structure at Court Square location.
LEFT » Study models of various
configurations for wayfinding structure.

A system of physical directional devices stakes out territory and establishes a graphic identity for this community's nascent cultural district. The project aims to create an iconic image that will become the symbol of Long Island City culture, immediately legible and memorable to local residents and visitors alike.

The wayfinding structures bear maps and signage at scales legible to both motorists and pedestrians, clearly communicating the locations of various institutions and giving directions on how to best reach them—on foot, by car, bicycle, or bus, or on the subway. The structures will also house interchangeable signage and display boards to provide information about specific institutions, exhibitions, performances, and events. An important part of the ongoing project is selecting optimal sites for the structures throughout Long Island City—which has nearly 500 city blocks and an area of 1,664 acres.

» LOUISE NEVELSON PLAZA

> MANHATTAN , 84 William Street
> SMITH-MILLER + HAWKINSON ARCHITECTS
> Department of Transportation, 2010

ABOVE » Louise Nevelson Plaza, Manhattan.

Louise Nevelson Plaza is part of a study of open space—titled "Strategic Open Spaces" that Smith-Miller+Hawkinson created for the Lower Manhattan Development Corporation (LMDC) after the devastation of September 11, 2001. The plaza is managed, owned, and operated by multiple government agencies including the Federal Reserve Bank of New York, the New York City Department of Transportation, the Department of Parks and Recreation, and the LMDC.

RIGHT » Aerial view.
BOTTOM RIGHT » Guard booth
and glass benches.
BELOW » Looking towards the
Federal Reserve Bank.

Post 9/11 federal funds were allocated by a joint city/state corporation for the Plaza to be re-designed as a center for the increasingly residential, mixed-use neighborhood of Lower Manhattan. The shift in the fundamental nature of the area around the Plaza required a redesign of the available open space for evening and weekend use.

Inventive new street furniture integrated with new landscaping encourages foot traffic through the area. Adjacent open space along Cedar Street, facilitated by the proposed changes at Liberty Plaza and Chase Plaza, establishes a pedestrian link between the World Trade Center site and William Street.

The plaza also serves as a 24-hour security check point for the Federal Reserve Bank. The custom designed black glass and steel guard booth is located on the plaza to facilitate vehicle inspection. The project team also included Ralph Lerner Architect and Quennell Rothschild & Partners Landscape Architect.

>> MYRTLE AVENUE PLAZA

> BROOKLYN, Myrtle Avenue, between Emerson Place and Hall Street
> AECOM TECHNOLOGY CORPORATION
> Percent for Art: Matthew Geller
> Department of Transportation, 2015

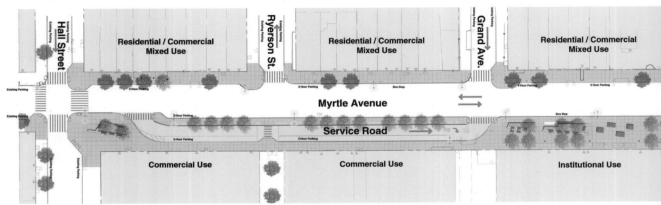

OPPOSITE, TOP » Plaza Corridor.
ABOVE » Bus stop.
BELOW » Plan.

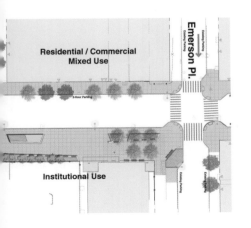

The Myrtle Avenue Plaza project converts two blocks of an existing service road between Grand Avenue and Emerson Place into a pedestrian plaza in the Clinton Hill, Brooklyn. Part of the New York City Plaza Program, initiated by PlaNYC 2030, the project reclaims an underutilized portion of the public right-of-way, transforming an access road into public space. It will also make crossing Myrtle Avenue safer through a series of pedestrian improvements.

The design creates a new public plaza, providing greenery and a new form of social gathering space for the neighborhood.

The main objectives are to increase pedestrian safety through curb extensions, widening the narrow sidewalk and median strip, narrowing the existing service road between Hall Street and Grand Avenue, and providing infrastructure for a future signalized crossing at the Grand Avenue intersection.

Sustainable practices were applied during the design process, introducing permeable paving, establishing planting areas, and continuous tree pits to the streetscape, intercepting stormwater, and reducing the urban heat island effect.

Myrtle Avenue Plaza is designed as an open and flexible space, relating directly to the surrounding buildings and the neighborhood building fabric. New pedestrian lighting is included as an amenity for the plaza area between Grand Avenue and Emerson Place.

» PARK ROW AND CHATHAM SQUARE

> MANHATTAN, Park Row by City Hall Park
> THOMAS BALSLEY ASSOCIATES / STANTEC / WEIDLINGER ASSOCIATES
> Department of Transportation and New York Police Department

Emerging security requirements for the New York City Police Headquarters created an extraordinary opportunity to re-imagine Park Row and Chatham Square as a new promenade and public plaza.

Park Row will be narrowed to create a lush pedestrian and cycling corridor connecting Chinatown to Lower Manhattan. Native grasses and perennials will form bioswales for the corridor's stormwater and surround seating covers furnished with distinctive red lounge benches throughout the landscape.

The corridor terminates with a new plaza, which will provide amenities for shopkeepers, tourists, and residents. The plaza has been designed with a new sculptural water feature, ginkgo groves, and garden plantings and trees. The lower plaza will surround the Kim Lau Memorial Arch. The upper plaza is a series of shaded and sunny spaces which are tied together by a long, sinuous red bench. The black granite sculptural fountain and plaza steps tie the upper and lower plaza together.

LEFT » 3-D study of perforated steel banquette.
RIGHT » Overall aerial perspective of Park Row and Chatham Square.

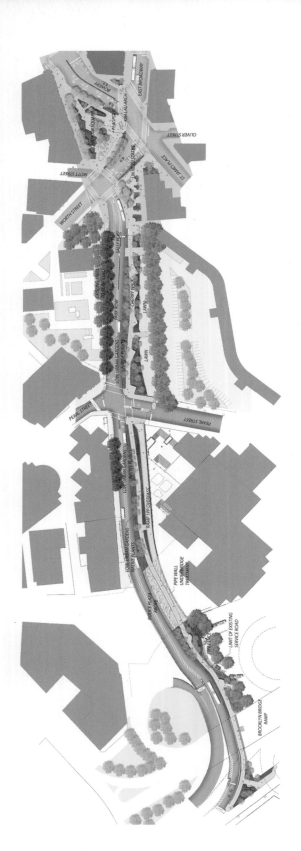

LEFT ≫ Park Row and Chatham
Square site plan.
BELOW ≫ Proposed view.
toward Police Plaza tunnel.

ABOVE » Proposed view down
Park Row toward City Hall.
LEFT » Pedestrian bridge to
Police Plaza. BELOW » Study
section of Chatham Square fountain.

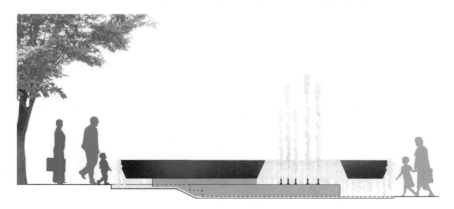

» PERSHING SQUARE

> › MANHATTAN, Park Avenue between 41st Street and 42nd Street
> › URS CORPORATION, with Quennell Rothschild and Partners
> › Department of Transportation, 2015

BELOW » Rendering of new plaza looking towards Grand Central Terminal.

The reconstruction of Pershing Square will provide a public gathering space near one of the most active transit and retail hubs in New York City. The project will permanently close the street to vehicular traffic to create a landscaped pedestrian plaza with movable tables and chairs, benches, lighting, and other public amenities. The new plaza will also include a terraced outdoor dining area for the adjacent Pershing Square restaurant.

Development of the plan involved significant community input through a series of design workshops. Materials used in the plaza, including bronze railings and granite site features, have been chosen for how they echo the historic Grand Central Terminal building. The design also incorporates sustainable elements, such as a rain garden that will capture runoff from much of the site.

The project has required coordination with the departments of Parks and Recreation, Environmental Protection, and Cultural Affairs, Public Design Commission, Metropolitan Transportation Authority, Community Board #5, and the Grand Central Partnership, which will ultimately provide maintenance and programming for the site.

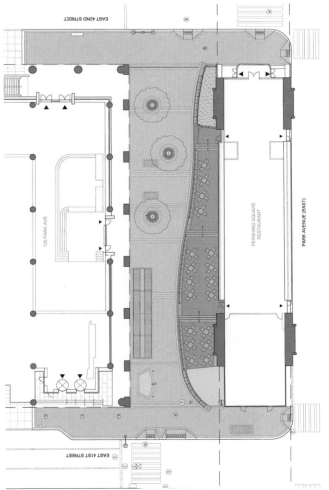

TOP » Rendering of new plaza viewed from Grand Central Terminal. LEFT » Site plan drawing of new plaza. ABOVE » Existing plaza looking towards Grand Central Terminal and 42nd Street.

ROBERTO CLEMENTE PLAZA

> THE BRONX, Willis Avenue and 149th Street
> GARRISON ARCHITECTS
> Percent for Art: Tim Rollins and K.O.S.
> Department of Transportation, 2015

Roberto Clemente Plaza is a primary shopping district for Bronx residents. To revitalize the area, an undulating, bench-lined stone planter strip will provide a waiting and loading zone for bus commuters and form an open, flexible-use plaza. The strip's geometry and fountain placement create a variety of seating zones within the plaza, such as an open zone for café tables and civic gatherings, as well as several subtly defined intimate seating spaces. When the water is idle, the fountain also serves as a stage for public events. Convenient access

LEFT » Bird's eye view from 149th Street and 3rd Avenue. ABOVE » Overhead view of water feature.

paths provide a permeable filter that provides plaza users with some shelter from the noise and traffic without squelching the energy of The Hub.

This project has various sustainabile features, as it follows the High Performance Infrastructure Guidelines of DDC and the Department of Transportation. The Willis Avenue median strip is a bio retention swale to contain runoff. The planter strip serves as a stormwater holding zone, containing runoff and reducing

ABOVE >> Bird's eye view.

irrigation needs for the plants. Reflective paving reduces albido and heat island effect. Ultimately, durable high life-span components and materials minimize maintenance efforts and costs. Native, low maintenance plants and trees absorb noise and air pollution, and provide a habitat for wildlife.

TOP RIGHT » Section diagram.
RIGHT » Diagram of site conditions.

⟫ TIMES SQUARE

> ⟩ MANHATTAN, Broadway and Seventh Avenue between 42nd and 47th streets
> ⟩ SNØHETTA; WEIDLINGER ASSOCIATES
> ⟩ Department of Transportation, 2015

OPPOSITE ⟫ Aerial view rendering of Broadway at 45th Street looking south. BELOW ⟫ Diagram and plan of bench layout.

While Times Square has long been an icon for entertainment, culture and urban life, the physical and operational conditions of the streets and sidewalks have deteriorated over time.

In 2009, the New York City's Department of Transportation's "Green Light for Midtown" pilot project used temporary paving and street furniture to close Broadway to vehicular traffic between 42nd and 47th streets, an initiative originally intended to improve safety and alleviate traffic. The hugely successful pedestrian public spaces moved DOT to permanently redefine Times Square with a three-fold purpose: to upgrade crucial utility infrastructure, provide event infrastructure for new and expanded public events, and make permanent improvements that the City piloted in 2009. The project site, known as the Bowtie, forms the heart of the Times Square theater district, and is bounded by Broadway and 7th Avenue between 42nd and 47th streets. The project will completely

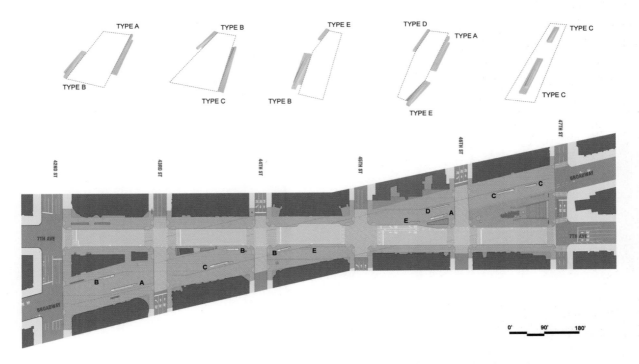

ABOVE » Paving mockup.
BELOW » View looking downtown
from Times Square.

reconstruct the roadways in Times Square, which have not been structurally repaired in decades, and provide new below-grade infrastructure, including new water and sewer mains.

Snøhetta's design for the area's pedestrian plazas is inspired by the grittiness of Times Square's past and its rich entertainment history—a duality that influenced both the larger concept and the project's details. According to Craig Dykers, Snøhetta's co-founder: "Our goal is to improve the quality and atmosphere of this historic site for tourists and locals, pedestrians and bicyclists, while reducing the traffic impediments so the 'center of the universe' will retain its edge while refining its floor."

The design creates uncluttered pedestrian zones and a cohesive surface that reinforces the Bowtie's role as an outdoor stage. This clear and simple ground surface, made of pre-cast concrete pavers, creates a strong anchor for the space, allowing the excitement of Times Square's commercial components to shine more brightly above.

RIGHT >> Understanding Times Square, early research by Snøhetta.

These pavers are embedded with nickel-sized steel discs to reflect the neon glow from the signs above. In addition to simplifying the ground surface by consolidating both movable and permanent sidewalk and street elements, Snøhetta's redesign also addresses practical issues such as drainage, maintenance, and programmatic flexibility.

Ten granite benches oriented along Broadway will define and frame the area's public plazas. These benches will create an infrastructural spine for events, and provide a clear orientation device for tourists and locals alike. New power and broadcast infrastructure embedded in the granite benches will reduce the use of diesel generators and enable swift and efficient set-up and break down of events.

PARKS
+
RECREATIONAL
FACILITIES

⟫ ASSER LEVY PARK AMPHITHEATER

> BROOKLYN, 302 Sea Breeze Avenue
> GRIMSHAW
> Department of Parks and Recreation, no date

This versatile 8,000-seat amphitheater in nine-acre Asser Levy Park is part of a major revitalization of the famous amusement park and beach community of Coney Island. The music arena and performance space will serve as a gateway to the area and a symbol of its new identity. The amphitheater is intended to be an entertainment destination for performers at all levels and encourage concert promoters to bring bands and artists to Coney Island.

The program for the Asser Levy Park Amphitheater is intended to accommodate a variety of performance types and sizes, with seating that will accommodate a variety of uses and performances throughout the year. In the off-season, much of the seating area will revert to park use.

LEFT ⟫ The aerial view illustrates the location of the amphitheater to the existing park land. ABOVE ⟫ Interior rendering illustrates the venue in use during a night time performance.

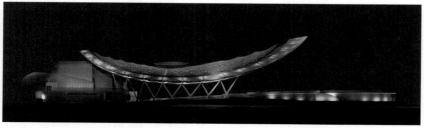

Sustainable design practices are being used wherever possible. Strategies include habitat restoration, green roofs, and environmentally conscious materials. The protection and restoration of the large open spaces and existing parkland will further support the cultural and ecological functions of the site.

ABOVE >> In the off-season, much of the seating area will revert to park use such as a skating rink. LEFT >> Nighttime elevation of the amphitheater. OPPOSITE, TOP >> The proposed program for the Asser Levy Park Amphitheater accounts for a variety of performance types and sizes. Seating is designed with a maximum amount of flexibility, allowing for a variety of uses and performances throughout the year. OPPOSITE, BOTTOM >> Visitors can play or relax on the park grounds surrounding the venue.

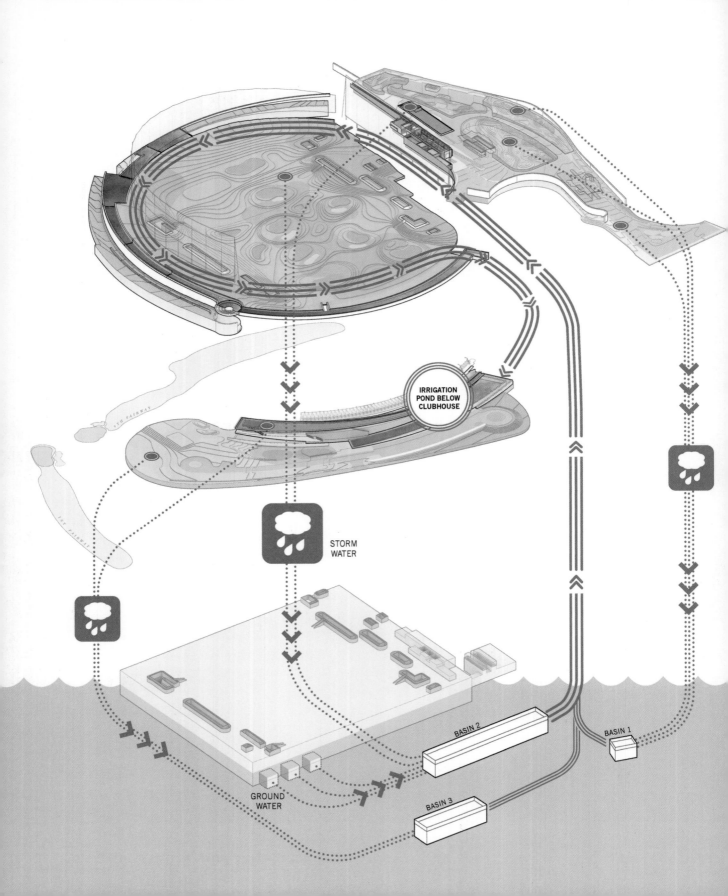

IRRIGATION
POND BELOW
CLUBHOUSE

STORM
WATER

BASIN 2

BASIN 1

BASIN 3

GROUND
WATER

≫ CROTON WATER FILTRATION PLANT DRIVING RANGE AND CLUBHOUSE

> THE BRONX, 3651 Jerome Avenue
> GRIMSHAW
> Department of Parks and Recreation and Department of Environmental Protection, 2017

OPPOSITE ≫ The diagram illustrates the process of how water is supplied to the plant. BELOW ≫ A green roof will cover the water filtration plant and will be equipped with a new public driving range.

The complex balance between the New York City Department of Environmental Protection's underground Croton Water Filtration Plant and the above ground, 32-acre public space is at the heart of this design. By incorporating the natural beauty of the surrounding environment, Grimshaw has created a unified, sustainable site for the Department of Parks and Recreation's new driving range and the buildings on top of the filtration plant.

ABOVE » The clubhouse will provide facilities to the new driving range. BELOW, LEFT » Site plan. BELOW, RIGHT » The map explains where the Croton Watershed is located in relation to the water filtration plant.

Water determined the site planning and building design strategies. Storm and groundwater is collected and redistributed through a system of landscape interventions and site subtractions. Through the use of bioswales and runnels, the water will be directed to collection ponds and filtering locations. All surface water will flow naturally, by gravity without the use of pumps, pipes, or valves. These collection ponds also serve as a security boundary to protect plants, eliminating the need for unsightly fencing.

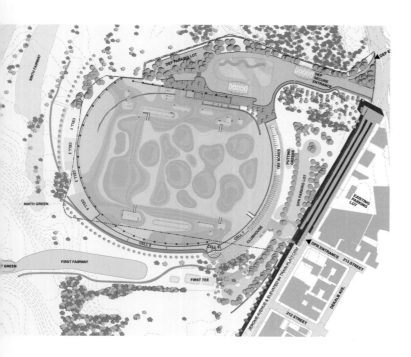

» GERTRUDE EDERLE RECREATION CENTER

> MANHATTAN , 232 West 60th Street
> BELMONT FREEMAN ARCHITECTS
  Bargmann Hendrie + Archetype, Inc., Associated Architects
> Department of Parks and Recreation, 2013

BELOW » North elevation.

The Gertrude Ederle Recreation Center project entailed the renovation of a historic 1906 bathhouse and construction of a 10,500-square-foot addition. It revitalizes a community facility that has served its neighborhood for more than a century.

The center has been a vital resource since its inception, serving first as a bathhouse for the surrounding working-class tenement districts for the purposes of public hygiene and recreation, and adapting over the years to serve the changing population of the neighborhood with opportunities for indoor and outdoor recreation. The renovation and expansion allows the New York Department of Parks and Recreation to continue to provide accessible and low-cost programs for healthy living, with updated facilities that address the needs of the 21st century user.

ABOVE » East elevation.
BELOW » Section.
OPPOSITE » North elevation.

The bathhouse has been completely renovated, with a restored indoor swimming pool, a refurbished gymnasium, a new multi-purpose community room, and new electrical, plumbing, and HVAC systems throughout. The addition contains locker rooms, a youth activities center, a computer classroom, an aerobics studio, a fitness center, a rock-climbing room, and comfort stations for the new playground.

>> MACOMBS DAM PARK

> THE BRONX, River Avenue to Ruppert Plaza between 157th and 161st Streets
> STANTEC / THOMAS BALSLEY ASSOCIATES
> New York City Economic Development Corporation and
Department of Parks and Recreation, 2012

OPPOSITE >> An whimsical quote marks the former center field wall and sections of the old stadium façade installed at the park level provide a backdrop to a new little league field. ABOVE >> The design for the 13-acre park features three dedicated ballfields and multi-use event space wrapped within a rich landscape bordered by Ruppert Plaza.

Yankee Stadium is a longtime landmark for the Bronx. Despite having the iconic field in their own backyard, many residents around the stadium had limited access to quality recreational space. When the City permitted the Yankees to build a new stadium, they made a promise to the community to not just replace parkland lost to the new venue, but to surpass it, with new amenities and a commitment to the long-term sustainability of the new facilities.

The design for the new 13-acre park includes three ballfields and a multi-use event space bordered by dramatic landscaping that creates formal and informal gathering spaces for visitors and spectators alike. Ruppert Plaza unites the entire park, linking ground level and rooftop portions of Macombs Dam Park in a seamless, fully accessible and intuitive fashion. The plaza and its promenade provide access to all major park elements—including an exercise loop, a dynamic playground, and water play feature—as well as the new stadium and public transportation. Surrounding the park are a number of bold and subtle features that pay homage to the former stadium's history.

Given its significance, the site's cultural importance also had to be integrated in the new park's design. The resulting interpretive program was not meant to place the focus on the New York Yankees, but rather reflect on the history of

ABOVE, LEFT » A sloped walkway and a sledding hill create a subtle, free-flowing ascent. ABOVE, TOP RIGHT » Custom features throughout the park recognize the former stadium's rich history. Granite bench tops fashioned as ticket stubs commemorate historic events. ABOVE, BOTTOM RIGHT » Commemorating the site's rich history, 49 etched granite plaques fit into the hexagonal paving pattern honoring sports, entertainment, civic and cultural events and personalities.

the site and instill pride in the neighborhood. The commemorative treatments include two frieze panels from the original stadium, distinctive plaques, a series of viewfinders providing 3D glimpses of past events, and an indelible field overlay woven into the turf of the main baseball field to faintly outline where the old stadium once stood without disrupting an active playing field now has its own renewed place to play.

The construction team raised the elevation of the field by five feet, allowing stormwater retention underneath. The fill from another local project provided the sub-base for the field and improved access to the street grid.

Macombs Dam Park ensures a community defined by, yet detached from, sports history within the walls of the old and new stadiums.

›› ROCKAWAY BEACH

> QUEENS, Beach 86th, 97th, and 106th streets
> MCLAREN ENGINEERING GROUP with Sage and Coombe Architects;
> Mathews Nielsen, Landscape Architects; Pentagram, Graphic Designers
> Department of Parks and Recreation, 2013

ABOVE ›› View from 97th Street to 86th Street after Hurricane Sandy. OPPOSITE, TOP ›› Beach 86th Street at boardwalk elevation. OPPOSITE, BOTTOM ›› Beach 106th Street view from Shorefront Parkway. FOLLOWING SPREAD, TOP LEFT ›› Beach 106th Street beachside seating made from recycled boardwalk. FOLLOWING SPREAD, TOP RIGHT ›› Beach 86th Street. FOLLOWING SPREAD, BOTTOM ›› Plan showing Rockaway rehabilitation sites and relevant issues.

In December 2012, after extensive damage from Hurricane Sandy, the design team developed a series of raised platforms or "islands" at the elevation of the former boardwalk to allow access to and from the street and beach. Each island provides outdoor showers, shading from the summer sun, and access to concession facilities.

Three primary sites at Beach 86th, 97th, and 106th streets were the focus of the project with a secondary site at Beach 116th Street. Spanning more than 1.5 miles, the architects sought to restore amenities and create a visual link between the sites—without the benefit of a connecting boardwalk. Design and construction were conceived and completed within five months.

Facilities that survived the storm were maintained at the existing elevation and pile supports for the boardwalk were left exposed to stabilize the dunes. A pair of ramps was constructed to bring beachgoers to each island: one from the street side and one from the beach. The beach side was also connected to the sand by a series of tiered platform steps, providing a theatrical setting for visitors to lounge and enjoy the vista.

Each facility was wrapped in a graphic element with an overlaid area map of the Rockaways, providing a visual icon orienting the visitor along the length of the beachfront.

SHORE FRONT PARKWAY

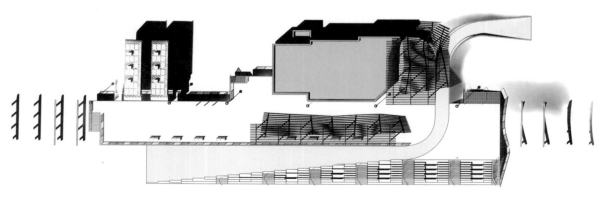

BEACH

N

SHORE FRONT PARKWAY

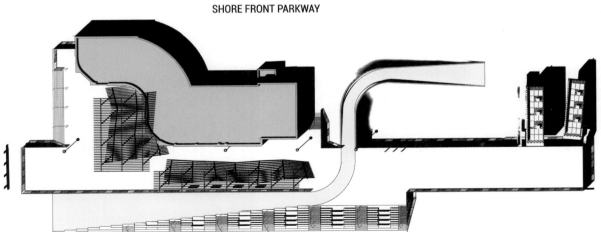

BEACH

⟩⟩ MODULAR BEACH STRUCTURES

⟩ 35 MODULARS in Rockaway Beach (Queens), Coney Island, Brooklyn,
and Staten Island
⟩ GARRISON ARCHITECTS
⟩ Department of Parks and Recreation, 2013

After Hurricane Sandy devastated much of the infrastructure of New York City's beaches, City agencies undertook the restoration of the ocean front in the seven months between the storm and Memorial Day 2013. Garrison Architects' contribution to this effort was the design of rapidly built, resilient, and sustainable comfort and lifeguard stations raised above the 500-year flood level.

To meet such an extraordinarily short design and construction schedule, all of the buildings were designed as modular structures that could be fabricated off-site in a factory while foundations and utilities were being installed on the beach. The buildings were planned as pairs, with space between and below to allow views of the beach and sky.

An integrated sustainable approach dictated narrow profiles, double exterior skins, and continuous clerestories to provide natural light and ventilation. Photovoltaic cell supplement energy requirements, and special stainless steel alloys are used to prevent salt air corrosion.

ABOVE ⟩⟩ Coney Island Comfort Stations, View from the boardwalk.
ABOVE, RIGHT ⟩⟩ Modular beach structures.

» OLMSTED CENTER

> QUEENS, 117-02 Roosevelt Avenue, Flushing Meadows-Corona Park
> BKSK ARCHITECTS
> Department of Parks and Recreation, 2014

OPPOSITE, TOP » An elevated boardwalk over a rain garden leads visitors to the center's new main entrance. OPPOSITE, BOTTOM » The site's water channel system is on full display along the path to the center's secondary entrance. BELOW » These stormwater diagrams illustrate the impact of new flood control strategies before implementation (left) and after (right).

This renovation and expansion of the Olmsted Center provides an opportunity for the use of innovative, pioneering sustainability strategies. The existing facility is a pre-engineered structure built by Skidmore, Owings & Merrill for the 1964-65 World's Fair as an administration center, which was later inherited by the New York City Department of Parks and Recreation. The agency's desire to remain at this location, which sits four feet below Federal Emergency Management Agency's 100-year flood plain, coupled with its need for more program space led to ambitious efforts in addressing the issue of rising currents. (The site was navigable by boat after Hurricane Sandy.) To achieve a sustainable site (the project is aiming for LEED Gold certification) that both celebrates the beauty of water systems and works in tandem with extensive flood control strategies, a network of structured and natural features will be implemented. These include wetland detention areas showcased as rain gardens and a raised water channel system that will convey, treat, and exhibit storm water runoff throughout the property. Meanwhile, the new 10,000-square -foot addition, raised to a height above the flood plain, celebrates the engineering ingenuity of the 1964 structure with its exposed steel structure that is incorporated into the exterior architecture of the building. Once completed, the new administration center will be a symbol of the Department's civic role as the steward of New York City's public parks.

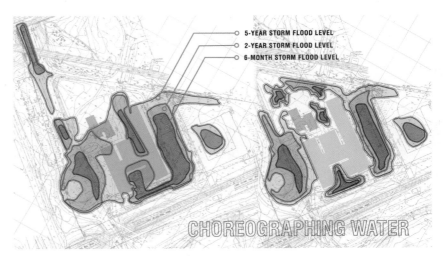

5-YEAR STORM FLOOD LEVEL
2-YEAR STORM FLOOD LEVEL
6-MONTH STORM FLOOD LEVEL

CHOREOGRAPHING WATER

≫ WEST HARLEM PIERS AND PARK

> ⟩ MANHATTAN, between 129th and 133rd streets along the Hudson River
> ⟩ W ARCHITECTURE AND LANDSCAPE ARCHITECTURE
> ⟩ Economic Development Corporation, 2008

A narrow 69,000-square-foot parking lot was expanded through creative planning into a 105,526-square-foot park that re-imagines the threshold between
the City and the Hudson River in a sustainable and meaningful way.

No wider than a tennis court, the site had been cut off from the neighborhood by adjacent traffic and the highway above. This point of access to the river,
historically a natural cove between adjacent bluffs, and more recently an industrial port, had become a paved and fenced parking lot.

Working closely with the community, the architects created a master plan
for the adjacent 40-block area. The first phase of the plan was the creation
of West Harlem Piers Park which transformed the adjacent road to promote
pedestrian access, new community piers, and the total re-envisioning of the
parking lot.

LEFT ≫ West Harlem Piers and Park.
ABOVE ≫ View of the Hudson River.

The piers follow sand bar formation patterns, rather than historic pier configurations. Additionally, the piers enable various activities including fishing, excursion boating, and general recreation. The upland plant material creates two ecologies: a woodland with mixed deciduous trees, low understory and perennial ground cover, and a cove which features colorful 300-foot-long seaside perennial beds at either end of the park and a sloped lawn. A bikeway edges the park and the narrowed Marginal Way with new sidewalks connects the street to the rest of the neighborhood.

The project involved phased construction to narrow the existing adjacent highway without disrupting traffic flow. Piers and roadway were the first phase, while upland improvements completed the park during phase two.

CULTURAL FACILITIES »

» **MUSEUMS + THEATERS + ART**

» **LIBRARIES**

New York City is a world-renowned cultural center, although when most people think of what it has to offer, they think of major institutions in Manhattan. Most of the museums, libraries, and theaters built in recent decades, however, have gone up in other boroughs. Many are devoted to specific interests, intended to serve surrounding neighborhoods or particular ethnic groups. Examples of these include the Studio Museum in Harlem, El Museo del Barrio in Upper Manhattan, and the Weeksville Heritage Center in Brooklyn.

In Queens, a number of museums and other cultural centers on the old World's Fair Grounds have recently been expanded and redesigned, including the Queens Theatre in the Park, the New York Hall of Science, and Queens Museum of Art. On the western edge of Queens, there is the Museum of the Moving Image and in Long Island City, the Noguchi Museum and a new entry pavilion to the MoMA PS 1. There are new buildings at the Staten Island Zoo, and new facilities at Historic Richmond Town and Snug Harbor.

Public libraries are a vital part of the modern city. These buildings are part of the cultural fabric and act as community centers in an era of dwindling, non-commercial public space. Libraries in Manhattan, the Bronx, and on Staten Island are part of the New York Public Library. Brooklyn, which was an independent city until 1898, has its own very large and impressive library system, as does Queens.

Among these three independent library systems are more than 200 individual branch libraries, spanning every neighborhood of the City. These include more than 60 branch libraries built as a gift to the City by Andrew Carnegie in the early 1900s.

MUSEUMS
+
THEATERS
+
ART

⟫ BRIC ARTS MEDIA AND URBANGLASS

> BROOKLYN, 647 Fulton Street
> LEESER ARCHITECTURE
> Department of Cultural Affairs, 2013

This renovation transforms an underutilized theater into a center for digital media and arts exploration. The re-imagined building will provide performance theaters, television recording studios, art galleries, classrooms, administrative spaces, and a glass blowing facility for two arts organizations, BRIC Arts Media and UrbanGlass.

The design was influenced by the theater's location in one of New York City's emerging cultural centers—the Brooklyn Academy of Music Cultural District. The primary objective of this project is to visually open the 1918 Strand Theater to the street signifying the building's rebranding as a cultural institution.

Throughout the design process, Leeser Architecture worked with both arts organizations to create a unified space that meets the complex programmatic demands of highly specific uses. Both groups are identified on the exterior of the 61,000-square-foot building, with windows allowing for passersby to view the unique creative processes within. BRIC's television studios are visible from the street, as well as within the building, visually educating and intriguing students and visitors. The spaces are designed with a flexible infrastructure, allowing them to evolve as the users' needs grow and change. The 250-seat main flexible theater accommodates performances ranging from dance to rock concerts.

The project received an Excellence in Design award from the Public Design Commission of the City of New York in 2010.

ABOVE ⟫ The exterior façade redesigned as an inviting and accessible community facility.
LEFT ⟫ Stage interior.
OPPOSITE ⟫ Elevation.

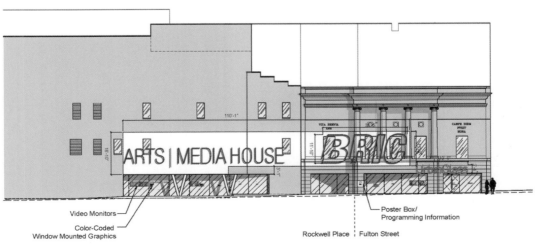

Video Monitors

Color-Coded
Window Mounted Graphics

Poster Box/
Programming Information

Rockwell Place | Fulton Street

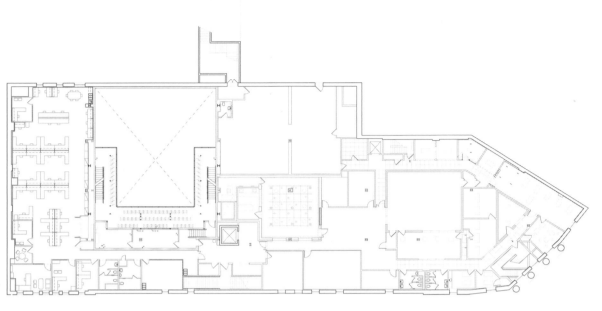

OPPOSITE, TOP » Second floor plan.
LEFT » The façade of the ground floor
is designed to increase the visibility and
accessibility of the cultural organizations
housed within the building. TOP RIGHT »
A television recording studio visible from
the lobby. ABOVE, BOTTOM RIGHT » The
theater is an educational tool designed
for flexibility. The design of the theater
accommodates many different user groups
whether it be students, a local performance group, or a musical act.

➤ BRONX RIVER ART CENTER

> ⟩ THE BRONX, 1087 East Tremont Avenue
> ⟩ SAGE + COOMBE ARCHITECTS
> ⟩ Department of Cultural Affairs, 2015

OPPOSITE ➤ Bronx River Art Center as seen from the elevated subway platform. BELOW ➤ Developed elevation.

The Bronx River Art Center occupies a four-story former warehouse bordering the Bronx River Greenway. It has a clear mission: to foster arts education within a framework of environmental stewardship. Taking this as design inspiration, Sage and Coombe Architects developed environmental and architectural strategies that work in tandem. The project has been registered with the United States Green Building Council with the goal of achieving LEED Silver certification.

The design includes classroom studios, a media lab, a pottery studio, and several multi-purpose classrooms. Offices for the staff are placed in counterpoint to the open classrooms for supervision and to create a sense of community, while rental studios and tenant offices provide the institution with income. On the ground floor, a public event space opens onto the garden and the Bronx River. The public gallery faces Tremont Avenue, providing the Center with a strong and visible presence that links to the community it serves.

To take advantage of the project's visibility from Tremont Avenue and the Greenway, as well as from the elevated subway that circumnavigates the site, the building will be wrapped with a supergraphic that announces the Center and its mission.

The project received an AIA Merit Award for Unbuilt Design in 2011 and an Excellence in Design award in 2010 from the Public Design Commission of the City of New York.

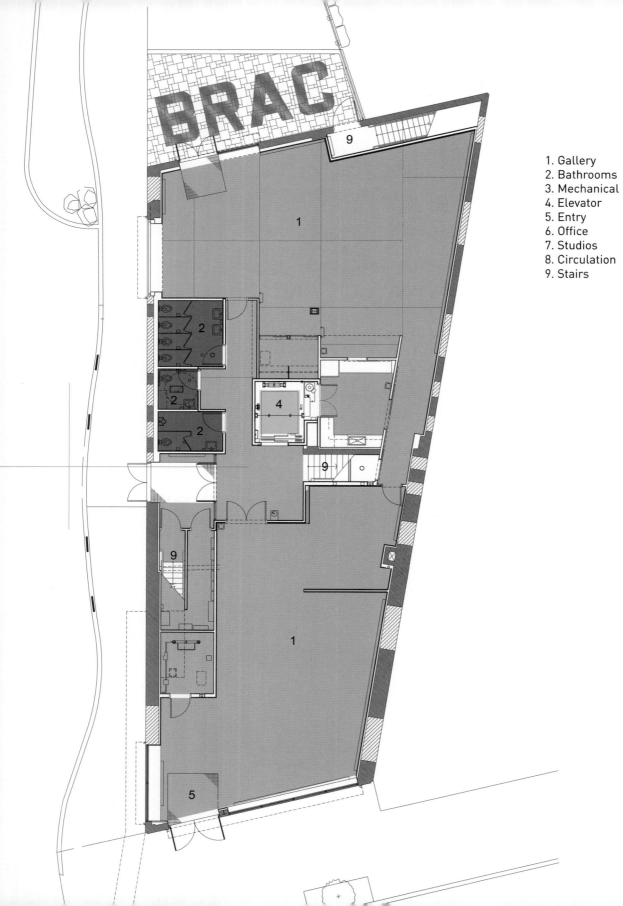

1. Gallery
2. Bathrooms
3. Mechanical
4. Elevator
5. Entry
6. Office
7. Studios
8. Circulation
9. Stairs

OPPOSITE » Bronx River Art Center - Entry and gallery level plan. RIGHT » Bronx River Art Center as seen from river banks. BELOW, LEFT » Second floor plan: offices and classroom studios. BELOW, CENTER » Third floor plan: artist studios. BELOW, RIGHT » Fourth floor plan: classroom studios.

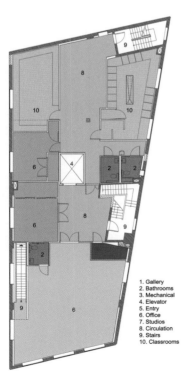

1. Gallery
2. Bathrooms
3. Mechanical
4. Elevator
5. Entry
6. Office
7. Studios
8. Circulation
9. Stairs
10. Classrooms

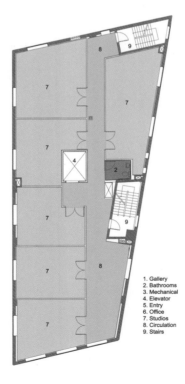

1. Gallery
2. Bathrooms
3. Mechanical
4. Elevator
5. Entry
6. Office
7. Studios
8. Circulation
9. Stairs

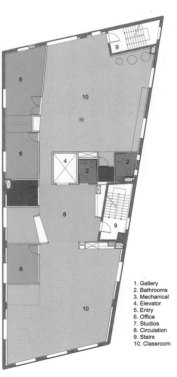

1. Gallery
2. Bathrooms
3. Mechanical
4. Elevator
5. Entry
6. Office
7. Studios
8. Circulation
9. Stairs
10. Classroom

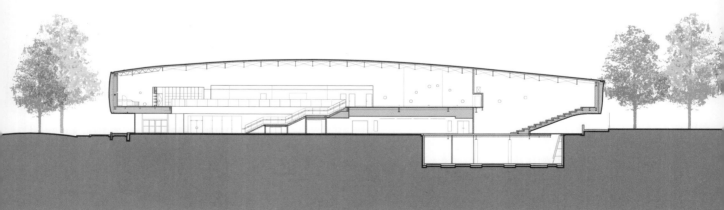

≫ BROOKLYN CHILDREN'S MUSEUM

> BROOKLYN, 145 Brooklyn Avenue
> RAFAEL VIÑOLY ARCHITECTS
> Department of Cultural Affairs, 2008

Serving a growing audience of children and families, the Brooklyn Children's Museum wanted a new public presence that would contribute to the vitality of the surrounding community. Rafael Viñoly Architects achieved this goal by creating a new 56,000-square-foot structure that differs from its context in color as well as physical form, yet remains welcoming and deferential to the museum's existing structure. The architecture of the new building is inviting to children, with a glittering envelope of yellow ceramic tiles that create a landmark attraction in the ethnically diverse residential neighborhood of Crown Heights.

The design expanded and reconfigured the existing 1977 museum. Two stories of new construction added a library, exhibition galleries, a café, and classrooms. The new plan and second floor galleries are integrated with the existing structure through open staircases and vertical circulation cores. The design provides access to the existing rooftop terrace and outdoor theater, linking these spaces directly to the second-floor Kids' Café. Throughout the building, specially designed features ensure that it remains accessible to children. Additional wooden handrails are mounted at a low level, and porthole windows punctuate the building envelope at a variety of heights and angles.

The Brooklyn Children's Museum is New York City's first LEED-certified museum and the first to tap geothermal wells for heating and cooling purposes. Wherever possible, construction used rapidly renewable and recycled materials and incorporated high-performance and sustainable features. Photovoltaic cells on exterior walls convert solar energy directly into electrical power, and energy-saving sensors control the interior lighting and ventilation systems.

ABOVE ≫ Perspective view from Brooklyn Avenue and St. Marks Avenue. OPPOSITE, BOTTOM ≫ Building section.

BELOW, TOP ⟫ An outdoor terrace on the existing museum roof provides the opportunity for play, performance, and dining. RIGHT ⟫ The undulating form and brilliant color of the 8.1 million yellow ceramic tiles on the façade. BOTTOM ⟫ Aerial view of the museum with the New York City skyline in the background.

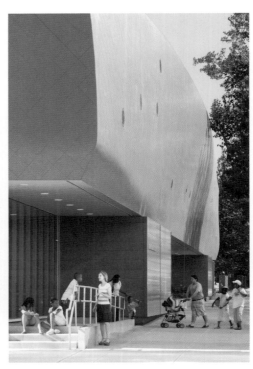

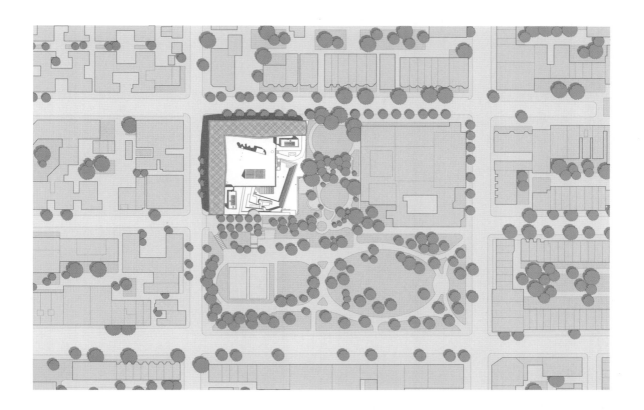

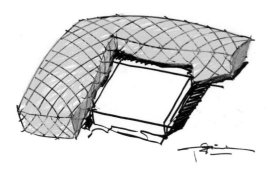

TOP >> Ground floor plan: reception, administrative offices, main hall, classroom. ABOVE >> Concept sketch. RIGHT >> Museum lobby with view to the southern wing. The entrance of the existing museum was renovated to deliver a spacious, light-filled, and child-friendly space.

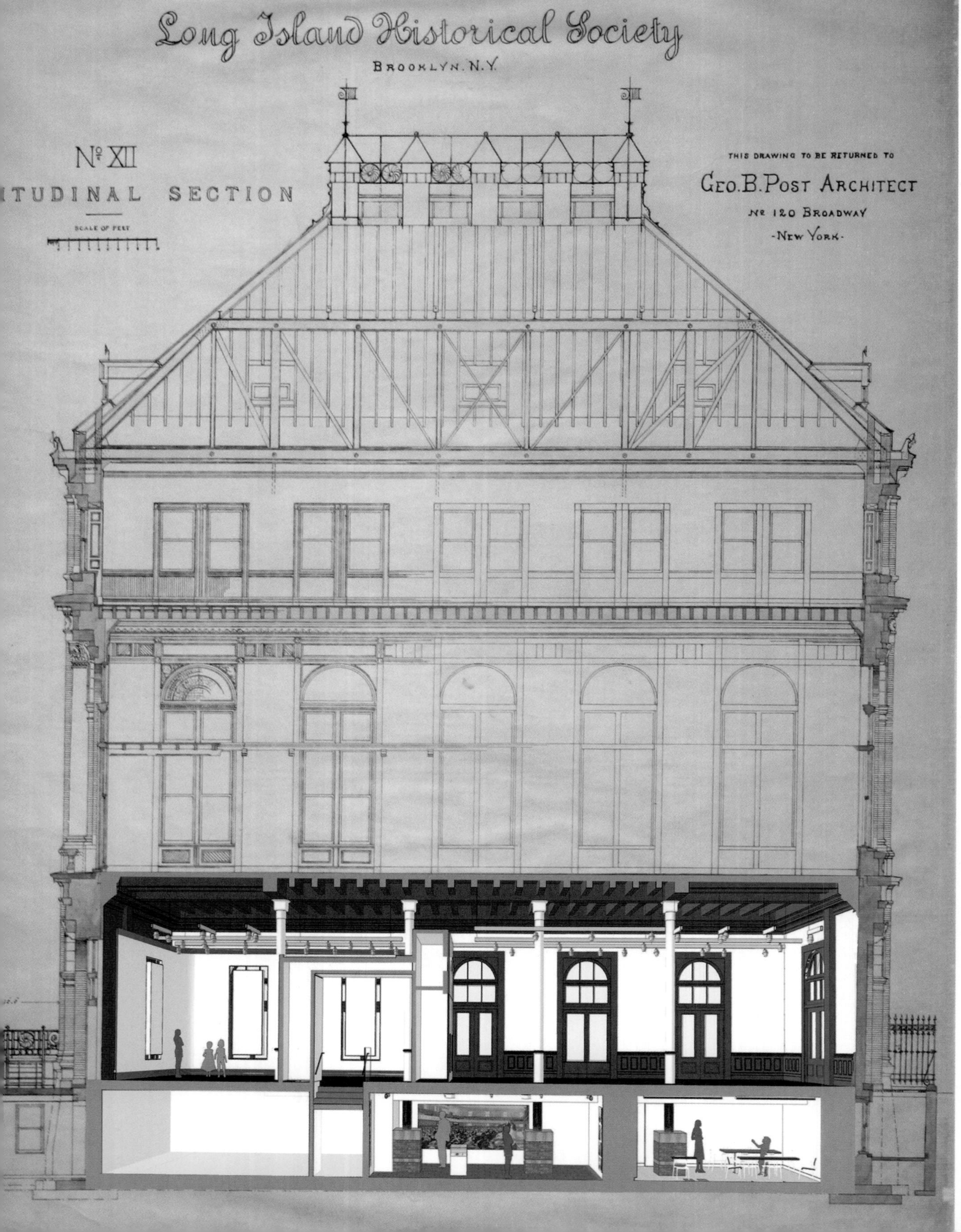

Long Island Historical Society

BROOKLYN. N.Y.

Nº XII

ITUDINAL SECTION

SCALE OF FEET

THIS DRAWING TO BE RETURNED TO

Geo. B. Post Architect

Nº 120 Broadway

-New York-

⟫ BROOKLYN HISTORICAL SOCIETY

> BROOKLYN, 128 Pierrepont Street
> CHRISTOFF:FINIO ARCHITECTURE
> Department of Cultural Affairs, 2015

OPPOSITE ⟫ Rerouting ductwork in and behind walls keeps focus on the original architecture.
BELOW ⟫ The building circa 1890, and today.

To create a modern gallery and event space in this landmark building, the architects first needed to restore the ground level and basement spaces back to their original 19th century architecture. Next, a new wall surface was designed to float free of the original ornate wood detailing on the walls, floors, and ceiling. This added layer will accommodate the mechanical services in the space between old and new. Abstracted forms of ornament—a new reception desk, and black aluminum mosaic floor will update the building.

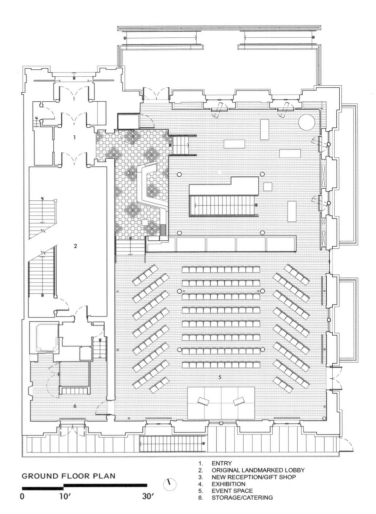

GROUND FLOOR PLAN

0   10'   30'

1. ENTRY
2. ORIGINAL LANDMARKED LOBBY
3. NEW RECEPTION/GIFT SHOP
4. EXHIBITION
5. EVENT SPACE
6. STORAGE/CATERING

TOP LEFT ≫ View from the new reception and gallery. TOP RIGHT ≫ Ground level plan. RIGHT ≫ Lower level classroom. OPPOSITE, TOP ≫ The original event space. OPPOSITE, BOTTOM ≫ View of reclaimed event space.

 **CARRIAGE HOUSES**

> STATEN ISLAND, 145 Arthur Kill Road
> RICE+LIPKA ARCHITECTS
> Department of Cultural Affairs, 2015

This project will provide exhibition and storage facilities for the Staten Island Historical Society's 62 historic carriages, as well as an exhibition gallery, a restoration area, and a multi-purpose space for educational programs and events. Departing from the original program for a single 3,000-square-foot metal building that could only partially house the collection, Rice+Lipka Architects organized the functions in three, arched-steel buildings that will provide the full 10,000 square feet needed to house the entire collection. The deeply corrugated arch spans were sized to maximize storage capacity.

The multiple houses are carefully situated to frame a series of spaces for the organization's frequent outdoor events. Brightly colored end walls create playful event backdrops with covered porches designed as platforms for outdoor activities. This will open programming and create a new identity for the Staten Island Historical Society.

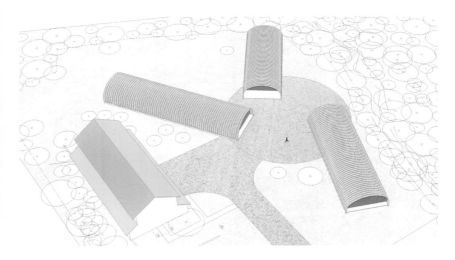

LEFT ≫ View of colored end walls.
ABOVE ≫ Birds-eye view of three storage structures arranged around a central gravel courtyard.

LEFT » View of colored end walls.
BELOW » View of central courtyard.
OPPOSITE, TOP » Site elevations.
OPPOSITE, BOTTOM » General site
plan of existing building and three
new storage facilities.

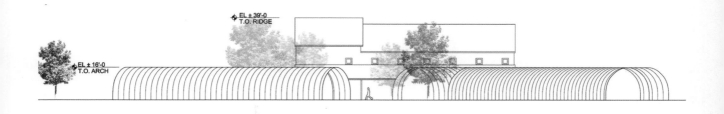

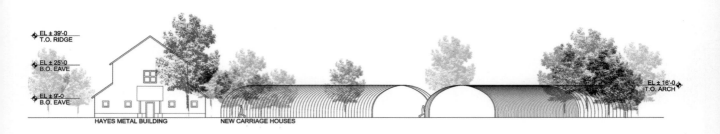

HAYES METAL BUILDING NEW CARRIAGE HOUSES

EL ± 39'-0 T.O. RIDGE
EL ± 25'-0 B.O. EAVE
EL ± 9'-0 B.O. EAVE
EL ± 16'-0 T.O. ARCH
EL ± 39'-0 T.O. RIDGE
EL ± 16'-0 T.O. ARCH

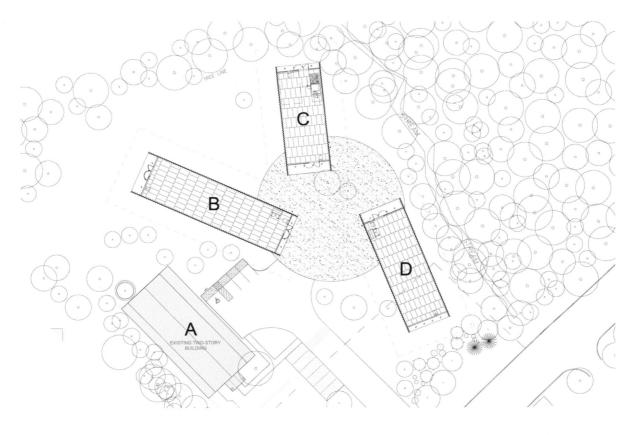

≫ EL MUSEO DEL BARRIO

> MANHATTAN, 1230 Fifth Avenue
> GRUZEN SAMTON ARCHITECTS (now part of IBI Group)
> Department of Cultural Affairs, 2010

OPPOSITE ≫ Detail of Fifth Avenue lobby interior. BELOW ≫ Detail of courtyard interior.

Gruzen Samton Architects planned, programmed, designed, and provided construction administration for the renovation of a prominent Hispanic organization located in the historic Heckscher Foundation for Children Building on Manhattan's Museum Mile. The design team worked closely with the client to fulfill its goal of creating an open and inviting new public face for the museum through comprehensively rethinking of the facility—most significantly through the redesign of the courtyard, lobby, galleries and, the design of an additional café.

The original courtyard was an enclosed space at sidewalk level with an uninviting wrought-iron fence entrance on Fifth Avenue offering the only public access. The design team completely redesigned the courtyard to accommodate

a wide variety of activities, from music and dance to dining and lounging. The courtyard was raised distancing visitors from traffic and commotion. The design features a multicolored floor finish of blue and beige-pigmented concrete combined with pink and yellow pavers laid out in an irregular grid.

The original exterior masonry wall of the eastern side of the courtyard was replaced with a new glass wall extended further to the west. This move significantly enlarged the interior lobby space to create a feeling that the exterior courtyard and interior lobby are one large room. This new glass enclosed space, called the Link, floods the lobby with natural light and connects the Fifth Avenue lobby to the café and gallery. The lobby's ash-slatted ceiling offers a visual counterpoint to the metal ceiling of the Link and exterior canopy, whereas the new terrazzo floor connects the lobby to the café and courtyard. The new museum shop is incorporated into the lobby by two glass and two wood-lined walls. An operable glass partition divides the lobby as needed for special events.

The design team completely gutted the interior space to create modern new facilities. The scope of work included significant improvements to gallery spaces, offices, and other important functional zones, along with extensive upgrades to the facility's lighting, audiovisual, security, fire protection, and elevators. The entrance's original figurative faience tile panels, designed by William Grueby, were carefully removed and remounted in the building's 104th Street lobby.

BELOW » Building section.

LEFT » Detail of entrance.
BELOW, LEFT » Main lobby.
BELOW, TOP » Doorways.
BELOW, BOTTOM » Gallery space.

⟫ IRISH REPERTORY THEATRE

> MANHATTAN, 132 West 22nd Street
> GARRISON ARCHITECTS
> Department of Cultural Affairs, 2014

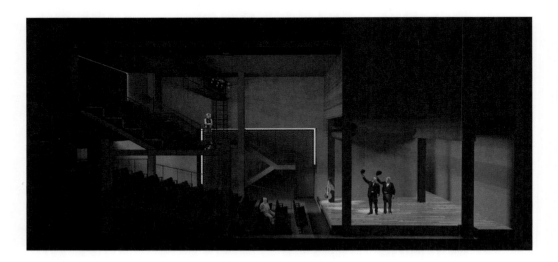

The Irish Repertory Theatre is located in the Stanwick Building in New York City's Chelsea neighborhood. During the 23 years that the IRT has been presenting plays in the current space, the biggest challenge has been the awkward relationship of the side seating to the stage. Although the 30 side seats offer close proximity to the performance, they give only a peripheral view of the stage and are often the target of audience criticism.

The renovation project involves all of the theater's performance and backstage spaces. Improvements include removing portions of the floor above to create a balcony, thereby replacing the side seating and freeing up more usable back stage area. The balcony addition will seat 40 audience members with direct, unobstructed sight lines. The new two-story space created by this alteration will improve the spatial quality and acoustics of the main theater and reflect the high caliber of the performances.

The proposed redesign will also improve the existing mechanical systems and resolve all code compliance issues, including accessibility, fire protection and egress. It will use regional and recycled materials, and low-emitting adhesive, paints, flooring, and composite wood products. With the project's Green Power program, low flow fixtures to reduce water use by 20%, construction waste management, and a construction IAQ management plan, the project is on schedule to achieve LEED Silver certification.

OPPOSITE » Section perspective.
TOP » View from stage.
BOTTOM » Top balcony.

» MOMA PS1

> QUEENS, 22-25 Jackson Avenue
> ANDREW BERMAN ARCHITECT
> Department of Cultural Affairs, 2011

Andrew Berman Architect designed a structure for entry, ticketing, and art display at MoMA PS1, an exhibition space of contemporary experimental art. Visitors to the museum will enter in, and then pass through this building the main courtyard on their way to the galleries. The approach to this project flowed from the nature of the site itself-the geometry and materials. The construction is of cast concrete with doors assembled of hot rolled steel and glazed with surface-applied laminated glass sheets.

The building won an American Institute of Architects New York Merit Award in 2012.

LEFT » MoMA PS1 entrance building.
ABOVE » Detail.

OPPOSITE, TOP LEFT ≫ Door detail.
OPPOSITE, TOP RIGHT ≫ Interior.
OPPOSITE, BOTTOM ≫ Courtyard doors.
ABOVE ≫ Interior, bookstore.

» MUSEUM OF THE MOVING IMAGE

> Queens, 36-01 35th Avenue
> LEESER ARCHITECTURE
> Department of Cultural Affairs, 2011

Housed in one of the buildings that comprised the Astoria Studio complex in the 1920s, the Museum of the Moving Image contains a comprehensive collection dedicated to educating the public about the art, history, technique, and technology of film, television, and digital media. Leeser Architecture's expansion and renovation of this unique museum allows for the interplay of rich moving image history with innovative technology and edge design.

Visitors enter the building through a portal of semi-transparent, mirrored glass, displaying the museum logo. The lobby is shaped by a surface strategically cut and folded to offer space for the projection of moving images. Its faceted interior indicates access to the major program elements, which begin adjacent to the lobby and move throughout the building, including a 267-seat theater, education center, screening room, changing exhibition gallery, collection storage facility, special events space, and courtyard. The exterior features another cut-and-folded surface, wrapping the addition in an innovatively designed pattern of triangular metal panels.

ABOVE, LEFT AND RIGHT TOP »
Museum's exterior.

The expanded museum integrates the existing structure with the new addition through a grand hallway, which connects the two. It is an environment where complexity is created from the convergence of imposing, enduring architecture and the fleeting transparency of the filmic image.

The detailing on the façade is as minimal as possible, yet it clearly defines edges, joints, surfaces, folds and cuts. The thinness of material is emphasized

LEFT » The glass entry way creates a bright portal between the museum experience and the outside world. BELOW, TOP » The white walls of the entrance provide a seamless backdrop for a 50-foot-long panoramic projection exhibit. The lobby is shaped by the underside of the main theater, efficiently using the space while creating a dynamic ceiling below. BELOW, BOTTOM LEFT » Throughout the museum, color is used in stark contrast to the white finishes to provide a heightened experience of space. Each punch of color harkens a portal into a new programmatic element, such as a theater or exhibition space. BELOW, BOTTOM RIGHT » The museum gift shop was redesigned focussing on the customer experience.

LEFT »The main theater uses a similar system of open joints to make surfaces appear suspended in space. Here, the softness required to accomplish acoustic dampening of sound is expressed through the softness of the individual woven felt, vacuum formed panels.

through open joints; no caulking is used on the exterior. A complex system of rain gutters behind the façade panels allows for this effect of weightlessness and sharp precision.

The museum uses reflective roofing, recycled and regional materials, air quality measures, electrical efficiency, and water efficiency to achieve LEED Silver certification. The project won the Starnet Design Grand Prize, an Excellence in Design award from the Public Design Commission of the City of New York in 2011,and the Red Dot Design Award in 2013.

ABOVE, LEFT » Video editing booths encourage visitors to participate in the world of film production. ABOVE, RIGHT » The history of cinema is showcased through memorabilia and artifacts in an intimate exhibition space.

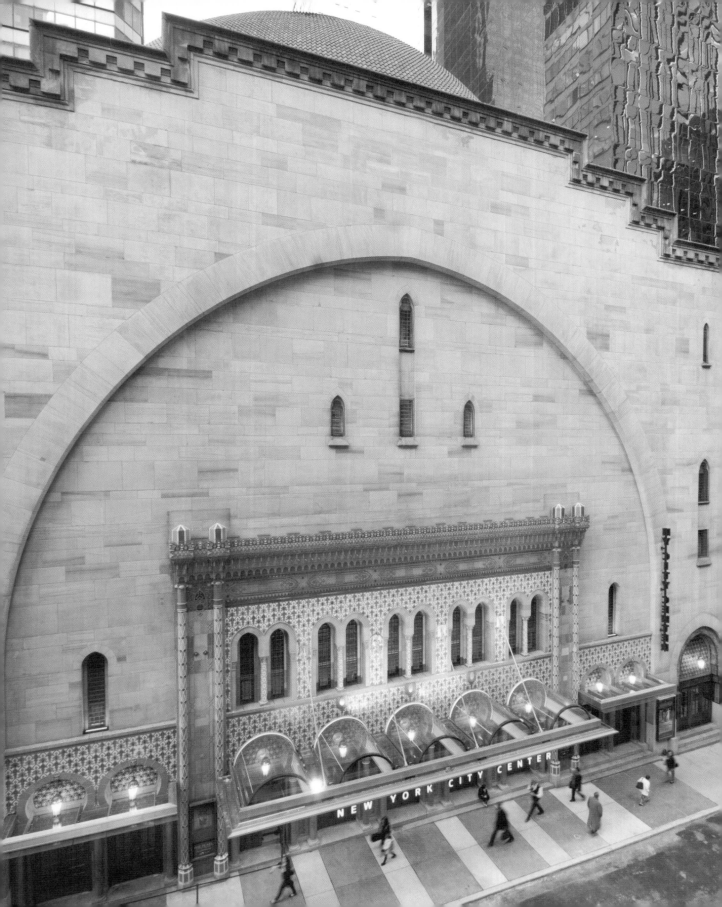

» NEW YORK CITY CENTER

> MANHATTAN, 131 West 55th Street
> DATTNER ARCHITECTS
> Department of Cultural Affairs, 2011

OPPOSITE AND BELOW » New York City Center façade renovation.

Dattner Architects designed the façade restoration and roof replacement for the landmarked New York City Center. With its unique neo-Moorish façade, it was built in 1923 as a meeting hall for the members of the Ancient Order of the Nobles of the Mystic Shrine. After reverting to City ownership, the building was saved from destruction by Mayor Fiorello LaGuardia and New York City Council President Newbold Morris, who created Manhattan's first performing arts center: a 2,750-seat home for theater, music, and dance.

Dattner Architects renovated the West 56th Street elevation, which is primarily brick, in a variety of bonding patterns with glazed terracotta and small amounts of stone for copings and other details.

Construction was phased to allow the building to remain in operation throughout the restoration. Ennead Architects designed the interior restoration.

NEW YORK HALL OF SCIENCE GARDEN OF SCIENCE

> QUEENS, 47-01 111th Street
> BKSK ARCHITECTS
> Department of Cultural Affairs, 2007

This 30,000-square-foot Garden of Science doubles the size of the New York Hall of Science's original "Kidpower!" teaching park to accommodate an increasing number of visitors with young children. The design was informed by the latest research on the developmental abilities of preschool-age children, specifically by how children's play contributes to the early formation of cognitive skills. The challenge was to create a playground and exhibit that both encourages activity and sparks the imagination. The result is an "outdoor classroom" for new educational programming that enables young learners to engage with the natural and built environment.

ABOVE » A nest constructed of ropes woven through a metal armature is a natural environment for a child's imagination. RIGHT » Aerial view of the garden.

OPPOSITE, TOP LEFT ≫ A small neighborhood of open framed wood houses. OPPOSITE, TOP RIGHT ≫ Architect's sketch of the Garden's meandering paths, which change in character as they cut through the landscape, crossing low hills and moving through a small mysterious forest shrouded by mist. OPPOSITE, BOTTOM ≫ The water vortex encircled by steel drums. ABOVE ≫ Exploratory play encourages cognitive development in addition to providing an outlet for physical activity.

In an age of ecological awareness, it was deemed important to provide a space to heighten young visitors' connection with the landscape and, by extension, with their surrounding world. Since children are physically close to the ground, the varying terrain and surfaces became keydesign elements. Plantings extend the range of sensory stimulation and change throughout the seasons, providing a wide palette of colors and scents.

A meandering path, textured with a snake-skin pattern of inset stone chevrons, runs through a valley between low, lushly planted hills. In contrast to the landscaped environment, white walls of structural steel pilings are set perpendicular to the path. They channel activities into distinct areas that encourage discoveries related to shelter, sound, texture, light, and materiality.

It received a Design Award from the American Institute of Architects New York Chapter in 2008.

≫ NEW YORK HALL OF SCIENCE

> QUEENS, 47-01 111th Street
> ENNEAD ARCHITECTS (formerly the Polshek Partnership)
> Department of Cultural Affairs, 2004

The juxtaposition of the luminous folded planes of this expansion with the undulating cellular concrete and dark cobalt cast glass frame of the iconic Harrison & Abramovitz 1964 World's Fair pavilion, creating a new identity for the New York Hall of Science. This expansion redefined and enlarged the exhibit space, modifying the visitor's overall experience. Translucent fiberglass panels wrap around the hall for a transparency that contrasts with the opacity of the original building. The north end of the exhibit hall is a glass prism which admits direct sunlight through its curtain wall and skylight, activating a glass sculpture commissioned as part of the City's Percent for Art program. A transparent base on the north allows glimpses into the Hall's interior, furthering the museum's goal of accessibility.

The Discovery Labs, adjacent and open to the new exhibition spaces on the upper and lower galleries, are given visible identity to draw in visitors. Also connected to the new hall, an exhibition space for traveling shows is provided in a light-controlled gallery. Outside, the luminous addition provides an anchor for the newly landscaped area that is home to the renovated Rocket Park and also accommodates outdoor programming. At night, the addition becomes a subtly glowing lantern in Flushing Meadows Park.

LEFT ≫ The translucent Hall of Light
hovers over the glass enclosed base.

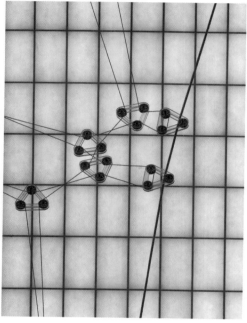

LEFT, TOP ≫ The exposed structural steel frame allows all building systems to be revealed and is a fitting armature for the exhibitry. LEFT ≫ Stair connecting exhibit halls within existing plinth. ABOVE ≫ Detail of curtain wall. OPPOSITE ≫ The north end of the Hall of Light is a glass prism that admits direct sunlight and and activates an art piece designed specifically for the hall by James Carpenter.

≫ NEW YORK HALL OF SCIENCE "KIDPOWER!" PARK

> QUEENS, 47-01 111th Street
> BKSK ARCHITECTS
> Department of Cultural Affairs, 1997

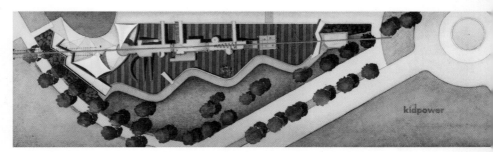

In the early 1990s, the director of the New York Hall of Science became increasingly convinced that a child's ability to understand basic principles of science could be furthered through play activity. This pioneering teaching park is the architectural realization of that vision. It was conceived through collaboration between architect and educator, and ultimately came to involve a fruitful melding of interdisciplinary contributions from landscape, exhibit, structural, child development, and safety consultants. A 30,000-square-foot permanent outdoor wing of the museum, it is the largest science park in the country and a signature element for this popular and well-attended facility. The dramatic sculptural quality of the park's built structure invites the community to discover the museum.

LEFT ≫ A series of steel pylons support a continuous metal and suspended walkway, while below an outdoor dining terrace is framed by a bold red retaining wall.
ABOVE ≫ Site plan.

The original Hall of Science building was built for the 1964 World's Fair and the character of this park was seen as a renewal of the World's Fair spirit that still pervades the site after more than 30 years. The large-scale elements of the park structure act as exhibits that raise intriguing questions about physical phenomena. A series of steel pylons carry a continuous metal tube and a suspended walkway alongside the Hall of Science terrace. The structure becomes an organizing element for the exhibits, with the regular rhythm of pylons providing a subtle sense of order within the exuberance of the shapes and colors that are the physical activities. Likewise, the alternating stripes of the resilient surfaces speak of order amidst the fun. An outdoor dining area is carved into the earth with a robustly scaled sheet piling retaining wall.

ABOVE, LEFT ≫ A series of connected rods and balls shows the physics involved in the "coupled torsion pendula" of an energy wave. ABOVE, RIGHT ≫ With the Whisper Dish a visitor can communicate to a friend on the other side of the playground. OPPOSITE ≫ The playground demonstrates the scientific principles of movement, the wind and sun, sound, and simple machines.

>> NOGUCHI MUSEUM AND SCULPTURE GARDEN

> QUEENS, 9-01 33rd Road
> SAGE AND COOMBE ARCHITECTS
> Department of Cultural Affairs, 2015

This project presented an unusual challenge in historic preservation: the museum, when renovated, was to look as if no work had taken place. Yet significant design changes to the facility's public spaces and gallery, teaching, offices and support spaces, infrastructure and building systems were required. In an effort to modernize the museum, large areas of the facility needed to be entirely rebuilt in three phases.

The first phase, completed in 2004, included the reconfiguration of galleries, design of a new bookstore and café, installation of 900 helical piles for structural stabilization, the lowering and dewatering of the cellar to form program space. The introduction of cooling and heating to all spaces was needed to ensure the Museum could remain open year-round.

For the second phase, completed in 2009, Sage and Coombe Architects replaced the garden façade in its entirety, creating an acclimatized gallery for traveling exhibits, and redesigned and rebuilt the museum's entry pavilion.

LEFT >> Main Gallery.
ABOVE >> Sculpture Garden.

ABOVE ≫ Entry pavilion.
BELOW, LEFT ≫ Garden from above.
BELOW, RIGHT ≫ Noguchi Garden
Museum. OPPOSITE ≫ View Into
upper gallery.

Matching brick to the existing weathered façade and selecting replacement windows with customized profiles to mimic the historic windows, the museum's garden façade was reconstructed without significant appearance of change. The entry pavilion was demolished and rebuilt and the interior ticketing and waiting areas were redesigned. Upstairs, the gallery renovation required the reconstruction of the existing exterior and interior envelopes to provide a thermal enclosure suitable to sustain 50% relative humidity at 70 degrees. A new mechanical room was created to house equipment and an integrated building management system was added. With climatic closure on the interior face, the gallery has become a contemporary exhibit space for visiting exhibitions.

The third and last phase of work includes the design and restoration of the Sculpture Garden and its surrounding enclosure, concluding the work to restore the museum as one of New York's most original and essential institutions.

» THE PUBLIC THEATER

> MANHATTAN, 425 Lafayette Street
> ENNEAD ARCHITECTS
> Percent for Art: Ben Rubin
> Department of Cultural Affairs, 2012

OPPOSITE » View of restored façade and new glass and steel canopy. BELOW » View of restored principal façade.

The most recent phase of Ennead Architects' ongoing renovation of The Public Theater—a new entry and lobby redesign—further revitalizes the identity of this New York City institution. The Renaissance Revival building was originally designed by Alexander Saeltzer and constructed in 1853 as the first Astor Library. In 1967, theater director Joseph Papp re-envisioned it as the home of The Public Theater.

Design goals for the 36,000-square-foot project were to preserve the historic structure and enrich the theater experience with modern amenities for patrons and a dramatic new entry and lobby. To complement the building's brownstone façade, the new stairway and ramps are made of monolithic granite. A new glass and steel canopy enhances the theater's presence on the street, providing shelter for patrons and a clear view of the newly restored and lighted façade above.

BELOW ≫ Entry lobby with new central bar and The Shakespeare Machine above by Ben Rubin. OPPOSITE, TOP ≫ View of lobby from new mezzanine. OPPOSITE, LEFT CENTER ≫ Detail of glass canopy. OPPOSITE, LEFT BOTTOM ≫ Mezzanine. OPPOSITE, FAR RIGHT ≫ View of lobby.

In the lobby interior, plasterwork on the ceilings and walls has been carefully restored, and the original archways have been reopened. The lobby features a chandelier sculpture by artist Ben Rubin, with radiating arms on which LED lights display quotes from Shakespeare. Stairs lead from the lobby to a new public mezzanine and balcony overlooking the main level. This gathering space reorganizes The Public's interior, orienting theatergoers by providing a visual connection with the various venues within the building. The centrally located box office and an entry to Joe's Pub further reinforce the the lobby's importance.

The design's careful blend of modern and historic elements reflects the nature of the acclaimed theatrical work—both traditional and experimental—for which The Public Theater is renowned.

» QUEENS BOTANICAL GARDEN VISITOR AND ADMINISTRATION CENTER

> QUEENS, 53-50 Main Street
> BKSK ARCHITECTS
> Department of Cultural Affairs, 2009

The new Queens Botanical Garden Visitor and Administration Center is the centerpiece of an ambitious capital improvement program for this institution, which occupies the former wasteland described by F. Scott Fitzgerald in *The Great Gatsby* as a "valley of ashes." It was the first garden in the country devoted to sustainable environmental stewardship. Its visitor center was the first public building in New York City to achieve a LEED Platinum certification.

At approximately 16,000 square feet, the new Queens Botanical Garden Visitor Center accommodates a reception area, auditorium, garden store, gallery space, meeting rooms, and administrative offices, with an additional 4,500 square feet of outdoor, covered event space. The building was conceived as a part of the garden landscape—not as a destination in itself, but as a backdrop to the experience of the surrounding topography, flora, fauna, and its seasonal change.

The Garden's main entrance building resembles a land-form with a sloping green roof that welcomes, shades, and offers a unique overview of the garden.

LEFT » The building was conceived as a backdrop to the seasonal changes of the garden. ABOVE » The new center was the first public building in New York City to achieve a LEED® Platinum certification.

From the building's forecourt, it appears to be a sheltered outdoor event space—a habitable grove of slanted columns that form a canopy. Entering the building involves crossing a stream of captured rainwater. From within, views are framed and walls slide away, so that staff members seem to inhabit a tree house. The resonance of these nature-inspired architectural strategies is palpable, on a site that 50 years earlier was an ashen landscape. The architecture,

ABOVE » A view of the green roof and the moat of collected rainwater.

landscape, structural, and mechanical systems of the building all play a role in making sustainability visible and tangible to the public.

The garden is located at the nexus of the most ethnically diverse county in the United States, where more than 130 languages and dialects are spoken. Community programs include gardening for children and seniors, seasonal celebrations, weddings, daily tai chi practice, and classes for visitors and professionals on everything from renewable energy to green landscaping and composting. Interpretive touchscreens display a presentation on the new building and grounds, including real-time energy data. Touchscreens and signage are translated into four languages.

The building design is the result of a community-driven planning process, which emphasized the importance of water as a resource vital to all cultures. Both the building and its site are imbued with the presence of flowing water, its abundance varying with the season to demonstrate the value of conservation and re-use.

LEFT » The forecourt's canopy is designed to funnel rainwater into a cleansing biotope basin filled with gravel and native wetland plant species. ABOVE » One of several assembly spaces at the new center, the canopied forecourt helps shape the visitor's experience of the gardens. BELOW » Site plan.

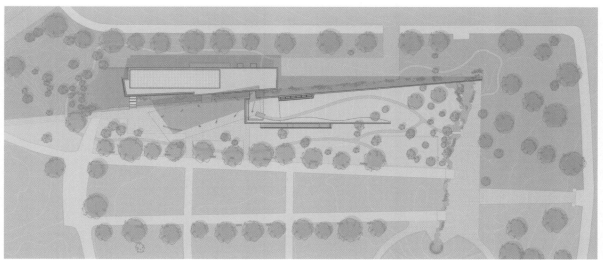

≫ QUEENS MUSEUM OF ART

> QUEENS, Flushing Meadows-Corona Park
> GRIMSHAW with Ammann & Whitney
> Department of Cultural Affairs, 2013

This project to integrate the Queens Museum of Art with Flushing Meadows Corona Park on the east, appearing vibrant and inviting from the highway on the west, while creating an interior space with room for growing permanent collections, temporary exhibition galleries, and expanded educational and public events spaces.

The 105,000-square-foot expansion allows the museum to occupy the entire building, the only structure remaining from the 1939 World's Fair. A new suite of six galleries, ranging from 800 to 2400 square feet, surrounds a central large works gallery that can accommodate concurrent exhibits and flexible curatorial choices. The central gallery is marked by a light reflecting lantern composed of glass ribs that appear to float beneath a large skylight. This crucial element allows visitors a glimpse of the sky above while directing the trajectory of natural

LEFT ≫ The west façade is equipped with glass panels that are backlit by LED lighting. Each panel bears a fritted dot pattern that distributes the fully programmable lights.
ABOVE ≫ Exterior.

BELOW ›› The west entrance will serve as the main entry point for visitors, which includes a drop-off plaza. OPPOSITE, TOP ›› Brand new skylights allow natural light to enter the space while strategically aligned louvers are positioned to diffuse the light appropriately into the galleries. OPPOSITE, CENTER ›› Cross section. OPPOSITE, BOTTOM LEFT ›› Competition sketch. OPPOSITE, BOTTOM RIGHT ›› Gallery diagram.

light entering the space. The surrounding four galleries are further shaded by a series of strategically aligned louvers, as well as two blackout galleries. A fluid glass staircase that works with the existing geometry of the building leads to additional spaces on the building's second floor. The redesign adds new exhibition spaces, as well as back of house facilities that include art storage, exhibit preparation space, and a wood shop.

A new ceremonial entry, visible from Grand Central Parkway, beckons visitors to the site and serves as a gateway to the park beyond. This new west façade is distinguished by a sculptural metal entry canopy and a series of glass panels that span the length of the building. Backlit by LED lighting, each panel has a fritted dot pattern that distributes the fully programmable lights. The glass façade serves not only as a beacon for the museum, but as a dynamic new canvas for commissioned works of art. The museum intends to commission new works for the façade on a regular basis.

The museum also has a significant educational component. The expansion has several new classrooms and support spaces allowing the museum to enhance its outreach to schools and the community, positioning the museum as a cultural center for the entire borough.

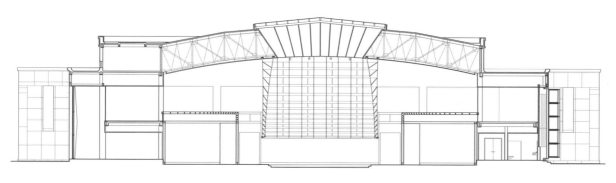

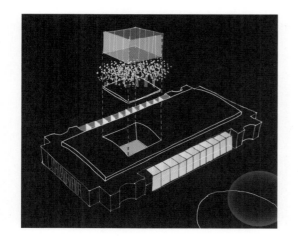

>> QUEENS THEATRE IN THE PARK

> QUEENS, 14 United Nations Avenue South,
  Flushing Meadows-Corona Park
> CAPLES JEFFERSON ARCHITECTS
> Department of Cultural Affairs, 2011

The Queens Theatre builds upon the playful circular geometries of the original 1964 Philip Johnson World's Fair complex. The new structure is a 600-person reception room, standing on axis with the giant oval of Johnson's New York State Pavilion. This nebula room is a transparent viewing pavilion from which to appreciate the park's past structures—the Unisphere, the Johnson observatory towers and the pavilions. It is a representative room for the borough, with rich materials and sunset colors that represent the festive, wide cross-section of the 109 ethnic cultures of Queens. Using the principles of Gestalt psychology and the art of perspective, a structurally glazed wall with metal fins projects at each vertical joint. The spiraling slope of the 'horizontal' mullions further intensifies the perception of curved movement in space.

LEFT >> Building in World's Fair context at dusk.
ABOVE >> Aerial view.

ABOVE, LEFT ≫ Interior concept sketch. ABOVE, RIGHT ≫ Nebula interior. BELOW ≫ Section. OPPOSITE ≫ Interior view with circular "Oculus" skylight revealing the older Philip Johnson structure beyond.

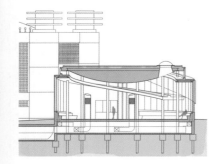

The design of the curtain wall uses a broad array of contemporary technologies including low emulsion coatings to reduce solar heat gain, silicone sealant joints in lieu of metal mullion caps, gas-filled insulating units to reduce heating costs, and laminated glass outer lights to increase unit size and provide vandalism resistance. Digital design techniques enabled fabrication of more than 5000 separate and unique glass panels that work in concert to create the illusion of perfect roundness.

This project has received several awards including Municipal Arts Society of New York 2011 MASterworks Award for Best Restoration, an A|L Design Award with special citation for Best Use of Color, the 2010 New York Construction Cultural Project of the Year, a Queens Chamber of Commerce Award and a NOMA National Award of Excellence in Architecture.

As described in the AIA Guide to New York City: "One of the few pavilions of 1964 that attempted to use fresh technology as generator of form. In this case tubular perimeter columns (as well as those supporting the observation deck) were slip-formed of concrete in a continuous casting operation that proceeded vertically. The roof, originally sheathed in translucent colored plastic, is a double diaphragm of radial cables separated by vertical pencil rods to dampen flutter. It was the architectural star of the fair; a happy park building working with park space. The reconstructed Queens Theater in the Park has brought sleek architecture and new vigor to this under-utilized complex."

⟫ QUEENS THEATRE IN THE PARK CIRCULAR LOBBY

> QUEENS, 147 United Nations Avenue South, Flushing Meadows-Corona Park
> PKSB ARCHITECTS
> Department of Cultural Affairs, 2015

BELOW ⟫ Plan.
OPPOSITE, TOP ⟫ Circular lobby.
OPPOSITE, BELOW ⟫ Carpet pattern.

The 1964 World's Fair ushered in an era of progress, invention, and an excitement for the future that deeply influenced popular culture and the aesthetics of everything from architecture and interior design to amusement parks and science fiction films. Four decades later, the fairgrounds stand as a modern relic. PKSB Architects' design will elevate the existing facility to match the quality of the recent Caples Jefferson addition and restore the spirit of the original "Theaterama," designed by venerated modernist architect Philip Johnson. An intergalactic-inspired carpet, designed by PKSB, evokes the geometry of the

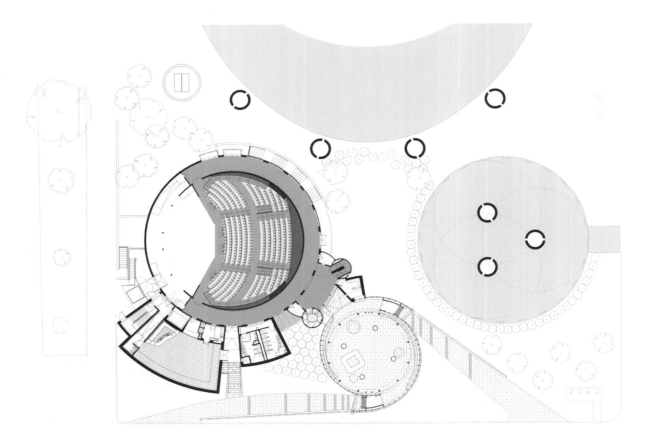

new lobby while referencing the fascination with space travel that permeated the 1964 World's Fair. The carpet will extend from the circular lobby into the main auditorium where a new raised seating platform and theatre seating will provide better sight lines, ensuring that every seat has a stellar view. Other improvements include renovating existing dressing rooms and restrooms, and adding audiovisual capabilities. These renovations, combined with the recent addition, will ensure that the theatre continues to thrive and maintain the spirit of innovation in which it was conceived.

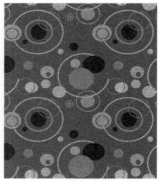

>> SNUG HARBOR CULTURAL CENTER, BUILDING E

> STATEN ISLAND, 1000 Richmond Terrace
> FREDERIC SCHWARTZ ARCHITECTS
> Department of Cultural Affairs, 2013

OPPOSITE >> Restored north façade.
BELOW >> East elevation.

Building E is the easternmost building in the row of five landmark Greek Revival style structures facing Richmond Terrace. This structure, completed in 1879, was built as a dormitory to house a then burgeoning population. In an effort to reduce operating costs in the 1950s, Sailor's Snug Harbor began demolition of certain buildings and relocated the remaining residents to the new home of Sailor's Snug Harbor in North Carolina. To prevent the possibility that further structures would be demolished and the site sold for development, City officials and private individuals combined forces on a plan of action to preserve the remaining buildings and grounds for public use.

The prime objective of this 24,000-square-foot historic preservation project was to prevent further deterioration of the building envelope of the landmark structure for the Snug Harbor Cultural Center. Design services started with providing an existing conditions evaluation and scope of work recommendations for this building, which appears on the National Register of Historic Places and was among the first buildings in New York City designated as a Landmark by the New York City Landmarks Preservation Commission.

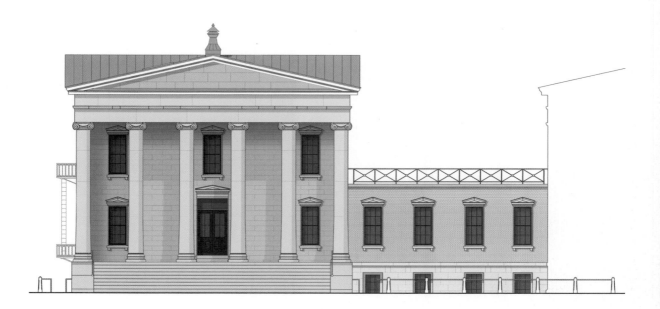

Frederic Schwartz Architects provided full design and construction-phase services including coordination of the subconsultants, preservation experts, engineering team, permitting, zoning, specification, schematic design, design development, construction documents, construction administration, shop drawing review, and on-site inspections.

Strict standards and attention to detail were required given the historic significance of the building. A new copper roof and vent details were installed and the masonry façade was cleaned, fully repointed, and rebuilt in deteriorated areas. Exact specifications for mortar type and mix, as well as appropriate cleaning and paint removal processes were required. All existing wood doors and windows were meticulously restored to match the existing details. Specific areas of the interiors that had been fire-damaged were repaired and replaced, including wood joists and flooring. The existing stormwater management in the building was upgraded and site drainage was improved.

BELOW, TOP LEFT » Fire escape.
RIGHT » Before: View of ground
floor corridor and existing interior
conditions. BELOW, RIGHT » Site
plan. BELOW, BOTTOM » Restored
east façade.

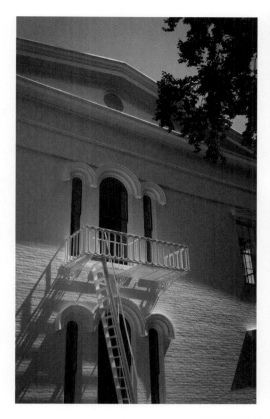

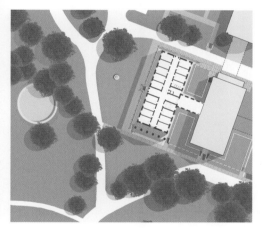

⟫ STATEN ISLAND CHILDREN'S MUSEUM

> STATEN ISLAND, 1000 Richmond Terrace
> PRENDERGAST LAUREL ARCHITECTS
> Department of Cultural Affairs, 2001

Located at historic Snug Harbor Cultural Center, the Staten Island Children's Museum occupies a three-building complex designed over a 25-year period. The emerging museum occupied a 19th century Italianate brick building in 1985, which the architects transformed to house children's exhibits and events. Ten years later, an expansion of the museum was initiated. The program included the addition of both interior and exterior exhibit space, a café, party rooms, staff offices, a loading dock, and storage rooms. The first phase incorporated an adjacent 1890's era barn while the second phase added the new connector building, which links the barn to the original museum building. The goal of this project was to join these diverse structures into an architecturally coherent series of spaces and experiences.

The historic brick barn had a basilican plan, including a roof with a central high "nave" and clerestory windows. The design positions a large flexible gallery on the upper floor to take advantage of the natural light and dramatic ceiling form. The roof structure was supported by a series of heavy timber wood trusses that were restored as a featured element. The ground floor, originally intended for housing sheep, required structural modifications to lower the floor level to create comfortable ceiling heights for a café, event space, staff offices, and restrooms. The stair connecting the two levels, inspired by a trussed drawbridge, refers to the maritime history of the site.

The connector building joins the museum and barn with a transparent steel-and-glass structure designed to maximize views of the bucolic campus and complement the historic masonry structures. The building is notched into the site to minimize its visual impact and connect the exhibit plaza to the lower level of the barn. Angled steel girders and arched beams are covered by a curved lead-coated copper roof that echoes the surrounding rolling terrain and creates transitions between the upper and lower plazas. In the galleries, either wood flooring or black slate contrast with whitewashed walls. Track lighting pro-

RIGHT ⟫ Exterior view of
connector and plaza stair, night.

vides flexible exhibit illumination. The upper plaza incorporates glass block and pre-cast concrete paving to bring natural light to a subterranean gallery, loading dock, and storage facilities on the lower level. The link to the barn is articulated by an agrarian silo structure housing an elevator. Vertical window slots allow glimpses of the plaza during travel between floors. Opportunities to connect the buildings to the site are intended to allow children to balance "controlled" exhibit tours with "running wild" in the park-like setting.

The complex offers children lessons of architectural discovery, presenting the contrasts between the textures and symmetries of the historical buildings and the playful asymmetry and transparency of the modern connector.

The Staten Island Children's Museum was selected by the New York City Art Commission for the Design Excellence Award in 2001, and received the 2004 Design Honor Award from the Staten Island Chapter of the American Institute of Architects.

OPPOSITE ≫ Barn gallery. ABOVE, TOP LEFT ≫ Upper plaza. ABOVE, TOP RIGHT ≫ Connector interior. ABOVE, BOTTOM LEFT ≫ Gallery below upper plaza. ABOVE, BOTTOM RIGHT ≫ View from original museum building to connector and barn addition.

⟫ STATEN ISLAND CHILDREN'S MUSEUM LIGHTWEIGHT STRUCTURES

> STATEN ISLAND, 1000 Richmond Terrace
> MARPILLERO POLLAK ARCHITECTS
> Department of Cultural Affairs, 2013

OPPOSITE ⟫ Meadow structure.
ABOVE ⟫ Wind scoop in fabrication by Goetz Boats.

This project implements environmental strategies that challenge the limits of traditional approaches to sustainability. Four new lightweight structures—unique in size and function—each realize a specific environmental initiative. The meadow structure is a freestanding tensile structure integrating translucent, photovoltaic thin film solar panels that support low voltage lighting. Renovations of two existing skylights integrate wind devices that ventilate the existing building and produce wind energy. Their bird-like forms, animated by the wind's fluctuations and directions, act as icons, strengthening the identity of the museum within the Snug Harbor campus.

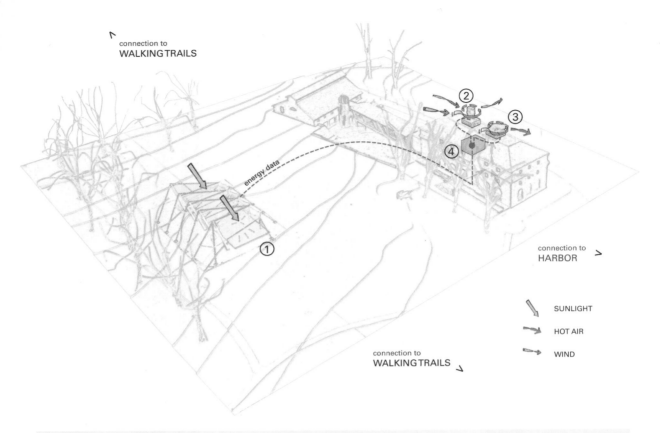

connection to
WALKING TRAILS

energy data

connection to
HARBOR

connection to
WALKING TRAILS

SUNLIGHT

HOT AIR

WIND

① **MEADOW STRUCTURE**
Integrated thin-film photovoltaic panels capture sunlight to power low-voltage lighting. The canopy shelters a 2,200 sf platform, providing program space and anchor for physical activity.

② **CUPOLA WIND TURBINE**
Generates energy to power the Interactive Display acting as an icon within the Snug Harbor campus.

③ **SKYLIGHT WIND SCOOP**
Passively ventilates the building via stack effect, acting as an icon within the Snug Harbor campus.

④ **INTERACTIVE DISPLAY**
Collects and displays data from Meadow Structure, Wind Turbine, and Wind Scoop in a new exhibition about renewable energies.

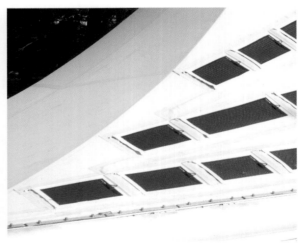

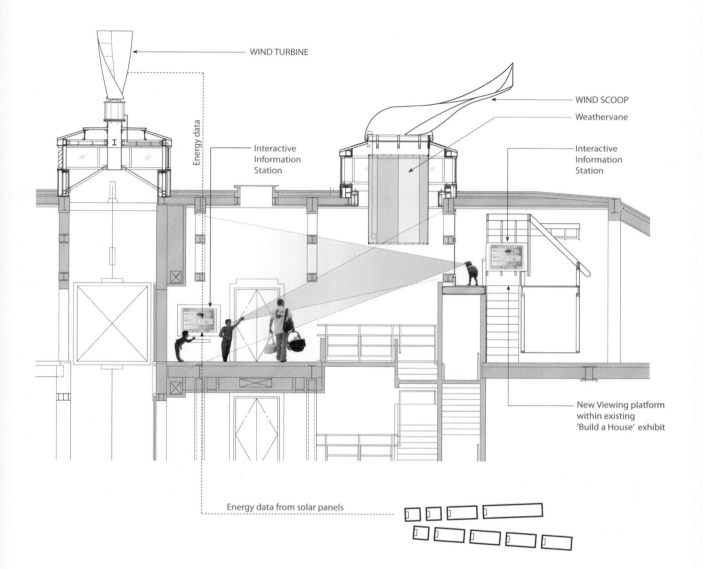

WIND TURBINE

WIND SCOOP

Weathervane

Energy data

Interactive
Information
Station

Interactive
Information
Station

New Viewing platform
within existing
'Build a House' exhibit

Energy data from solar panels

OPPOSITE, TOP ≫ Site plan and
energy strategies. OPPOSITE, BOT-
TOM LEFT ≫ Wind scoop refreshes
air supply in the museum and cools
passively. OPPOSITE, BOTTOM
RIGHT ≫ Flexible photovoltaic fabric
assembly. ABOVE ≫ Cross section
through the museum, environmental
systems and exhibit.

STATEN ISLAND CHILDREN'S ZOO CAROUSEL AND LEOPARD EXHIBIT

> STATEN ISLAND, 614 Broadway
> SLADE ARCHITECTURE
> Department of Cultural Affairs, 2013

For the redesign of the existing Children's Zoo in Staten Island, Slade Architecture created a new children's farmstead including entry building, bookstore and educational center, enclosure for the new carousel, farm exhibits, and a new outdoor leopard exhibit. This provides a welcoming public face for the zoo on Clove Road and marked the entry to the farmstead exhibit areas.

The proposed entry building also creates a public plaza that incorporates a landscaped amphitheater and a new duck pond. From here, a visitor has the option of going into the new farmstead or towards the main zoo structures and the new leopard exhibit. The circulation for the farmstead is structured to offer a variety of interconnecting paths allowing the visitor to create his or her own didactic experience. In addition to the farm animal exhibits where children can pet and feed the animals, there are a series of farm-related objects and buildings including barns, a tractor, a windmill, water features and a working garden. The main structure within the farmstead is a teaching barn where children can enter for a "behind the scenes" look at the interior.

LEFT >> Aerial plan.
ABOVE >> Deck.

A new transformable enclosure provides housing for a themed carousel ride. The jewel-like structure offers transparent views into the carousel. The enveloping glass façade is 50 percent operable for passive natural ventilation in the summer housing. During winter, the transparent plastic roof takes advantage of the sun's rays to warm the enclosure. Throughout the new area, trees become an important feature in terms of aesthetics and visual quality of the zoo.

In the leopard enclosure, the goal of creating an immersive experience is delivered through careful scripting of views. Through incorporating existing and newly introduced landscaping elements, including the characteristic trees, visitors view the leopards from different angles with unobstructed views.

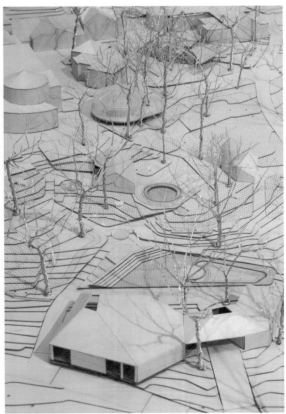

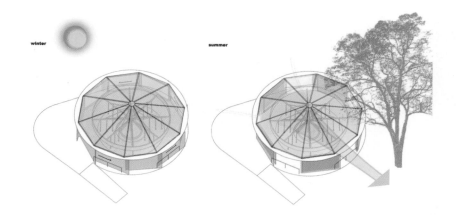

winter   summer

OPPOSITE, TOP » Carousel interior. OPPOSITE, BOTTOM LEFT » Site model. OPPOSITE, RIGHT CENTER » Leopard exhibit model. OPPOSITE, BOTTOM RIGHT » Carousel model. ABOVE » Summer and winter diagram. BELOW » Plan.

≫ STATEN ISLAND ZOO
THE CARL F. KAUFFELD HALL OF REPTILES

> STATEN ISLAND, 614 Broadway
> GRUZEN SAMTON ARCHITECTS (now IBI Group) with Curtis + Ginsberg
> Percent for Art: Steve Foust
> Department of Cultural Affairs, 2007

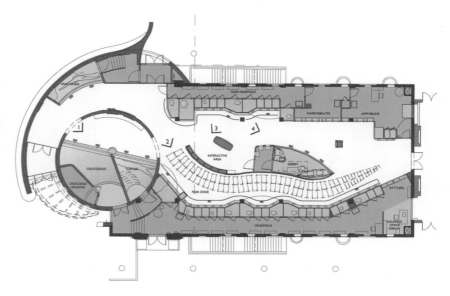

The extensive renovation and expansion of the Staten Island Zoo Hall of Reptiles, originally constructed in the 1930's, reinforces the facility's global reputation as a progressive herpetological center. Located in the heart of the wooded zoological grounds, the reconstructed building serves as the new main entrance to the expanded reptile and amphibian exhibit area. The curvilinear building form uses patterned brickwork and metal roofing to create a distinctive and harmonious focal point for the institution.

OPPOSITE ≫ Interior reptile wing exhibits.
ABOVE ≫ Reptile wing floor plan.

The facility was named in honor of the late, legendary curator of reptiles and Staten Island Zoo Director Carl Kauffeld (1936-1973). Mr. Kauffeld had an international reputation in herpetology. The "Fear Zone: A Snake Encounter" display, a focal point of the renovation and expansion, is where visitors confront their own fear of snakes. Using theatrical lighting, background audio and various color, tactile and visual components, visitors are introduced to a non-threatening, full-sensory experience that highlight misconceptions about snakes and why people fear them.

≫ WAVE HILL HOUSE

> THE BRONX, 675 West 252nd Street
> DATTNER ARCHITECTS
> Department of Cultural Affairs, 2013

Wave Hill House was built in 1843 by William Lewis Morris and has been home to Theodore Roosevelt, Mark Twain, and Arturo Toscanini. The estate, which is on the National Register of Historic Places, was deeded to the City of New York in 1960. Wave Hill, Inc., was formed in 1965 as a non-profit corporation to administer the 28-acre garden and cultural center, which overlooks the Hudson River and the Palisades.

Dattner Architects designed renovations to the 20,850-square-foot structure. Exterior restorations include the replacement of the slate roof and work on all windows and lintels. Structural repairs improve visitor flow and accessibility through a replanning of public spaces with the addition of an elevator. The lighting and finishes in the historic Armor Hall and children's program spaces in the Kerlin Learning Center were also upgraded. The restoration designs were approved by the New York City Landmarks Preservation Commission.

OPPOSITE AND BELOW ≫
Wave Hill House.

>> THE WAVERTREE

> MANHATTAN, East River Pier 16, South Street Seaport
> W ARCHITECTURE AND LANDSCAPE ARCHITECTURE
> Department of Cultural Affairs, 2015

ABOVE >> Historic image of the Wavertree.
OPPOSITE >> Existing deck of the Wavertree.

The Wavertree was built at Southampton, England, in 1885 for R.W. Leyland & Company of Liverpool and named after the Wavertree district in Southampton. It is a 279-foot-long, 2,170-ton, full-rigged ship, being restored as a living artifact moored at the South Street Seaport Museum's East River Pier 16. Today, she is the largest ship of her kind afloat.

The Wavertree was first employed to carry jute, used in making rope and burlap bags, between eastern India and Scotland. At less than two years old, she entered the trades, taking cargo around the world. After sailing for a quarter of a century, in December 1910, she was dismasted off Cape Horn. Rather than re-rigging her, her owners sold her for use as a floating warehouse at Punta Arenas, Chile, and she was converted into a sand barge at Buenos Aires, Argentina in 1947.

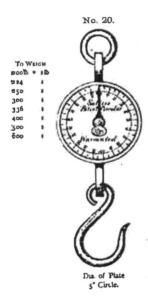

No. 20.

To Weigh
200lb • 1lb
224 1
250 1
300 1
336 1
400 1
500 1
600 1

Dia. of Plate
5" Circle.

Since being acquired by the Seaport Museum in 1968, the Wavertree has undergone considerable restoration and maintenance work. This project will make the ship structurally stable and begin the work necessary to make the Wavertree suitable for public exhibits. To determine the work required for structural stability, it was necessary to assess its existing conditions and understand how it will be used in the future. A master plan was developed to meet access requirements and visitor circulation needs, which determined the location of the new deck in the cargo hold, and other structural improvements.

The Seaport Museum intends to make the Wavertree the centerpiece of its collection of historic sailing vessels—a dockside attraction featuring public exhibitions on the ship's top weather deck and the mizzen deck below. After the ship is preserved, restored, and adapted, new interactive exhibit spaces will be created to tell the story of the seaport and the ship.

MIZZEN TOPMAST   MAIN TOPMAST   FORE TOPMAST

MIZZEN MAST   MAIN MAST   FORE MAST.

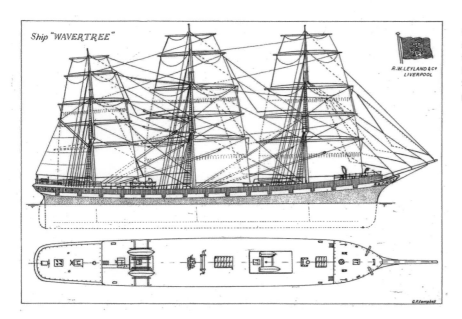

Ship "WAVERTREE"

R.W. LEYLAND & Cº
LIVERPOOL

G.F. Campbell

OPPOSITE, TOP ≫ Sketch of hanging scale. OPPOSITE, BOTTOM ≫ Wavertree with Financial District beyond. LEFT ≫ Ship plan. BELOW, LEFT ≫ Ship exterior detail. BELOW ≫ Floor plan and section.

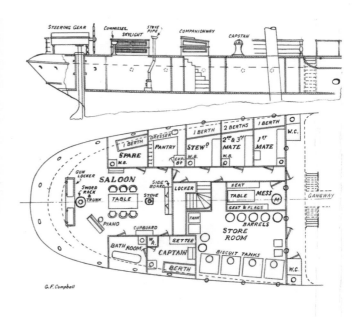

STEERING GEAR   COMPASSES, SKYLIGHT   STOVE PIPE   COMPANIONWAY   CAPSTAN

1 BERTH   DRESSER   1 BERTH   2 BERTHS   1 BERTH   W.C.
SPARE   PANTRY   STEWᴰ   2ᴺᴰ & 3ᴿᴰ MATE   1ˢᵀ MATE
N.B.   CUP.Bᴰ   W.B.   N.B.
GUN LOCKER
SALOON   SIDE BOARD   LOCKER   SEAT
SWORD RACK & TRUNK   TABLE   STOVE   TANK   TABLE   MESS   GANGWAY
PIANO   SEAT & FLAGS
CUPBOARD   BARRELS
BATH ROOM   W.R.   SETTEE   STORE ROOM
CAPTAIN   BISCUIT TANKS
BERTH   W.C.

G.F. Campbell

⟫ WEEKSVILLE HERITAGE CENTER

> ⟩ BROOKLYN, 1698 Bergen Street
> ⟩ CAPLES JEFFERSON ARCHITECTS
> ⟩ Percent for Art: Chakaia Booker
> ⟩ Department of Cultural Affairs, 2013

Weeksville Heritage Center sits on the site of the historic African-American village of Weeksville, Brooklyn. It is the curator of the three remaining original Weeksville homes, which date to the 19th century. The architects' brief was to create a new, 1.5-acre landscaped outdoor space to further the appreciation of the Weeksville homes, and construct a new gateway building to house classrooms, offices, an exhibition gallery, a performance space, and a small library. The center requested a building that would serve as a modern counterpoint to the historic site, have open views of the Weeksville homes, bring the public in along the village's original dirt road, and weave African-American art and patterns into the fabric of the structure.

The new building is kept at a low elevation in deference to the historic homes. The project's sustainable features include a geothermal heating and cooling system and the extensive use of controlled natural light. Design elements include the use of African hardwood, mottled purple-and-green slate, zinc roofing, and an atrium structure with etched glass that casts basket-weave-patterned shadows across visitors' paths. The project seeks to achieve LEED Gold certification.

Weeksville received a Citation in 2007 from the American Institute of Architects New York Chapter, a Design Award in 2006 from the Art Commission of the City of New York, and a Citation in 2004 from the National Organization of Minority Architects.

OPPOSITE ⟫ Street level view of the center's main entrance.
ABOVE ⟫ Center's landscaped courtyard.

LEFT » Seating in the courtyard.
BELOW » Patterns from the center's fence reflected on the sidewalk.
BELOW, BOTTOM » Balcony overlooking the courtyard.

ABOVE » A glass gallery connects the administration spaces to the performance space and additional public areas.
RIGHT » The center with Hunterfly residences in the background.

⟫ WYCKOFF HOUSE MUSEUM

> ❯ BROOKLYN, 5816 Clarendon Road
> ❯ nARCHITECTS
> ❯ Department of Cultural Affairs, 2015

nARCHITECTS is designing the Wyckoff House Museum in East Flatbush, Brooklyn, the site of New York State's oldest house and the city's first designated landmark. The new building will house cultural education complex offices and event space. Conceived as a portal between its present-day environment and the ca. 1650s Dutch Wyckoff House, the new building will frame views of the original house and provide a covered outdoor area for events and a variety of cultural programs. The project is seeking LEED Silver certification.

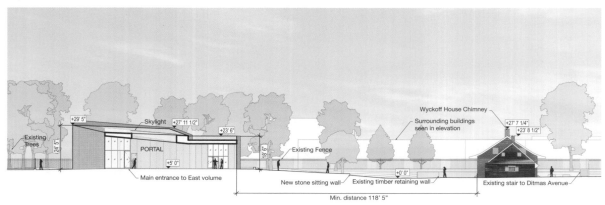

OPPOSITE, TOP ≫ The Wyckoff House Museum. OPPOSITE, BOTTOM ≫ Building plan. ABOVE ≫ The portal building and the landscape looking northeast. RIGHT ≫ View of the historic Wyckoff House through the portal building.

LIBRARIES

>> BRONX LIBRARY CENTER

> THE BRONX, 310 East Kingsbridge Road
> DATTNER ARCHITECTS
> Percent for Art: Iñigo Manglano-Ovalle
> New York Public Library, 2006

BELOW >> Dusk view from Kingsbridge Road. OPPOSITE >> Windows allow a connection between the street, the lobby, and lower level. The stair to the concourse level features "Portrait of a Young Reader" by Iñigo Manglano-Ovalle.

The Bronx Library Center adds architectural interest to the neighborhood and provides community space. The design features a transparent, façade. Each floor is conceived as a rational, rectangular public space surrounded by service, circulation, and smaller program spaces fitting into the irregularities of the site.

Circulation through the 78,000-square-foot building is an important part of the visitor's experience. Each public stair is unique and provides a different processional experience; the staircase from the concourse level to the ground floor incorporates site-specific artwork by Iñigo Manglano-Ovalle depicting the DNA sequence of a young reader, rendered in colored glass.

OPPOSITE, TOP LEFT >> Fourth floor adult reference area and computers. OPPOSITE, TOP RIGHT >> Third floor collections and reading area. OPPOSITE, BOTTOM >> Fourth floor reference area with view to mezzanine. ABOVE >> Second floor children's storytelling area. BELOW >> Second floor children's programming room.

The Bronx Library Center also houses the Latino and Puerto Rican Cultural Center, which has extensive bilingual collections, educational and cultural programs, and multi-media exhibits. A 150-seat auditorium, conference rooms, and computer labs are located on the lower concourse level. These spaces are grouped around a public gallery suitable for events. The project was the first library in the New York Public Library system to receive LEED Silver certification.

>> EAST ELMHURST LIBRARY

> QUEENS, 95-06 Astoria Boulevard
> GARRISON ARCHITECTS
> Queens Library, 2015

This project called for the expansion of a Brutalist-style, single-story, 7,500-square-foot brown brick library built in the a 1970s on a busy boulevard.

To reveal and celebrate the activities of the library, and create an attractive and independent environment for teens, the existing building will be enclosed in a continuous glass room along the street. This strategy treats the existing building as an artifact, displayed along with the newly added program elements, to create a coherent whole.

The design provides 4,390 square feet of additional space for the growing population of young adults, a quiet reading area, and an independent multi-purpose assembly space for 120 people that serves a wide variety of community needs.

The existing and new spaces are organized around an interior landscaped courtyard. A large skylight allows generous light into the formerly dark spaces of the existing library and provides a green center visible throughout the library. This courtyard is terraced to accommodate the different floor elevations, which resulted from the sloping property. It will act as a flexible reading space for library patrons and as an entrance and breakout space for the community room.

OPPOSITE AND ABOVE, TOP ⟫ Exterior with new identity and overhang. ABOVE, LEFT ⟫ Interior courtyard. ABOVE, RIGHT ⟫ View from above.

The project meets the criteria for LEED Silver certification and contains several innovative sustainability features, including thermostatically controlled buoyant air natural ventilation in the courtyard skylight, carefully designed solar control, active heat recovery ventilation, and a high performance envelope with insulated glazing that uses a suspended plastic film to enhance its thermal resistance threefold. It was the recipient of an Excellence in Design award from the Public Design Commission of the City of New York in 2012.

» ELMHURST LIBRARY

> QUEENS, 86-01 Broadway
> MARPILLERO POLLAK ARCHITECTS
> Percent for Art: Allan McCollum
> Queens Library, 2013

The Elmhurst Library project is a community institution with diverse program spaces located both inside and out. A circulation spine brings the vitality of the street into the building, acting as a "trellis," traversing the landscape of the site toward an unexpected view into an interior block landscape, hidden from the street.

The entry includes a large open stair, prominently positioned before reaching the elevators. This stair occupies the center of the building and the site, connecting the two main floors of the library. It is enclosed in one of the two glazed reading rooms, fully visible from the adjacent sidewalks—the solid lower portion, a walk-in bookshelf, the lighter upper portion, an open truss cantilevered from above.

ABOVE » Elmhurst Library, view looking toward the main entrance.
LEFT » Garden perspective.

Wide landings on the main stairway connect all floors, with corner windows overlooking the park. From the stairway, horizontal and vertical circulation enhances the sense of connectivity between spaces by giving access to the library's diverse programs through colorful 'portals,' which provide identity as well as orientation.

Public art plays a significant role in the interior and exterior spaces. Artist Allan McCollum's "SHAPES" wall, in the reading room above the main entrance on Broadway, is visible from the street. This artwork is an integral part of the building's conceptual and social agenda.

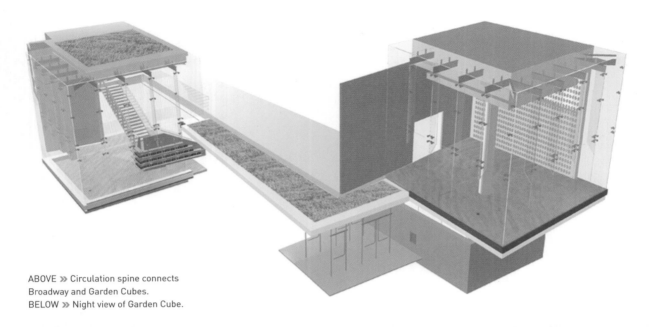

ABOVE » Circulation spine connects
Broadway and Garden Cubes.
BELOW » Night view of Garden Cube.

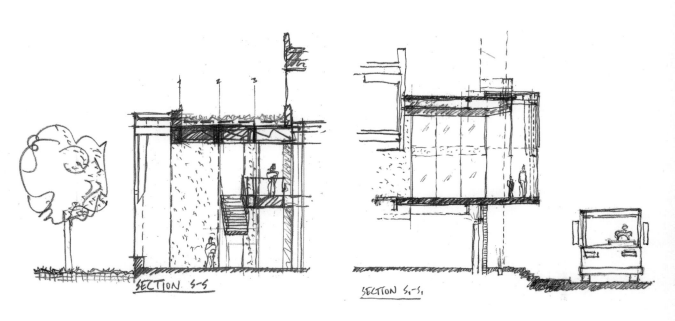

SECTION S-S

SECTION S₁-S₁

TOP » View of main reading room and monumental stair.
BOTTOM » Section sketches through cube in the park and cube overlooking Broadway.

>> FAR ROCKAWAY LIBRARY

> QUEENS, 1637 Central Avenue
> SNØHETTA
> Queens Library, 2016

Public Library, Far Rockaway, N. Y.

OPPOSITE >> Far Rockaway Library, daytime rendering. LEFT >> The original Far Rockaway Library was damaged in a fire in 1962.

At the turn of the 19th century, Far Rockaway was a summer retreat where New Yorkers could escape the heat of the city. The original Carnegie library, which burned in 1962, had long been a valuable resource for Far Rockaway, a community which has been home to many accomplished intellectuals including Nobel laureates Richard Feynman, Baruch Blumber, and Burton Richter. Snøhetta's design focuses on important community resources, replacing and expanding the existing library and teen center facilities, and serving as a catalyst for community change.

The building is a simple volume clad in fritted, colored glass, with a gradient of color reminiscent of the nearby coastal sky. The simplicity of form and skin provides a calm contrast to the retail outlets located along the rest of the intersection. The translucenct glazed façade suggests the activity within the library while providing a degree of privacy for occupants. The central atrium space allows for natural light and a view of the sky from within the building.

The building will seek LEED Silver certification, and will achieve a 25 percent minimum energy cost reduction.

ABOVE AND BELOW ≫ Building studies. LEFT ≫ Façade elevation study. OPPOSITE, TOP ≫ Far Rockaway Library, interior atrium. OPPOSITE, BOTTOM ≫ Far Rockaway Library, nighttime rendering.

⟫ GLEN OAKS LIBRARY

> QUEENS, 256-04 Union Turnpike
> MARBLE FAIRBANKS
> Percent for Art: Janet Zweig
> Queens Library, 2013

This new 18,000-square-foot structure doubles the size of the original Glen Oaks library. The building includes adult, young adult, and children's reading areas and collections, a community meeting room, digital workstations, an outdoor reading garden, and a landscaped plaza. To relate the building to the scale of the surrounding residential community and to meet zoning requirements, half of the interior space is below grade. A double-height space adjacent to the building entry provides abundant natural light for the lower level. Skylights in the plaza bring light through a contoured ceiling to define specific reading areas below.

ABOVE >> Glen Oaks Library sits at the juncture of a low scale commercial area and a residential neighborhood.
LEFT >> Time lapse sequence of the word "search" as it travels across the façade during the course of the day.

LEFT » The contoured ceiling shapes intimate reading areas lit by skylights in the plaza above. BELOW » Adult reading room, lower level.

OPPOSITE, TOP » The adult reading room on the lower level is connected to the main floor by an open stair. OPPOSITE, BOTTOM » Teen reading room and outdoor reading garden.

The building massing and materials respond to differing site conditions on each elevation, while the interior library spaces are open plans with reading rooms on all three levels. The exterior materials speak to the scale of the library and its residential adjacencies, and include channel glazing and fiber-cement paneling. A large picture window along the front elevation provides views into and out of the second floor children's area, while presenting a civic identity to the community.

The word "search" is projected onto the façade through natural daylight, with the size and intensity of the letters varying according to the season and the strength of available sunlight, creating a moving, ephemeral register of local site conditions. A frit pattern on the glass at street level includes the word "search" translated into the 29 languages spoken in Glen Oaks.

⟫ HUNTERS POINT LIBRARY

> QUEENS, Center Boulevard and 48th Avenue
> STEVEN HOLL ARCHITECTS
> Percent for Art: Julianne Swartz
> Queens Library, 2015

BELOW ⟫ The view across the East River of the new Hunters Point Library as it will be seen from Roosevelt Island.

A prominent site on the East River, the magnificent view of Manhattan, inspired this design, which carves the lines of the main interior circulation route into the west façade. A stair case rises up from the open arrival space and is flanked perpendicularly by reading tables in ascending sections backed with bookcases. While users may be on computers, the view from the entrance is of books, and the view on the way up the stairs is of the East River and Manhattan.

BELOW, TOP LEFT » Model detail of foamed-aluminum rainskin that will cover the exterior of the library. RIGHT » Model view of the bosque of Gingko trees that will occupy the public reading garden behind the new library. BELOW, BOTTOM » Design sketch for the new library depicting the elevations of the building.

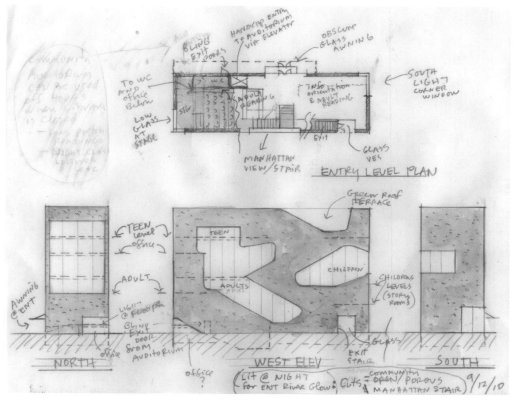

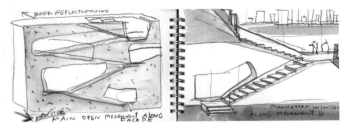

The program's separation into areas for children, teens, and adults, can be seen in the carved cuts of the east face of the 21,000-square-foot building. The new library is open and flowing, while the plan is compact, to provide the most energy-efficient design and the greatest amount of public space on the site. The library also has a cybercenter, conference room and an outdoor amphitheater.

Along the west side of the site, is an elongated reflecting pond of recycled water, which is edged in the natural grasses that once grew at the bank of the East River. Frogs, turtles, and fish inhabit this year-round natural water strip. On the east entrance side, the library and an office pavilion form a public reading garden with a bosque of gingko trees. At the top of the interior staircase is a rooftop reading garden with panoramic views. At night, the glowing presence of the new library along the waterfront joins the landmarked "Pepsi" sign and the "Long Island" sign at the old Gantry to become an inviting icon for the community.

The fabric-formed concrete structure is exposed and painted white inside, while exterior insulation and a foamed aluminum rainskin give the exterior a subtle sparkle and glow, without being overly shiny. As the material is 100 percent recycled aluminum, this outer layer relates to all the green aspects in the new facility. The project was the recipient of an Excellence in Design award from the Public Design Commission of the City of New York in 2010.

ABOVE, LEFT AND TOP RIGHT ≫ Interior views of Manhattan-view stair reading area. ABOVE, BOTTOM RIGHT ≫ Watercolor sketch of library circulation and Manhattan-view windows. ABOVE ≫ Watercolor sketch of of Manhattan-view stair reading area. OPPOSITE ≫ Library interior.

» KENSINGTON BRANCH LIBRARY

> BROOKLYN, 4211 18th Avenue
> SEN ARCHITECTS
> Percent for Art: Carol May and Tim Watkins
> Brooklyn Public Library, 2012

OPPOSITE » Main entrance.
BELOW » Building section.

With a welcoming civic presence, the new Kensington Branch Library brings to this neighborhood a much needed resource for educational support. With added programs, libraries have recently become community centers of sorts, and have seen increased use by all age groups.

Located on a busy avenue, the library has a transparency that reveals the reading spaces from the street. The first floor consists of the circulation desk, the main reading area, stacks, and a separate section for young adults. The cellar has a large meeting room, with direct access from the main stair, while the children's area is on the second floor. User friendly features include stroller parking near the children's area, inviting storytelling rooms, and a lobby featuring the work of local artists.

A main feature of the 20,000-square-foot library is a central skylit area on both levels. The large square skylight at roof level has a simple louver system above it to control the glare. A circular opening in the second floor brings light

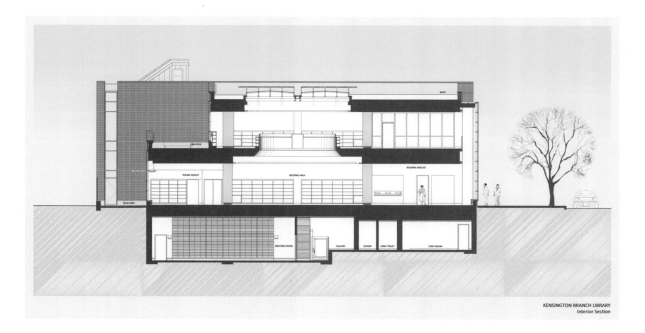

KENSINGTON BRANCH LIBRARY
Interior Section

ABOVE ›› First floor reading room. OPPOSITE, TOP LEFT ›› Storytelling room. OPPOSITE, TOP RIGHT ›› Second floor reading room - toddlers. OPPOSITE, BOTTOM LEFT ›› Second floor reading room. OPPOSITE, BOTTOM RIGHT ›› Main stairs.

into the heart of the first floor reading areas. The skylight, combined with the glazing on the north side, bathes the entire library with natural light throughout the day, virtually eliminating the need for artificial lighting. The glass on the east and south façades, protected with sunshade louvers, provides additional natural light.

The exterior of the building is a state-of-the-art rainscreen system. It is composed of open jointed terra cotta panels, manufactured in Germany. The open joint system allows for ventilation between the exterior and underlying in-sulated wall. Other sustainable features include a daylight dimming system and an efficient mechanical system, utilizing condensing boilers and VAV boxes. The building is seeking LEED Silver certification.

» KEW GARDEN HILLS LIBRARY

> QUEENS, 72-33 Vleigh Place
> WORK ARCHITECTURE COMPANY
> Queens Library, 2014

Kew Garden Hills Library, which was previously known as the Vleigh Branch, has long been a cornerstone of community activity with some of the best attendance and circulation figures of any library nationwide. To meet the growing needs of the library's adult, teenage, and child visitors, a comprehensive renovation and extension by WORK Architecture Company adds a perimeter of inviting community spaces along two edges of the building. The additional space is capped by a landscaped roof, completing a continuous, multi-faceted green loop in dialogue with the library's side gardens.

ABOVE » Daytime rendering.
RIGHT » Nighttime rendering.

The wavy, curtain-like concrete façade material is literally lifted up into an iconic band, framing the library's interior activities above expansive street-level windows. The apex reveals the main reading room at the most public corner, with a second "mini peak" at the children's room. Between these two peaks, the façade dips to provide privacy in the staff areas. The concrete band also provides structural support for the building's extension, requiring only two columns along its length.

An awning is created by folding a section of this façade up over the street, as one would mark one's place in a favorite book.

OPPOSITE, TOP » Interior view.
OPPOSITE, BOTTOM » Elevation.
BELOW, TOP LEFT AND RIGHT »
Concrete façade material detail.
BELOW, BOTTOM » Model.

» KINGSBRIDGE BRANCH LIBRARY

> THE BRONX, 291 West 231st Street
> PRENDERGAST LAUREL ARCHITECTS
> New York Public Library, 2011

BELOW » Exterior.
OPPOSITE » Upper atrium balcony overlook.

The original Kingsbridge Branch of the New York Public Library was designed by McKim, Mead & White, funded by Andrew Carnegie and opened in the Bronx in 1905 adjacent to the long buried Spuyten Duyvil Creek. Recently, the library occupied a 1950's era replacement. With the goal of expanding the facility, the Library recently purchased a neighboring corner lot. The mean grade of this unusual site is 12 feet below the sidewalk level and the site's south and east sides are defined by full-height fieldstone retaining walls.

The library program called for 12,000 square feet of space, including separate reading rooms for adults and children, book stacks, a community room, a children's storytelling room, and support offices. The two street façades are set

back from the stone walls, forming an L-shaped sunken courtyard, a "hidden urban garden". This outdoor space is landscaped with bamboo planting beds, textured paving and native schist "scholar's" stones.

The visitor to the library enters the building through a glass and concrete bridge overlooking the garden. The adjacent elevator tower anchors the entry portal and creates a campanile-like element in the complex. The community room is a curved-face metal-clad rhomboid which anchors the eastern corner and frames the northern boundary of the atrium

The building also features one of the Bronx's earliest sedum planted green roofs, which provides thermal insulation for energy conservation, stormwater filtration and retention, and makes a colorful contribution to the views of neighboring properties. A Fordham University research project is scheduled to begin study of the green roof's contribution to biodiversity in the Bronx.

The atrium provides daylighting to the interior, connects reading rooms to views of the stone walls and garden, showcases the interior of the library from

the street. Bathed in sunlight and focused on the interior garden extension, it is a pivotal point between the two levels.

The reading rooms are centrally located and equipped with custom baltic birch computer stations and tables wired for laptops. Traditional media is housed on color coded shelving with translucent recycled resin end panels. Produced by a local artisan, custom wool cushions provide children's seating in the storytelling and reading areas and reflect the rainbow theme of the shelving.

A polished concrete floor provides a durable, monolithic surface for the high traffic reading rooms. A suspended acoustic ceiling of recycled perforated aluminum floats above the reading room. Wood slat ceilings and acoustical wood wall panels are installed in the more intimate storytelling and community rooms. The north and west walls include both board-formed concrete and recycled ground-face concrete masonry laid in a staggered bond, adding textural interest and permanence.

The Kingsbridge Branch Library was selected by the New York City Art Commission for their Excellence in Design Award in 2005.

OPPOSITE, TOP » Stair with native stones. OPPOSITE, BOTTOM AND ABOVE » Adult reading room.

» MACON BRANCH LIBRARY

> BROOKLYN, 361 Lewis Avenue
> SEN ARCHITECTS
> Brooklyn Public Library, 2008

OPPOSITE AND BELOW » The library's extensive woodwork was restored to its original grandeur.

This branch library is located in the Stuyvesant Heights Historic District, a residential neighborhood of 19th century masonry buildings. The imposing symmetrical structure, designed by Richard Walker in the Classical Revival style, was one of several libraries funded by the philanthropist Andrew Carnegie at the turn of the 20th century.

The single-story building has all the elements of a Carnegie library, with red brick and limestone trim around the windows and entrances. The entrance leads to a raised paneled vestibule, where the circulation desk and main reading areas are reached by a staircase. The reading rooms have high ceilings with ornate plaster moldings, perimeter built-in wood shelving, and large high windows that flood the interior with natural light. The original lighting consisted of a pattern of pendants of various sizes, suspended from the high ceilings.

ABOVE, TOP ROW AND BOTTOM RIGHT ≫ Images from the historical archives of the Brooklyn Public Library. ABOVE, BOTTOM LEFT ≫ Interior.

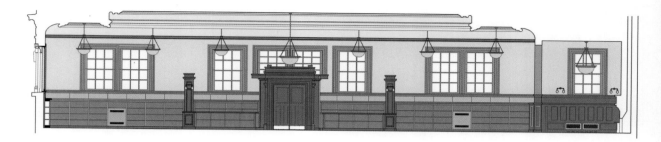

ABOVE » A section showing the new lighting pendants.

The building underwent several mechanical upgrades in the 1960s and '70s, when a grid of two-by-four fluorescent lights was suspended 10 feet below the original 21-foot ceilings, and air-conditioning ducts were installed in an ad hoc manner throughout the space, completely obliterating the effect of the high ceiling reading rooms and alcoves. Water damage to the interior had also destroyed a lot of the existing millwork.

After careful surveys of the remaining historical fabric, the original drawings and photographs, Sen Architects came up with an approach that carefully inserted new elements while preserving and restoring the old. This interior rehabilitation included the replacement of all lighting and mechanical systems and the creation of a separate area for an African American heritage center. The air-conditioning ducts were located in the attic space, and fan coil units were carefully integrated with the design of new built-in furniture. The new lighting was designed in the pattern of the original building, with high efficiency fixtures that meet current energy codes. The African American room entrance, through the reading room, was also designed to complement the restored millwork.

This project integrated the air conditioning, computer technology, and recent building code requirements into this century-old structure, restoring it as a public space that is actively used by the community.

⟩⟩ MARINERS HARBOR BRANCH LIBRARY

⟩ STATEN ISLAND, 206 South Avenue
⟩ ATELIER PAGNAMENTA TORRIANI
⟩ New York Public Library, 2013

The New York Public Library's new one-story Mariners Harbor Branch rests on the highest elevation of a 16,000-square-foot plot in the Mariners Harbor neighborhood. The design was inspired by a cracked open shell, rough on the outside, smooth and mother-of-pearl-like on the inside, in honor of the neighborhood's maritime and oystering history.

Atelier Pagnamenta Torriani created a cutting edge design, where the outside flows into the building, making it the first NYPL branch with a ground-level outdoor terrace.

Transparent glass walls and skylights minimize the need for overhead lighting during operating hours. Existing mature trees, preserved in the back garden, surround the terrace. The new building features views of the outdoors, self-checkout, and free wireless Internet service, with areas for reading and meeting. There are lounge areas for adults and young adults, as well as a storytelling area for children.

The project received an Excellence in Design award from the Public Design Commission of the City of New York and is seeking LEED Silver certification.

LEFT ⟩⟩ Section.
ABOVE ⟩⟩ Exterior view.
OPPOSITE ⟩⟩ Exterior.

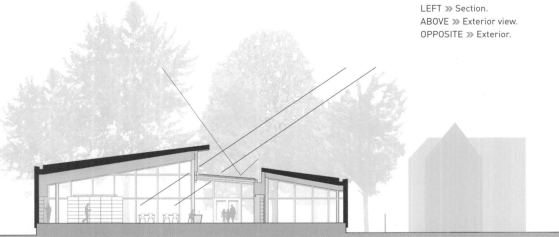

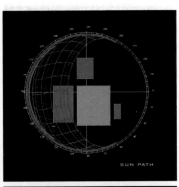

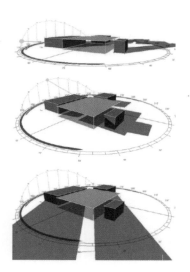

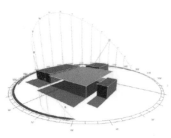

TOP ≫ Reading area.
LEFT ≫ Sun studies.
OPPOSITE, TOP ≫ Building evolution.
OPPOSITE, BOTTOM ≫ Materials.

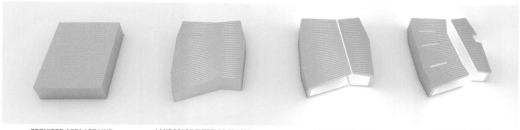

REQUIRED AREA LOT LINE   LANDSCAPE EXTERIOR SPACES   FUNCTIONAL AND CIRCULATION SEPARATION   NATURAL LIGHTS REQUIREMENTS

SHELL

the exterior shell is standing seam zinc cladding over insulated metal framing.

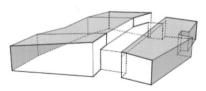

FACADE GLAZING

the facade glazing is low-e insulated glazing. A glare study was conducted to determine the fritting patter density required on the eastern and western exposures, in order to control heat gain modulate light, while allowing sufficient transparency for viewing. The resulting fritting pattern will also minimize the possibility of avian impact.

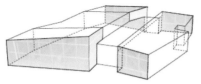

SKYLIGHT GLAZING

the skylight glazing over the circulation spine   is technical glazing with   integral louvers . The angle of the louvers is optimized to allowed northern light to penetrate, while deflecting direct light.

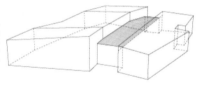

≫ RIDGEWOOD LIBRARY

> QUEENS, 20-12 Madison Street
> BEYHAN KARAHAN & ASSOCIATES, ARCHITECTS
> Queens Library, 2010

OPPOSITE, TOP LEFT ≫ Exterior, restored light fixtures and façade. OPPOSITE, TOP RIGHT ≫ Interior. OPPOSITE, BOTTOM ≫ Interior rendering. BELOW ≫ Floor plan.

This two-story, Neo-Tudor public library designed by Henry C. Buckner opened in 1929 after a decade of planning, as the first of its kind built entirely from municipal funds. Several major renovations took place since the building's original construction. Sometime between 1929 and 1963, the front entry area including the monumental stairway was enclosed and the building was extended to the west by about 36 feet. A mezzanine was also added to the main floor area to make room for the growing collection. In 1966, the entry area was revised again. At this time, the large historic windows were replaced by smaller and simpler ones.

Queens Library's desire to bring this branch to contemporary levels of technology and functionality drove this renovation. The approach was to research and restore as many of the original architectural features as possible for this unique public library while satisfying the program elements for the users. Original exterior light fixtures and façade ornamentation were meticulously restored, and the interior ceilings were raised to reveal the original plaster cove ornamentation and the radiating shelving system from the main service desk.

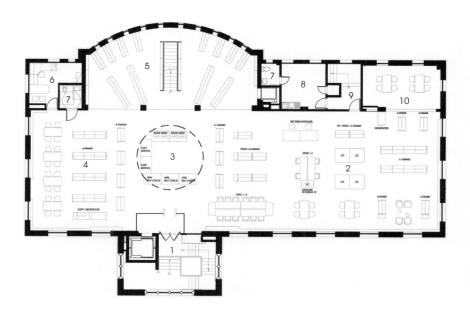

» QUEENS CENTRAL LIBRARY, CHILDREN'S LIBRARY DISCOVERY CENTER

> QUEENS, 89-11 Merrick Boulevard
> 1100 ARCHITECT
> Queens Library, 2011

LEFT » The perimeter wall has been thickened to incorporate quiet reading nooks and social spaces. RIGHT » The completion of the CLDC is the first phase of 1100 Architect's master plan for the renovation and modernization of the 275,000-square-foot Queens Central Library.

This white-walled, light-filled addition to the 1966 granite and limestone Queens Central Library provides a festive two-story building where children can curl up on upholstered chairs, kneel on colorful pillows, sprawl on benches, or settle into computer desks. Situated on a busy corner, the new glowing glass façade increases the library's visibility and reintroduces it as a cultural and social destination for the community.

The façade is composed of four different types of glass: transparent, translucent, opaque, and textured opaque. It opens the colorful interiors to the street, through its large transparent windows that admit abundant natural light.

Entry to the CLDC is from inside the bustling Central Library building, where bright red letters over the doorway invite kids to "Discover!" A collection of educational toys and books fill these spaces where children can relax,

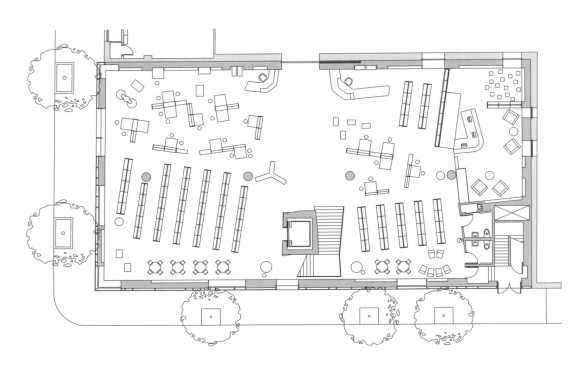

OPPOSITE, TOP » First floor plan.
OPPOSITE, BOTTOM » Phenome-
na-based exhibits are displayed in
science-themed plazas dispersed
throughout the library stacks.
These exhibits contribute to the
experiential learning environment.
LEFT » *The New York Times* architecture critic Michael Kimmelman
describes the CLDC as "part of a
quiet revolution reshaping the city's
public architecture."

receive instruction, or do science experiments on their own. Murals, mobiles, and brightly colored patterns on the floor entertain while guiding the children through the spaces.

The CLDC is seeking LEED Silver certification. The sustainable design strategy consists of a high-performance façade, energy-efficient mechanical systems and lighting, radiant floor heating, recycled and low-emitting ma-terials, and water conservation. Less than a year after it opened, the project received a Municipal Art Society MASterwork Award.

ABOVE, LEFT » The staircase acts
as a sculptural element in the space
and is strategically placed opposite
the entrance portal to make all
visitors aware that the children's
library occupies two floors and to
encourage the use of stairs rather
than the elevators. ABOVE, RIGHT »
"The CLDC has become an attractive
citywide resource that encourages
literacy as well as math and science
exploration. It gets kids out of the
homework world and into the world
of fun." Joanne King, Director of
Communications, Queens Library.

⟫ SCHOMBURG CENTER FOR RESEARCH IN BLACK CULTURE (CENTER FOR SCHOLARS)

> MANHATTAN, 515 Malcolm X Boulevard
> DATTNER ARCHITECTS
> New York Public Library, 2007

The renovation of the Schomburg Center for Research in Black Culture included the creation of the new Center for Scholars, as well as the re-envisioning of several key public spaces. A new glass façade, complete with a video wall viewable at night from Malcolm X Boulevard, and a prominent new entry announce the library to the neighborhood. A new street-level gallery was created by inserting a partial floor in the double-height reading room. The reading room, which can be seen from the gallery, was reconfigured to reveal a soaring ceiling topped with acoustic wood panels. The room is the dramatic setting for Aaron Douglas's four signature 1934 murals titled "Aspects of Negro Life."

The new Center for Scholars has an area for readings and lectures, private offices, and a conference room. The 16,000-square-foot project renovated the reading and reference areas, an electronic research area, photography print vault room, stacks, and the entrance lobby.

LEFT ⟫ New façade and projection video wall creates a new entry and iconic presence.
RIGHT ⟫ Entry lobby.

LEFT ≫ Center for Scholars.
BELOW ≫ Gallery view.
BOTTOM LEFT ≫ Gallery view.
BOTTOM RIGHT ≫ Circulation desk.
OPPOSITE ≫ Reading room.

» SCHOMBURG CENTER FOR RESEARCH IN BLACK CULTURE

- › MANHATTAN, 515 Malcolm X Boulevard
- › MARBLE FAIRBANKS
- › New York Public Library, 2015

The Schomburg Center for Research in Black Culture, a research unit of the New York Public Library, is a world-renowned institution dedicated to materials on the history and culture of people of African descent. The collection includes five divisions of materials: books and articles; arts and artifacts; manuscripts, archives, and rare books; moving images and recorded sound; and photographs and prints. The Center is an active hub of Harlem's cultural life, supporting research and engagement with issues around black life and experiences of the global African diaspora.

LEFT » Detail of east façade.
ABOVE » The southeast corner of the building at 135th Street and Malcolm X Boulevard includes a large scale video screen.

The design objective of the project is to enhance the way the Center inter-
faces with the public and with the surrounding Harlem community by displaying
portions of its vast collection at street level. Features of the design include high
definition LED display systems, interactive information panels, display windows
for historical artifacts, and a new landscaped plaza with distinctive paving, plantings, and seating adjacent to the display areas. The project also includes a gift
shop and conference room addition along with interior renovations for the Center's Manuscripts, Archives & Rare Books Division.

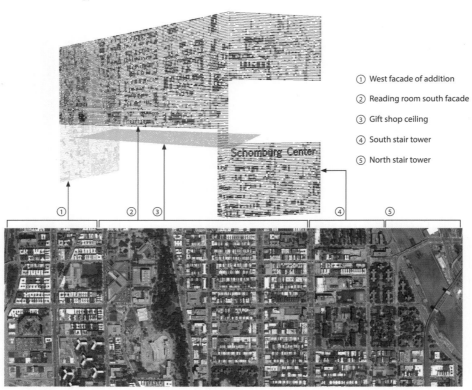

① West facade of addition

② Reading room south facade

③ Gift shop ceiling

④ South stair tower

⑤ North stair tower

Schomburg Center

OPPOSITE, BOTTOM » The pattern on the glass and metal panels is abstracted from a map of Harlem. ABOVE » The east façade displays The Schomburg Center's multi-media collection to the community through multiple scales of digital display systems. RIGHT » The landscaped plaza creates a shaded area for seating.

» STAPLETON LIBRARY

> STATEN ISLAND, 132 Canal Street
> ANDREW BERMAN ARCHITECT
> New York Public Library, 2013

BELOW » Stapleton Library, exterior.

This new 12,700-square-foot branch of the New York Public Library consists of a glass-walled, light-filled addition to a classical 1907 Andrew Carnegie Library, originally designed by Carrère and Hastings. The historic structure, which features a classical portico and tall arched windows, was completely renovated and is now the children's reading room. The library expanded onto a sloping empty adjacent lot where an additional entrance could be accessed without steps. Teen and adult reading and research areas are located in the new building, separated by a transparent community room.

In the 7,000-square-foot addition, glue-laminated Douglas fir posts, beams, and joists were used to create an efficient, warm, and exposed structure. The new timbers relate to the original oak casework and shelving of the Carnegie building. The facility was designed to be an open, accessible, and seamless connection of the new and old. The library now has bright reading rooms, desktop computers, and Internet accessibility.

Energy efficient elements, such as skylights and a curtain wall, maximize the natural sunlight in the building. A radiant heating system efficiently warms the space in the winter months.

The library, located in the northeastern corner of the island, was conceived as a lively modern public institution that will contribute to the revitalization of the urban center of Stapleton. The architects sited the new library to create a clear public space in front of the building, across the street from and with a strong visual and physical connection to Tappen Park, the Victorian center of the community.

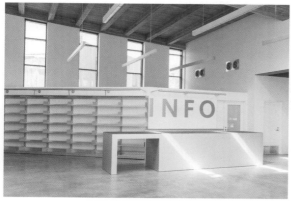

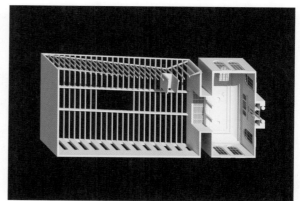

OPPOSITE ≫ Entrance detail.
ABOVE, TOP ≫ Adult reading room.
ABOVE, CENTER LEFT ≫ Informa-
tion desk. ABOVE, CENTER RIGHT ≫
Building plan. RIGHT ≫ Translucent
core within reading room.

≫ WOODSTOCK BRANCH LIBRARY

> THE BRONX, 761 East 160th Street
> RICE+LIPKA ARCHITECTS
> New York Public Library, 2015

This project reinvents 10,000 square feet of a McKim, Mead, and White-designed branch library in the Morrisania neighborhood of the Bronx. It creates a contemporary identity for the branch and a fully accessible interior environment. The project furthers the New York Public Library's mission to provide broad access to information, offer special programs, and to create a nurturing environment for teenagers and young children.

With this project, the architect developed a new paradigm for the renovation of a simple and powerful building by recovering its spatial and organizational strengths and by amplifying its extraordinary character through the insertion of vibrant, contemporary architectural and programmatic elements, which provide increased functionality and technology to support modern library functions.

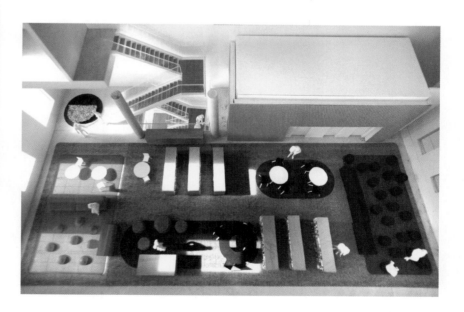

ABOVE ≫ View of main reading room and centralized open stairway beyond. RIGHT ≫ Physical model of first floor with adult and teen areas.

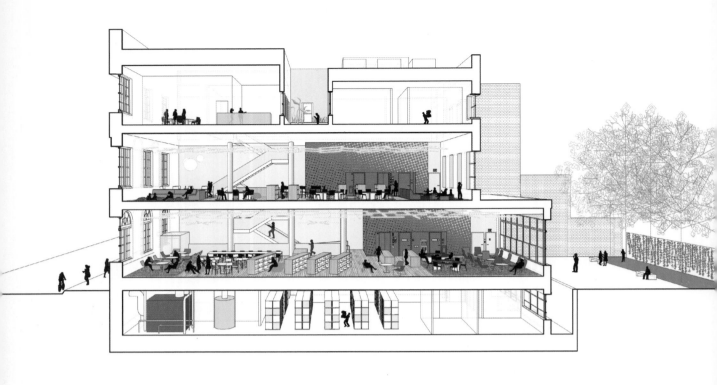

OPPOSITE, TOP ≫ Section perspective showing new multi-purpose space, adult and teen reading areas and children's floor. OPPOSITE, BOTTOM ≫ View from street. RIGHT ≫ Model of first floor adult reading lounge with open glazed stair. BELOW ≫ A new ramp makes the library accessible for wheelchairs and strollers. A new open stair opens up to the floors above while a circular LED info-board scrolls library announcements and activities.

HEALTH + HUMAN SERVICES

Buildings designed to accommodate various social services vary in program more so than other service or safety facilities. Unlike police stations, firehouses, museums, and libraries, these buildings are designed to serve a very specific and often time-critical health and well-being needs. These facilities include health clinics, service centers for homeless persons and families, animal adoption shelters, and social service facilities.

» CENTRAL HARLEM HEALTH CENTER

> MANHATTAN, 2238 Fifth Avenue
> STEPHEN YABLON ARCHITECT
> Department of Health and Mental Hygiene, 2008

OPPOSITE » The clinic's waiting room features wood and stone walls and a curved metal ceiling. BELOW » Ceiling simulates a skylight in the main lobby located within the building's core, creating a welcoming entrance to the health center.

Located in a landmarked McKim, Mead and White historic public health center building, this 7,000-square-foot clinic exudes tranquility and lessens the fear and public stigma associated with seeking testing, treatment, and counseling for HIV and AIDS and other sexually transmitted diseases.

The project included a new lobby and STD clinic, which is composed of a triage area, waiting and educational space with counseling offices, and clinical space with exam rooms and labs. The floor plan of the building provided a unique design challenge: the plan was broken up by the building's central lobby and cores with only a narrow connecting space along the back. This connector was transformed into a light-filled central waiting and educational area that links the counseling and clinical sides of the clinic. The connector's luminous

Organization

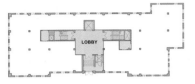

Existing Condition

Plan Organization

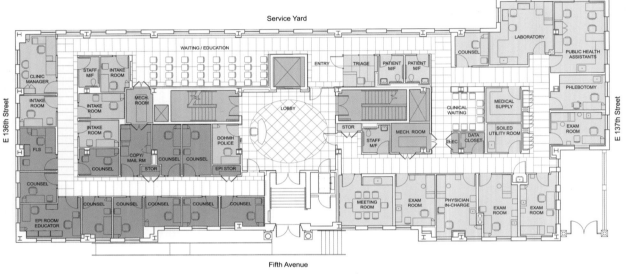

First Floor Plan

TOP » Floor plan.
BOTTOM » Interlocking "L"
section concept.

long back wall obscures views to a service area and organizes the circulation throughout the clinic, preserving patients' privacy and anonymity. The wall is composed of sliding translucent resin screens embedded with a colorful beaded mesh made by African women who have been affected by HIV and AIDS.

An interlocking L-shaped section concept, recognizable and consistent throughout the public circulation areas, further organizes the space. The walls of the outer "L" are finished in epoxy and its ceiling is made of curved aluminum ceiling panels. The complementing "L" features porcelain tiles and bamboo. This entire circulation system is indirectly lit, creating a soothing space. A luminous ceiling that simulates a skylight in the main lobby, a space without natural light, creates an uplifting experience immediately upon entering. The design conveys to patients that they will be treated with dignity and provided with the highest level of health care.

The project is designed to seek LEED Silver certification. Sustainable materials such include porcelain tile with recycled metal content, bamboo veneers, resin panels, linoleum floors, and ceiling tiles with high recycled content are used. Low VOC coatings and adhesives are used throughout, and low flow plumbing fixtures, highly efficient lighting and HVAC systems reduce energy consumption.

The clinic received a Design Excellence Award from the Society of American Registered Architects New York Chapter in 2011, Design Excellence Award for Healthcare Facilities Design from the Boston Society of Architects in 2010, and a Healthcare Environment Award from *Contract Magazine* in 2010.

TOP ≫ Waiting and education area.
BOTTOM ≫ Typical hallway.

>> CHELSEA DISTRICT HEALTH CENTER

> MANHATTAN, 2303 Ninth Avenue
> STEPHEN YABLON ARCHITECT
> Department of Health and Mental Hygiene, 2016

BELOW >> High-tech park pavilions concept. OPPOSITE, TOP >> Public lobby looking towards new stair. OPPOSITE, BOTTOM >> Waiting area.

In operation continuously as a free public health center since 1934, a landmark quality Art Deco style building in an urban park will be transformed into a contemporary, light-filled high-tech park pavilion, supporting New York City's ambitious goals to reduce the incidence of HIV through increased education, testing, and treatment. Once completed, the 23,600-square-foot facility will house the largest sexually transmitted disease clinic in the United States.

To encourage more community residents to seek testing and treatment for diseases often stigmatized in the community, the New York City Department of Health requires a welcoming and reassuring environment that also meets the demands of today's increasingly complex patient processing and treatment methods.

Curved wood ceilings and natural finish floors will be calming while park views in all of the waiting areas further reduce anxiety. Patient privacy and anonymity, critical to encouraging increased community use, will be achieved through self-directed patient flow throughout the facility. The architecture will play a key role in enabling this approach by providing orientation devices including park-facing "Green Walls", clad in a tile pattern inspired by the park's sycamore trees. An old fire stair will be replaced by a new, light-filled stairwell with a full building height glass curtain wall sliced into the rear of the building.

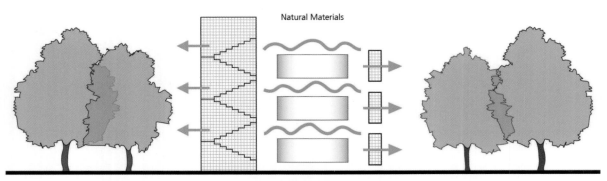

Natural Materials

New Park Stairwell   High-tech Pavilions   Green Wall

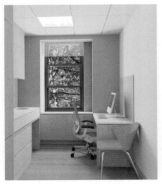

ABOVE » The new light-filled stairwell has park views and abundant natural light. The "Green Walls" in the stairwell, circulation areas, and waiting rooms are wrapped in a tile pattern inspired by surrounding sycamore trees. FAR LEFT » Office. LEFT » The corridors feature epoxy walls and wood ceilings.

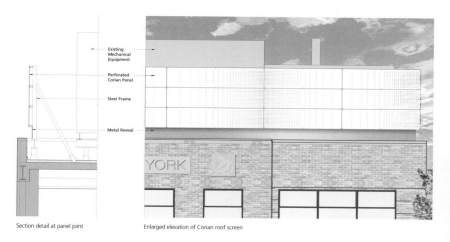

Section detail at panel joint   Enlarged elevation of Corian roof screen

Existing
Mechanical
Equipment

Perforated
Corian Panel

Steel Frame

Metal Reveal

TOP LEFT » The Corian roof screen hides existing and new mechanical systems on the roof. Its perforated pattern evokes the curved ceilings within the building. ABOVE » Existing conditions. BOTTOM LEFT » Renovated east elevation.

This will bring in abundant natural light to the interiors, provide expansive park views, and encourage patient and staff stair use.

Restoration and renovation of the exterior, including an innovative perforated Corian roof screen, a new accessible entry, and all new infrastructure are included in the scope. LEED Gold certification is anticipated for this project. The project was a finalist in World Architecture News Healthcare Awards program in 2012.

>> FOREST HILLS COMMUNITY CENTER

> QUEENS, 108-25 62nd Drive
> WXY (WEISZ + YOES) ARCHITECTURE
> New York City Housing Authority, 2009

OPPOSITE, TOP >> Multi-purpose room. OPPOSITE, BOTTOM RIGHT >> Classroom. BELOW >> Multi-purpose room plans.

WXY renovated four 200-square-foot classrooms and a 3,200-square-foot multi-purpose room at Queens Community House, in Forest Hills. The center, originally built by the New York City Housing Authority, was in need of new finishes and lighting. The goal was to provide well-lit, open spaces using indirect and direct lighting and a bright, colorful palette that would be appreciated by young and old alike. The multi-purpose room—which is used for ping pong, yoga, basketball, movies, and to serve meals to 300 seniors on weekdays—was fitted with a new poured sports floor and basketball backboards, acoustical buffers and metal halide lighting.

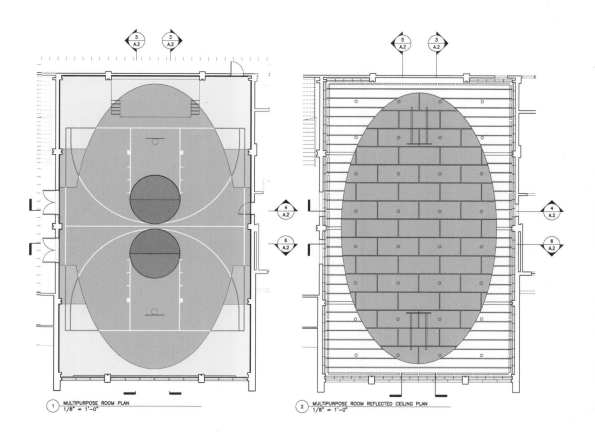

1. MULTIPURPOSE ROOM PLAN
1/8" = 1'-0"

2. MULTIPURPOSE ROOM REFLECTED CEILING PLAN
1/8" = 1'-0"

HELP 1 FAMILY RESIDENCE

> BROOKLYN, 515 Blake Avenue
> SLADE ARCHITECTURE
> Department of Homeless Services, 2015

BELOW » Elevation.
OPPOSITE » Courtyard.

These two large residential buildings, with 196 units and a community center, fill an entire city block. This renovation will replace all of the existing façades, which have experienced significant water damage, and do not provide sufficient insulation for the interiors.

Given the large footprint and visual presence of these buildings, the renovation provides an opportunity to create a positive impact for the community. On the façade, color and varying panel thicknesses will add visual interest and bring continuity to the existing building form.

This renovation will create a more energy-efficient structure by installing insulated operable windows to take advantage of cross ventilation. The stabilizing thermal effect of the building's concrete structure, will help maintain a cooler interior temperature during hot months. In the winter, the concrete will reduce heating requirements.

Several safety features will be upgraded as well, including an addressable fire alarm system and compliance with New York State regulations. Structural renovations include replacing exterior stairs and parapet structures. The existing exterior walkway and stairs foster activity and exercise in line with the *New York City Active Design Guidelines*.

» THE KALAHARI

> MANHATTAN, 40 West 116th Street
> FREDERIC SCHWARTZ ARCHITECTS
> Department of Housing Preservation and Development, 2008

OPPOSITE » 116th Street perspective.
ABOVE » Courtyard view.

This new, 250-unit, mixed-use condominium reflects the richness and variety of Harlem's vibrant African American heritage. A sustainable, affordable, market-rate development, it creates housing with generous amenities and green technologies for individuals and families of diverse backgrounds and income levels. The 475,000-square-foot project is divided into two separate 12-story buildings, joined by a lobby with 40,000 square feet of community and commercial space at the street level.

Located in the heart of the nation's largest African American community, the building proudly celebrates its culture. The brick patterns and colors of the public street façades and courtyard were inspired by the patterns painted on

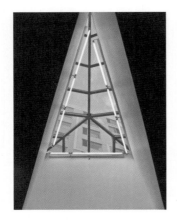

ABOVE » Skylight detail.
BELOW » Lobby.
OPPOSITE, TOP » Site plan.
OPPOSITE, BOTTOM » Typical unit living room.

desert homes of the Sub-Saharan Kalahari tribe. The undulating massing is a response to the city's zoning code, with its alternating rhythm of tower and wall heights along the building's 300-foot length.

Shared public green roofs, recycled materials, a high-performance building envelope and air filtration, heat recovery, and photovoltaic panels reduce the building's energy consumption by more than 30 percent below the energy code. Amenities include a large common outdoor green roof garden, children's playroom, meeting rooms, music practice rooms, and a free fitness center. The project harnesses solar power with rooftop photovoltaics, wind and hydrogen-generated energy (through energy tax credits) and features high-performance lighting fixtures, bamboo flooring, and furnishings created with sustainable materials. Its structural system is made of recycled steel and concrete. A fresh-air filtration system purifies interior air. The building complies with the United States Green Building Council's LEED Silver standards and uses 30 percent less energy than similar buildings.

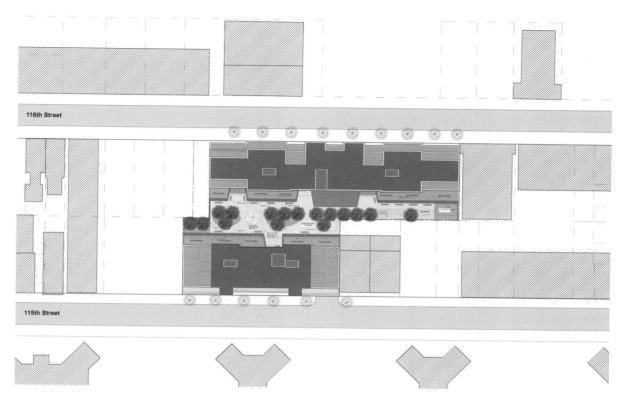

116th Street

115th Street

➤➤ MONTESSORI PROGRESSIVE LEARNING CENTER

> ❯ QUEENS, 195-03 Linden Boulevard
> ❯ SLADE ARCHITECTURE
> ❯ Administration for Children's Services, 2007

The interior renovation of the Montessori Progressive Learning Center in Queens included creating a library, reconfiguring the teachers' lounge, renovating all restrooms, minor classroom improvements, renovating two kitchens, and creating a new reception area. This project was subject to the New York City Sustainable Building Guidelines.

The renovation was completed while the building was occupied—the Montessori School has no periods of closure longer than a four-day weekend. Renewable,

low-toxicity products and methods were specified for the highly sensitive environment of a functioning nursery school. Working with the school and contractor, Slade Architecture coordinated the phasing to minimize the impact on school operations.

The scope called for the conversion of a small basement storage room to provide shelving for a small library. By imaginatively capturing underutilized and overlooked circulation space around the storage room, the architect created an amenity that exceeded everyone's expectations, all within the original budget. The space provides the required library shelving plus a reading area that can be used for larger school gatherings and presentations. It has become the central hub for teachers, students, and parents. Since the area designated for the new library is below grade, a sense of openness and brightness was implied by incorporating a reflective ceiling, bright murals, mirrors, and lighting. By aggregating and organizing existing circulation space, an amenity was created that no one thought was feasible within the confines of the allocated area.

≫ PATH (PREVENTION ASSISTANCE AND TEMPORARY HOUSING) FAMILY CENTER

> THE BRONX, 151 East 151st Street
> ENNEAD ARCHITECTS
> Percent for Art: Lane Twitchell
> Department of Homeless Services, 2011

OPPOSITE ≫ View from the southwest with public entry. BELOW ≫ The building as seen in the neighborhood context.

This welcoming and light-filled new building gives physical form to the City's progressive approach to overcoming homelessness: prevention, client service, permanence and accountability. The 76,800-square-foot structure is designed to facilitate an orderly and dignified flow to the clients as they are guided through the Department of Homeless Services' evaluation and assistance process. Throughout the building, large, south-facing spaces with abundant natural light house open administrative work areas for staff members, client waiting areas and interview rooms.

The building is located in an architecturally diverse area of the Bronx. The north and south façades reflect the scales and personalities of their distinct contexts, connecting with the community and surrounding neighborhoods.

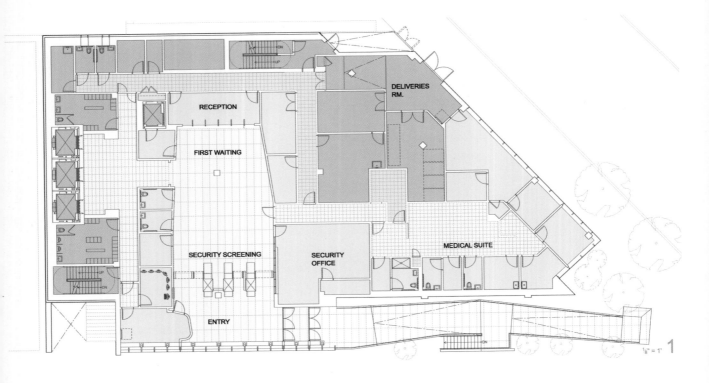

RECEPTION

FIRST WAITING

DELIVERIES RM.

SECURITY SCREENING

SECURITY OFFICE

MEDICAL SUITE

ENTRY

1/8" = 1'   1

ABOVE » First floor plan.
LEFT » Site plan.

FRANZ SIGEL PARK

FRANZ SIGEL PARK

GERARD AVENUE

EAST 151ST STREET

WALTON AVENUE

METRO NORTH TRACKS

Terra cotta references the brick architecture of the residential buildings in this community, zinc and metal trim evoke an industrial aesthetic of the nearby manufacturing district, and glass provides visibility and transparency.

High performance building systems are integrated throughout the building. Sustainable features include: green roof technology, rainwater collection, a rainscreen façade system, construction and demolition waste management, and materials with recycled content. The building achieved LEED Gold certification.

❯❯ RIVERSIDE HEALTH CENTER

> ❯ MANHATTAN, 160 West 100th Street
> ❯ 1100 ARCHITECT
> ❯ Percent for Art: Richard Artschwager
> ❯ Department of Health and Mental Hygiene, 2013

The renovation and expansion of the Riverside Health Center, a public facility managed by the New York City Department of Health and Mental Hygiene, will support the center's mission to promote the health of the Upper West Side community. Brightening the material palette and increasing the amount of sunlight provides enlivened spaces for clinical services, administrative functions, and learning.

The design team collaborated with several City agencies on the development of architectural solutions that encourage physical activity, the results of which became part of the City's *Active Design Guidelines* and led to the creation of a new LEED Innovation Credit. This project inspired an investigation of how the physical environment can support physical and men-

ABOVE ❯❯ Glazed-terracotta tiles by artist Richard Artschwager energize the façade and the main staircase. RIGHT ❯❯ Building functions were reorganized to provide a clear flow of spaces for visitors and staff. The first floor primarily consists of clinical spaces, the second floor consists of administrative offices, and the expanded third floor houses the Health Academy with classrooms and computer testing labs.

OPPOSITE » Section of the main staircase. TOP » Rendering of a new auditorium. BOTTOM » Rendering of the main lobby.

tal well-being. In the original 1960 design of the building, the main public staircase was hidden—its disuse a symbol of inactivity. The redesign encourages visitors to walk rather than take the elevator. In addition to this emphasis on the use of the stairs, an exercise room, showers, and bike rack constitute a comprehensive physical health program.

A mural by artist Richard Artschwager made of orange glazed-terracotta tiles covers part of the façade and the main staircase. The installation is part of the New York City's Department of Cultural Affairs' Percent for Art Program, which increases the accessibility and visibility of art throughout the city. The building is on track to receive LEED Silver certification and will reduce energy costs by at least 20 percent.

» DR. BETTY SHABAZZ HEALTH CENTER

> BROOKLYN, 999 Blake Avenue
> nARCHITECTS
> Department of Health and Mental Hygiene, 2008

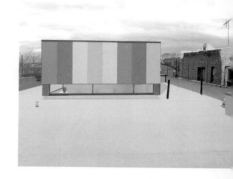

This 5,600-square-foot community health center serves as a one stop health clinic for the East New York community. This renovation and expansion project includes the addition of a mezzanine floor, façade repair, upgrade of the mechanical systems, and a reconfiguration that increases the number exam rooms and patient areas. The design features a new entrance and reception area on the opposite end of the current lobby to improve functionality and usability for the staff and patients, while maintaining the center's operations during construction. The public image of the center will be entirely renewed through a socially relevant graphic mural, glazing at the new entrance, and a new metal canopy.

OPPOSITE, TOP » View of southwest corner renovation with new main entrance. OPPOSITE, BOTTOM » Photo of existing building. LEFT » View of new reception area and waiting room. ABOVE, TOP » View of proposed mezzanine addition. ABOVE, BOTTOM » View of previous entrance, reconfigured as a staff room.

⟫ STATEN ISLAND ANIMAL CARE CENTER

⟩ STATEN ISLAND, 3139 Veterans Roads West
⟩ GARRISON ARCHITECTS
⟩ Department of Health and Mental Hygiene, 2015

OPPOSITE TOP AND BOTTOM ⟫ Exterior. ABOVE ⟫ View through façade.

To encourage the adoption of animals and reduce animal stress, this design turns the typical shelter programming inside out. The animals are "in the window," while offices and other functions are deeper inside. Since the exterior skin is translucent, both the animals and the interior spaces benefit from natural daylight. At night, the glow of the building is a presence in the neighborhood.

The 5,500-square-foot building is sheathed in highly insulated, tongue-and-groove multiwall polycarbonate paneling supported by a gold anodized aluminum frame. The roof over the perimeter, where the animals are housed, is higher than that over the interior, where other shelter functions are located. This bi-level arrangement creates an interior clerestory between the two roof levels that brings sunlight into the building from all directions regardless of the time of day. Dog runs surround the exterior which is shaded by trees.

The building is designed to achieve a LEED Silver certification. It will have temperature controlled passive ventilation, a heat recovery ventilation system, photocell controlled high efficiency lighting, recycled steel components, high fly ash concrete, recycled polycarbonate, recycling stations, a water recovery system, and solar thermal water heating.

OPPOSITE, TOP » Lobby.
OPPOSITE, BOTTOM » Exterior side.

Exploded Building Modules Axonometric

1. Concealed mechanical equipment.
2. Translucent perimeter.
3. Painted spiral duct.
4. Structure.
5. Cattery.
6. Core building functions.
7. Animal enclosures along perimeter.

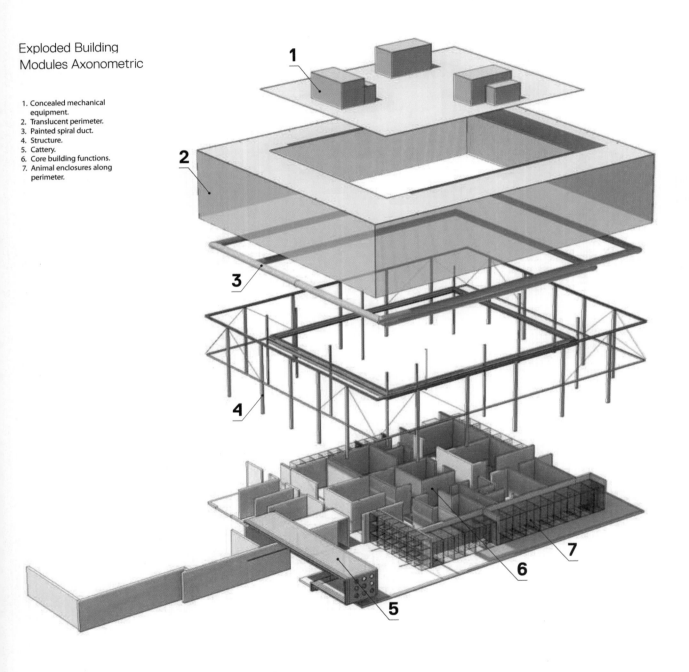

» 2 LAFAYETTE STREET

> › MANHATTAN, 2 Lafayette Street
> › BKSK ARCHITECTS
> › Department of Citywide Administrative Services, 2014

OPPOSITE, TOP » Rendering of the lobby of the new headquarters for the Department of Youth and Community Development. OPPOSITE, BOTTOM » Rendering of the lobby of the new Department for the Aging headquarters. BELOW » A floor plan for the Department of Youth and Community Development showcases a vibrant material palette that links the various program spaces within the sprawling headquarters.

This 110,500-square-foot renovation on seven floors of the historic Court Square Building is expected to achieve LEED Gold certification. This space will house two City agencies- the Department of Youth and Community Development and the Department for the Aging. A roundtable discussion early on with project leaders and representatives identified key attributes of a healthy, efficient, and sustainable office environment and how they could be woven through the new workplace.

The existing bones and infrastructure of the Court Square Building has posed opportunities for creating welcoming, natural light-infused spaces. New public spaces will be framed by expansive views of the City, reinforcing the agencies' connection to the communities and the importance of their efforts.

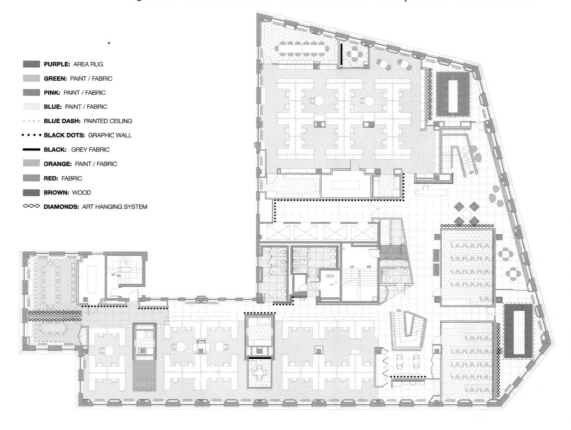

PURPLE: AREA RUG
GREEN: PAINT / FABRIC
PINK: PAINT / FABRIC
BLUE: PAINT / FABRIC
BLUE DASH: PAINTED CEILING
BLACK DOTS: GRAPHIC WALL
BLACK: GREY FABRIC
ORANGE: PAINT / FABRIC
RED: FABRIC
BROWN: WOOD
DIAMONDS: ART HANGING SYSTEM

PUBLIC SAFETY »»

» **POLICE STATIONS + CRIMINAL JUSTICE FACILITIES**

» **FIREHOUSES + EMS STATIONS**

During the last few decades, New York City has become an increasingly safe place. Modern public safety and first responder agencies require up-to-date facilities and equipment, but equally important is that such buildings are indeed visibly "public" and are seen as serving the community.

The recent building programs delivered by DDC for the New York Police Department, the Fire Department of New York, the court system, and the Department of Correction have helped ensure that the City's first responders are able to stay at the cutting edge of technology, while preserving the legacy of contemporary architectural quality that characterized these building typologies in eras past.

These projects include renovations and many new facilities, along with a major new police training academy, a new emergency call center, and a citywide integrated emergency command facility. The renovations ensure that the existing police stations and firehouses that are an important part of the City's historic fabric will continue to serve into the future, while the new facilities provide resources and accommodations befitting a 21st century force.

POLICE STATIONS + CRIMINAL JUSTICE FACILITIES

≫ KINGS COUNTY SUPREME COURTHOUSE

> BROOKLYN, 360 Adams Street
> CHRISTOFF:FINIO ARCHITECTURE
> Office of the Criminal Justice Coordinator, 2012

When the criminal court moved to a new building, the civil court could be reconfigured with more space. The redesign gathered all the public offices, previously scattered throughout the building, onto the main entry floor. Set behind glass, they immediately establish a more welcoming and accessible relationship between the City and its citizens. To further reduce the stress of going through a court system, each new courtroom has a dedicated, glass-enclosed conference space for consultations between client and counsel. These often sensitive meetings, which used to take place in public corridors, can now occur in an acoustically private, yet visible setting. All spaces—courtrooms, chambers, deliberation and robing rooms—have access to daylight.

OPPOSITE ≫ One of four new courtrooms.
RIGHT ≫ Behind the judge's bench.

OPPOSITE ≫ Floor plan. BELOW ≫
The main public corridor has a more
open and accessible feel.

ABOVE ≫ Benches for pre-trial counsel meetings.
BELOW ≫ View to the spectator's well.

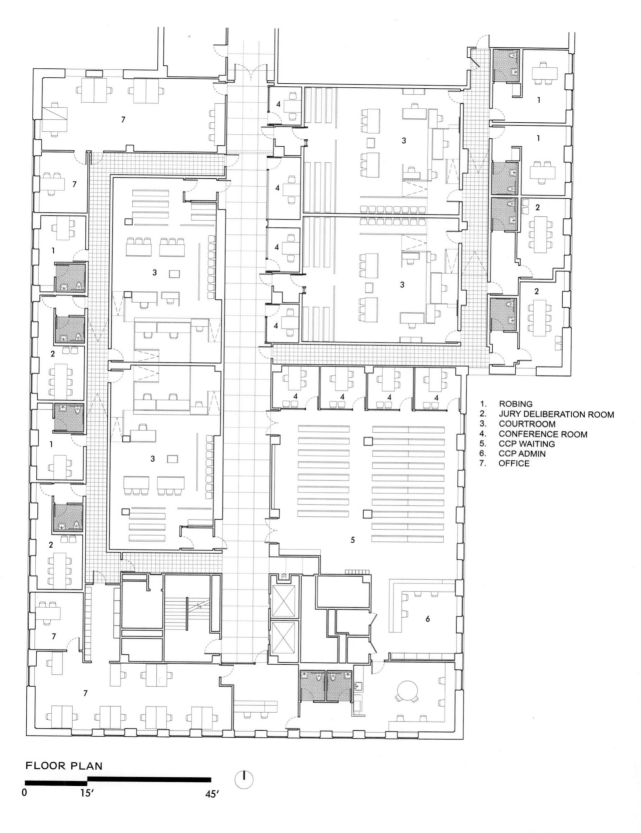

FLOOR PLAN

0   15'   45'

1. ROBING
2. JURY DELIBERATION ROOM
3. COURTROOM
4. CONFERENCE ROOM
5. CCP WAITING
6. CCP ADMIN
7. OFFICE

>> NEW YORK CITY POLICE ACADEMY

> QUEENS, College Point Boulevard and 31st Avenue
> PERKINS+WILL, Michael Fieldman Consulting Architect
> Percent for Art: Erwin Redl
> New York Police Department, 2013 (first phase)

OPPOSITE >> Court from east at dusk.
BELOW >> Four pedestrian bridges over
the existing canal connect the academic
and physical training buildings.

The largest public building project currently underway in New York City, which is also the largest project that DDC has ever undertaken, is a new police academy in northern Queens, just north of Flushing and across the bay from LaGuardia Airport. The project will create a model training facility for the country's largest police force and law enforcement agencies throughout the world. When complete, the 2,440,000-square-foot complex, located on the former site of a 35-acre police automobile pound, will serve thousands of recruits, civilians, active duty officers, and visiting police officers, in world-class learning and training environments.

The first phase will constitute 720,000 square feet. It includes a 370,000-square-foot instructional building with classrooms, offices, auditoria, and mock training environments designed to simulate the variety of conditions that police officers face in the field. The complex will include a 210,000-square-foot physical training building comprised of gymnasia, tactical training classrooms, a training pool, and a cafeteria. There will also be an outdoor muster deck to hold the entire recruit class, in addition to a running track, parking lot, and utility plant. Subsequent phases of the project will include the world's largest indoor firing range, a 450,000-square-foot "tactical village" that includes a subway car and mock street scenes, an eight-acre field for emergency vehicle exercises, rescue training facilities, an outdoor track, a museum, visiting lecturer and visitor accommodations, and additional parking space.

The highest density buildings are arranged in a c-shaped configuration, surrounding shared courtyard space, to allow for crossings between buildings and to minimize travel time and distances between the various destinations on campus. Two goals are achieved by physically arranging these components in this manner: the successful circulation of the 6,000 people on campus during the peak instructional hours, as well as maximum spatial flexibility for emergency staging and train-

ABOVE, LEFT » Atrium. ABOVE, CENTER TOP » Interior, dining area. ABOVE, CENTER BOTTOM » Auditorium.

ABOVE » Link and bridge.

ing. Throughout the design of the project, particular focus was placed on effective circulation across the campus to provide efficient, safe, and effective instruction, as well as achieve the client's desired degree of control and monitoring.

In addition to being a state-of-the-art training facility, the academy will be pioneering from the standpoint of both environmental and human health. The complex's sustainable features, many of which double as passive recreation space, include green roofs, rainwater harvesting systems for on-site reuse, biofiltration of stormwater runoff, energy efficient lighting, a high-performance building envelope with solar shading and daylight harvesting, and an energy-efficient utility plant. Sited on a former wetland that previously served as a dumping ground and drainage area, the overall campus design incorporates strategic landscaping approaches that ensure the complex's successful integration to its surroundings. The use of native plant species and reclaimed greenspace simultaneously blend the old and new environments, cool the site, and support improved air and water quality. The project is seeking a LEED Silver certification and incorporates several building design strategies from *New York City's Active Design Guidelines*.

>> PUBLIC SAFETY ANSWERING CENTER II

> SKIDMORE, OWINGS & MERRILL LLP
> New York Police Department, Fire Department of New York, and
  Department of Information Technology and Telecommunications, 2015

BELOW >> Aerial site rendering.
OPPOSITE >> Exterior view, day.

This 911 emergency answering center will be staffed by both the police and fire departments to create a new unified response center for the five boroughs of New York City. Its program required a highly secure and fortified architectural response.

The 240-foot cube of a building is securely sited through its setbacks, rotation on the site, and use of sculpted landscape. The serrated aluminum and charcoal-grey-toned metal façade give the building dynamism and visual anonymity. Depending on the viewer's perspective, traveling north or south on the adjacent parkway, the façade has a darker charcoal or lighter silver appearance.

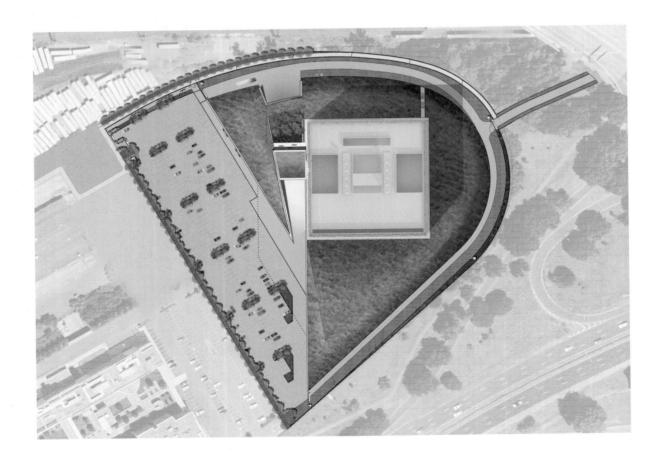

ABOVE » Glass pavilion
entrance rendering.
ABOVE, LEFT » Model elevation
of building exterior.

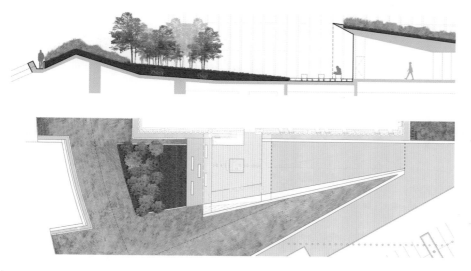

Windows and mechanical louvers inserted into the façade intentionally disguise the program behind them.

A courtyard garden provides an outdoor area for the employees of the emergency answering center. Reinforcing the idea of "approaching edges," the sloped entry and planted roof converge at this point to form the main gateway to the building. The glass entry pavilion stands at the intersection between the building and the open landscape beyond.

The cubic form of the call center offers flexibility and efficient planning for the functional demands of the 550,000-square-foot workplace inside. At the heart of the building is the 50,000-square-foot, 30-foot-high call center floor. The intense demands for communication information technology, and electrical and mechanical equipment are accommodated on adjacent floors. As an emergency answering center, the facility is designed to be self-sufficient, offering continuous service, even if utilities are interrupted.

An Active Modular Phytoremediation System was developed by the Center for Architecture, Science & Ecology, a multi-disciplinary research collaboration co-founded by SOM and Rensselaer Polytechnic Institute. This phytoremediation technology, which uses the roots of plants to clean the air and introduce nature to interior spaces, is being integrated into the lobby. As a secure, facility, the building offers limited opportunities as a sustainable and progressive workplace. Windows are restricted, even for the ground floor lobby and cafeteria areas. However, the project introduces sustainable features and exposure to nature for its users who are taking highly stressful calls at all times of the day and night.

ABOVE, LEFT » Section and plan showing employee courtyard.
ABOVE, TOP RIGHT » Active Modular Phytoremediation System.

≫ RIKERS ISLAND ADMISSIONS FACILITY

> QUEENS, 10-01 Hazen Street
> 1100 ARCHITECT AND RICCIGREENE ASSOCIATES JOINT VENTURE
> Department of Correction, 2018

This new 620,000-square-foot facility on Rikers Island will provide a central point of admissions for the majority of male adult inmates remanded to the Department of Correction. It will offer a more efficient intake process and, by replacing a number of outmoded temporary modular structures, maintain the current capacity on the island. Also, the reconfiguration will allow for future expansion in two locations.

The building will set a new standard for correctional facilities design through an emphasis on security, operational efficiency, and normative environments. The concept for the facility includes providing professional screening and evaluation for new arrivals, creating a basis for housing assignment that

LEFT ≫ Aerial view of the facility looking towards the south/west.
ABOVE ≫ View of the main staff entrance with housing units above.

accounts for both risk and need, and providing an environment where the expectation of orderly and respectful behavior is created through the use of environmental design, access to sunlight, views to the outside, good sightlines, acoustic dampening, year-round climate control, and security glass in lieu of steel bars.

The four-story structure is organized into two slender volumes separated by a central courtyard, aligned east-west to achieve maximum southern exposure. The façade is articulated with a variety of openings: larger for gathering areas and smaller for the admissions housing windows, arranged linearly to emphasize the long horizontal mass of the building. The courtyard, used by inmates for recreation, is bisected by a ramp that provides pedestrian and cart access to all floors of both sides of the building.

BELOW ≫ Diagram of sustainability features.

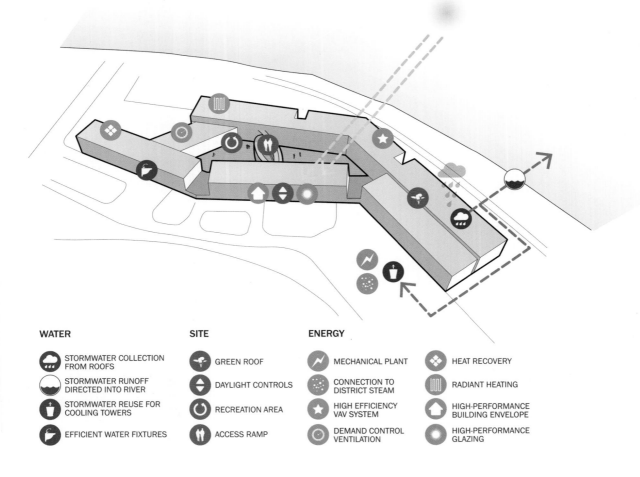

WATER

- STORMWATER COLLECTION FROM ROOFS
- STORMWATER RUNOFF DIRECTED INTO RIVER
- STORMWATER REUSE FOR COOLING TOWERS
- EFFICIENT WATER FIXTURES

SITE

- GREEN ROOF
- DAYLIGHT CONTROLS
- RECREATION AREA
- ACCESS RAMP

ENERGY

- MECHANICAL PLANT
- CONNECTION TO DISTRICT STEAM
- HIGH EFFICIENCY VAV SYSTEM
- DEMAND CONTROL VENTILATION
- HEAT RECOVERY
- RADIANT HEATING
- HIGH-PERFORMANCE BUILDING ENVELOPE
- HIGH-PERFORMANCE GLAZING

ABOVE ›› View of the facility from the East River looking south.

In addition to admissions, the facility will contain a public lobby, central control, administration, staff support, visitation, health services (including outpatient, specialty, and mental health clinics), gathering spaces for educational and religious services, outdoor recreation space, a barbershop, laundry, commissary, food services, and maintenance areas. Approximately 1,500 individuals will be accommodated in a combination of single cell, dormitory housing, and infirmary beds.

This project expects LEED Silver certification. The sustainable design approach includes emphasis on sustainable sites, water and energy efficiency, daylighting, and indoor environmental quality. Incorporating these durable, high-performance and sustainable strategies will result in long-term environmental benefits and operational cost savings.

⫸ 11 METROTECH SECURITY

> BROOKLYN, 157 Flatbush Avenue
> WXY ARCHITECTURE
> New York Police Department and Fire Department of New York, 2010

This project provided security enhancements for New York Police Department facilities and the Fire Department of New York headquarters at the Metrotech Center in downtown Brooklyn. The design included attractive and durable solutions, including six security booths, roadway barriers, and bollards.

The new parallelogram-shaped security kiosks challenge the notion that security enhancements automatically result in an aesthetic of unattractive, industrial materials and forms. The sculptural quality of this unusual booth enhances and softens its presence on the street. Moreover, the cladding, made from multi-layered glass panels, produces an ever-changing combination of shadows and reflections.

The design has been implemented in the context of the site improvements being put in place by Forest City Ratner for the contiguous Metrotech campus and planned streetscape improvements to Flatbush Avenue.

ABOVE, TOP ⫸ Security kiosk. ABOVE, BOTTOM ⫸ Kiosk at Tillary Street. OPPOSITE ⫸ Metrotech campus. BELOW ⫸ Kiosk plan.

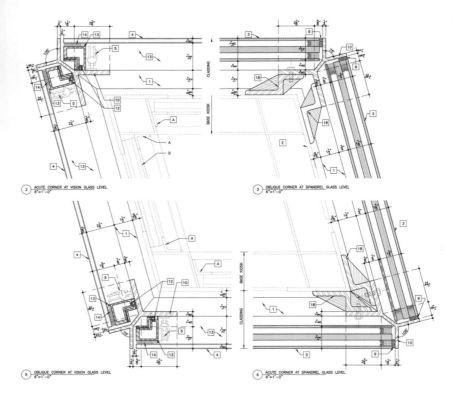

>> 121ST POLICE PRECINCT

> STATEN ISLAND, 970 Richmond Avenue
> RAFAEL VIÑOLY ARCHITECTS
> New York Police Department, 2013

ABOVE >> Exterior rendering.

The New York Police Department recognized the need for an expanded law enforcement presence that would cut response times and relieve the workload of the existing precincts on Staten Island. The new 52,000-square-foot 121st Police Precinct is the headquarter of the borough's first new precinct in decades.

The design solution responds to the challenges of an irregular site with two distinct building volumes—a two-story linear bar, gently arcing in plan and gradually increasing in height as it approaches Richmond Avenue and a separate one-story volume where the site extends outward to the south. The second floor cantilevers toward Richmond Avenue in a symbolic gesture of community engagement that defines the main entrance and creates a visual link between the main lobby and the street.

The two buildings are distinguished by varied heights, differing surface treatments—horizontal stainless-steel cladding on the long bar of the main building and gray brick on the one-story volume. A skylight over the interstitial space between them brings natural light into the ground-floor lobby. The long bar structure shields the residential neighborhood to the north from the police parking lot to the south. Outdoor mechanical services are concealed within the building. This project expects to achieve LEED Silver certification.

ABOVE » Model.
BELOW » Ground floor plan.

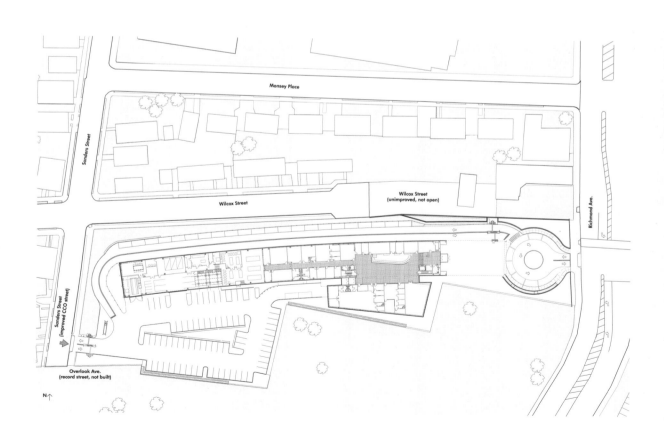

FIRE-HOUSES + EMS STATIONS

⟫ EMS STATION 27

> THE BRONX, 243 East 233rd Street
> WXY ARCHITECTURE
> Fire Department of New York, 2011

RIGHT ⟫ Apparatus bay.
OPPOSITE ⟫ Main south façade.

Built on the site of a former fire station in the northern reaches of the Bronx, this new building provides an ambulance station and emergency medical service facility on a busy main street backing on to a neighborhood of small homes.

The building program called for a three-vehicle service area, support zones, offices, a gymnasium and locker facilities, a training room, and a combined kitchen and lounge. The design for the 11,300-square-foot building addresses its relatively small site—about 2,900 square feet—and the need to dedicate much of the ground floor to EMS vehicles.

OPPOSITE » Stairs.
ABOVE, LEFT » Lounge overlook.
ABOVE, RIGHT » Stair.

The internal organization is driven by the need for visibility and immediate communication. Two interlocking functional blocks, each with a double-height space and interior vision panels, create openness and connectivity. A mezzanine with offices and life support facilities overlooks the ground-floor apparatus space. The third-floor locker area opens to a balcony with dining and meeting spaces in the lounge above.

Connecting these functional groupings is a central stair, color-coded with ceramic wall tile. Lot line windows allow for daylight and orientation to the stair. Reflecting the interlocking, paired floors inside, the four-level building reads as two stories from outside.

Responding to the site's conditions, the main façades are luminous while the sides are more matte. Each is distinct in proportion of zinc to masonry, and the striated glass openings vary from the front to the rear façade.

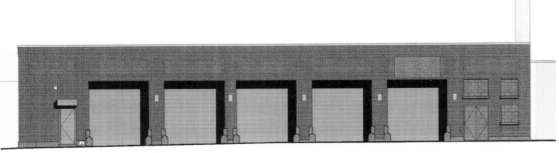

≫ EMS STATION 32

> BROOKLYN, 347 Bond Street
> BEYHAN KARAHAN & ASSOCIATES, ARCHITECTS
> Fire Department of New York, 2006

The Brooklyn Heights and Red Hook Emergency Medical Services Station is a 7,900-square-foot facility with division offices for the Fire Department of New York. The building was originally constructed in 1917 as an automotive garage.

This adaptive reuse is based on the prototypical program and spatial distribution of spaces built in various parts of New York City. A simple layer of metal paneling conceals deteriorated parts of the existing brick exterior of the building and creates a new modern composition for the façades. A slender new entrance canopy balances the flagpole and creates a modern and inviting new front entrance.

LEFT ≫ Exterior. FAR LEFT, BOTTOM ≫ Existing west elevation. LEFT, BOTTOM ≫ New west elevation. RIGHT ≫ Exterior.

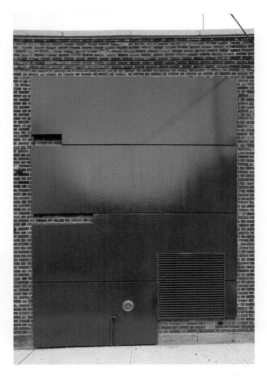

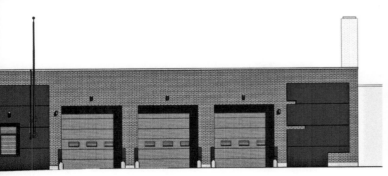

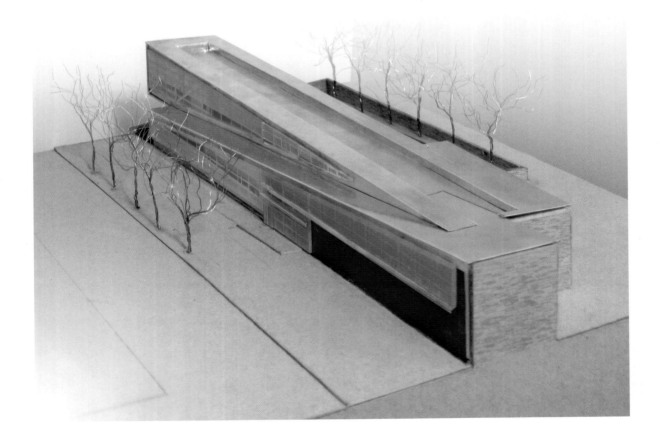

≫ EMS STATION 50

> QUEENS, 159-10 Goethals Avenue
> DEAN/WOLF ARCHITECTS
> Fire Department of New York, 2015

OPPOSITE, TOP ≫ Rendering showing cantilevered design. OPPOSITE, BOTTOM ≫ Model. ABOVE, TOP ≫ Concrete wall prototype. BELOW, CENTER ≫ North elevation. BELOW, BOTTOM ≫ South elevation.

This new 12,000-square-foot building on the Queens General Hospital campus will serve as the emergency medical service facility's new home. The station transforms the site's bi-directional slope, providing housing for vehicles, supplies, and changing areas for the men and women who provide emergency care to the community. The building rises up with an opposing angular volume that culminates in a dynamic cantilever overhanging the parking entry. This low-rise design maximizes the efficiency of the sloped site and mediates the disparate elevations of the surrounding neighborhood structures.

For the project's materials, long glass triangles in the window walls provide a translucent gradient that echoes the structure's angular forms. This theme is also expressed in the lightly carved pattern of diagonal slashes in the external concrete walls. Together, glass and rubber exterior surfaces create a crisp, open appearance.

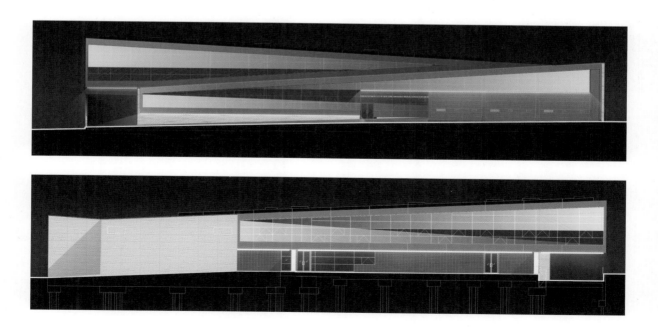

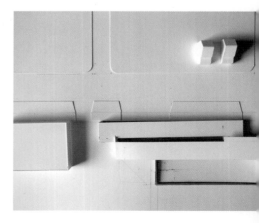

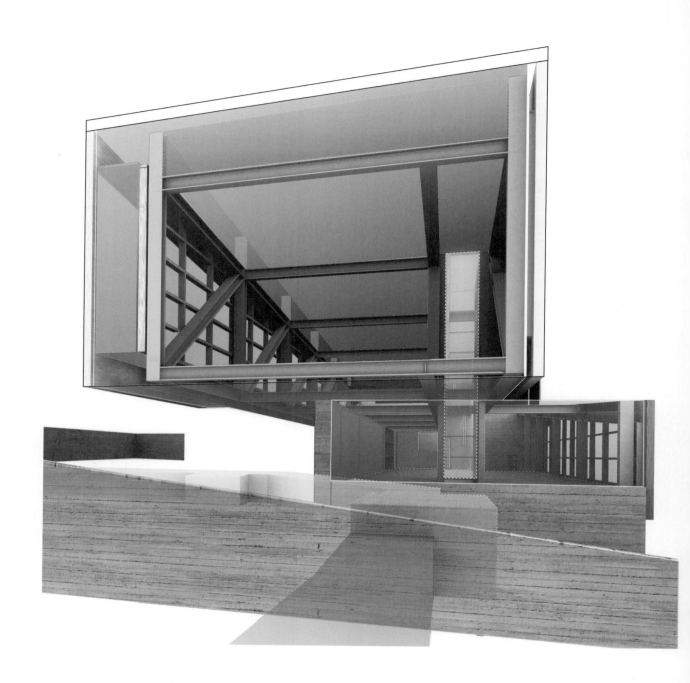

OPPOSITE, TOP LEFT >> Rendering
of an open office. OPPOSITE, TOP
RIGHT >> Rendering of atrium.
OPPOSITE, BOTTOM RIGHT >> Study
model. OPPOSITE, BOTTOM LEFT >>
Site bird's eye view.
ABOVE >> Section perspective
exposes the double volumes of
the building.

>> ENGINE COMPANY 63

> THE BRONX, 755 East 233rd Street
> THE GALANTE ARCHITECTURE STUDIO
> Fire Department of New York, 2013

This expansion doubles the building's size and meets Fire Department of New York guidelines—giving firefighters the room they need to perform their duties safely and effectively. The renovated building's exterior is clad in a gray terra cotta rainscreen, with inset cement board panels. A sunscreen incorporating the FDNY logo shades the structure's southern-facing windows.

The redesigned Engine Company 63 will have a completely new structure wrapped around the existing building. A new battalion bay, modern housewatch, decontamination area, commercial kitchen, and other elements will be located on the first floor. The second floor will house new dormitories, offices, training rooms, study rooms, bunk rooms, lockers, restrooms, and a fitness center.

LEFT >> *Bris soleil* fabrication.
ABOVE >> South façade.

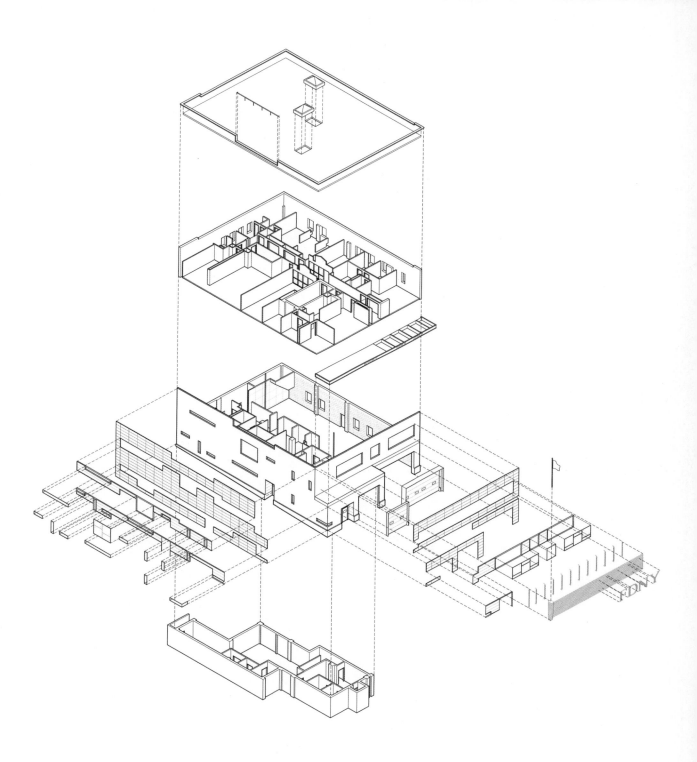

OPPOSITE, TOP » Rendering.
OPPOSITE, BOTTOM » West façade.
ABOVE » Exploded axonometric.

≫ ENGINE COMPANIES 97, 310, 320

> THE BRONX, BROOKLYN, and QUEENS, 1454 Astor Avenue;
5105 Snyder Avenue; 36-18 Francis Lewis Boulevard
> W ARCHITECTURE AND LANDSCAPE ARCHITECTURE
> Fire Department of New York, 2010

BELOW, TOP LEFT ≫ EC 310, Brooklyn. BELOW, TOP RIGHT ≫ EC 320, Queens. BELOW, BOTTOM RIGHT ≫ Construction in progress. BELOW, BOTTOM LEFT ≫ Construction in progress.

The primary objective of these renovations was to replace existing slab floors, built in the 1930s, to accommodate the increased weight of contemporary firefighting equipment. Services located on the first floor, including kitchens, restrooms, and the housewatch booth, were upgraded with modern amenities to contemporary barrier-free access standards. The design strategy was to work

with the existing historic fabric and insert new or rebuilt programs as contrasting elements.

For example, rebuilt programs elements were constructed largely out of bamboo plywood, a rapidly renewable material. Since lighting was important in the renovation, natural daylighting opportunities were maximized and energy efficient lighting was installed.

BELOW, TOP LEFT » EC 97, The Bronx. BELOW, TOP RIGHT » Model of Housewatch. BELOW, BOTTOM RIGHT » Site location, New York City. BELOW, BOTTOM LEFT » Construction in progress.

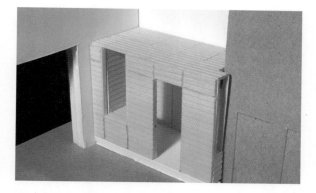

>> ENGINE COMPANY 217

> BROOKLYN, 940 Dekalb Avenue
> THE GALANTE ARCHITECTURE STUDIO
> Fire Department of New York, 2009

BELOW, LEFT AND OPPOSITE >>
Interior. BELOW, RIGHT >>
Restored stair.

This renovation added a new apparatus slab, complete with new drainage, fueling and truck maintenance systems, and a new exterior concrete truck apron. The apparatus slab was designed, in accordance with Fire Department of New York standards, to support a 90,000-pound fire truck. The basement can now house a number of different functions—a condition this firehouse had not seen in 50 years.

The 12,000-square-foot renovation also included a new commercial kitchen and lounge for firefighters, a housewatch with state-of-the-art FDNY technology, and fully renovated upper floors with office space, bunkrooms, and restrooms.

LEFT » Exterior.
BELOW » Housewatch.

OPPOSITE » Brick and masonry
exterior. RIGHT » New kitchen
and lounge.

≫ ENGINE COMPANY 235, BATTALION 57

> ⟩ BROOKLYN, 206 Monroe Street
> ⟩ THE GALANTE ARCHITECTURE STUDIO
> ⟩ Fire Department of New York, 2009

BELOW LEFT ≫ Housewatch.
BELOW ≫ Housewatch axonometric.
OPPOSITE ≫ Copper roof.

Engine Company 235 required a total renovation as years of deferred main-tenance had damaged this century-old structure. The roof and siding were damaged, and the drainage system was decaying. The original apparatus slab, designed to support four horses and a carriage, was weakening after years of serving trucks.

This 12,000-square-foot redesign addressed these issues. The historic details were retained as the building exterior was completely restored, a new historically appropriate copper roof was added to ensure that the building can provide another century of service. All of the masonry was tuck pointed with new mortar, preserving the period nature of the front façade. The new apparatus slab will support a 90,000-pound fire truck meeting Fire Department of New York standards. A new gear grid and housewatch were also installed.

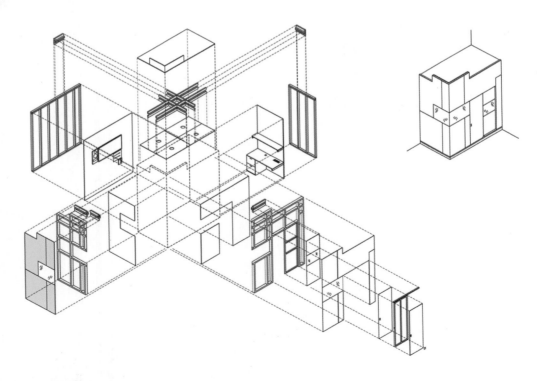

>> ENGINE COMPANY 239

> BROOKLYN, 395 Fourth Avenue
> BEYHAN KARAHAN & ASSOCIATES ARCHITECTS
> Fire Department of New York, 2008

OPPOSITE >> Exterior.
ABOVE >> Interior.

Built in 1895, this three-story, 7,000-square-foot brick and limestone structure, was typical of the firehouses serving low-to-medium density residential neighborhoods. It consisted of an apparatus room for fire engines, an office, a dormitory, a kitchen, and a lounge. The renovation adapted the interiors to the needs of 21st century fire fighting. The façade was restored, protecting and enhancing original details, including sculptural limestone carvings and decorative brickwork. A modern extension at the back of the building enlarged and seamlessly integrated the existing and new interior spaces.

New skylights over the stairway and the new kitchen and dining area introduced natural light into most of the work spaces of the building. The new south façade, with *brise soleil* and large glass openings, was also designed to bring in daylight while keeping the heat of the summer sun away from the interior, therefore reducing the energy consumption to comply with the current New York City energy guidelines.

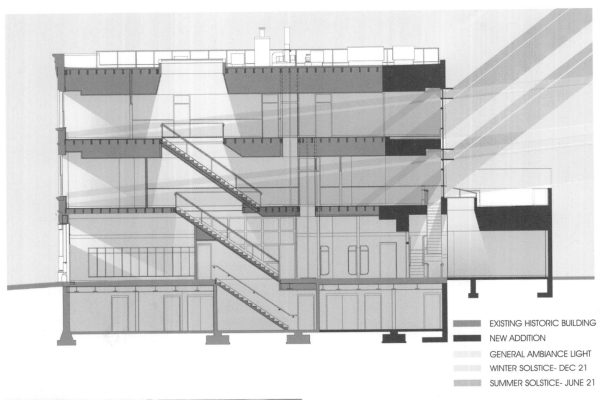

EXISTING HISTORIC BUILDING
NEW ADDITION
GENERAL AMBIANCE LIGHT
WINTER SOLSTICE- DEC 21
SUMMER SOLSTICE- JUNE 21

ABOVE ›› Skylights over the stairway and the new kitchen and dining area bring natural light into work spaces. The new south façade, with a *brise soleil* and large windows.
LEFT ›› Exterior. OPPOSITE TOP LEFT ›› Signage. OPPOSITE TOP RIGHT ›› Staircase detail. OPPOSITE BOTTOM LEFT ›› Façade. OPPOSITE BOTTOM RIGHT ›› Façade detail.

» ENGINE COMPANY 259, LADDER 128

> QUEENS, 33-49 Greenpoint Avenue
> ANDREW BERMAN ARCHITECT
> Fire Department of New York, 2009

ABOVE » Daylit lounge area.
BELOW, LEFT » Engine Company
259 Firehouse, Ladder 128. BELOW,
RIGHT » Dining room with stair to
roof terrace. OPPOSITE » Entrance
detail. FOLLOWING SPREAD »
Apparatus bay with stainless steel
housewatch.

This project involved the adaptive reuse of a classic New York City firehouse that could no longer accommodate the demands of modern firefighting equipment. The architects gutted and temporarily supported the brick shell of the original building to thread new structure, spaces, and mechanical systems into it.

Beyond solving the myriad of technological and logistical issues related to a modern firehouse, the project established coherent series of spaces suitable to the varied programmatic needs of the firefighters. The program included a garage for three trucks with fueling areas, as well as areas for cooking and dining, a lounge, offices, training rooms, locker rooms, a dormitory, a laundry, and an exercise facility.

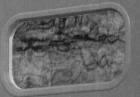

≫ GREENPOINT EMS STATION

> BROOKLYN, 332 Metropolitan Avenue
> MICHIELLI + WYETZNER ARCHITECTS
> Fire Department of New York, 2013

OPPOSITE ≫ Exterior night view. BELOW, LEFT ≫ Second floor split level. BELOW, RIGHT ≫ North-south linear atrium.

This two-story, 12,400-square-foot facility that supports the Fire Department of New York ambulance crews and vehicles has a strong, contemporary form occupying a prominent site on Metropolitan Avenue, near Bedford Avenue. This emergency medical services station is part of FDNY's plan to improve response time to medical emergencies throughout the City by increasing the number of stations and thereby reducing the distance ambulances travel to reach those in need.

The station's requirements led to a four-part division of the facility. Since the space for housing vehicles calls for a higher ceiling than in the rest of the station, one side of the building is taller than the other. This helps organize its functions. The east side of the ground floor has spaces for four vehicles and a vehicle support zone. The west side, in the lower bay, has offices and other administrative space.

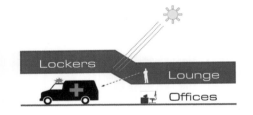

ABOVE, LEFT » View from vehicle bay. ABOVE, TOP RIGHT » Stair detail. ABOVE, BOTTOM RIGHT » Program diagram. OPPOSITE » Exterior corner detail.

Above the vehicle bay, on the second floor, are the locker rooms and restrooms for the personnel who maintain the station's three shifts. Across the atrium to the west is a fitness facility, training room, and a combined kitchen and lounge area. The first floor's different ceiling heights create different levels at the second floor and that shift in levels repeats at the roofline. The architects mark it with a skylight that extends from the front to the back of the building, bringing daylight to the second floor and, through an opening in the floor, to the ground level. The double height, glass-enclosed entry also marks the division between functions and is filled with natural light.

On the exterior, roll-up red doors on the vehicle side introduce bright color for what is otherwise a primarily cool, glass façade, provides a diagonal sculptural break, covered with perforated aluminum panels, that runs parallel along the street façade, connecting the entrance with the second floor. The 90-foot-long, second-story translucent glass wall, with a honeycomb pattern set into the glass, appears to float above the ground floor and is part of the building's strong identity.

≫ RESCUE COMPANY 3

> THE BRONX, 1647 Washington Avenue
> ENNEAD ARCHITECTS
> Fire Department of New York, 2009

BELOW ≫ Detail of principal façade.
OPPOSITE ≫ Principal façade.

This high performance structure is one of five new special operations rescue facilities in New York City. In addition to firefighting, these elite companies respond to specialized emergency situations, such as building collapses, subway emergencies, and scuba diving operations, and therefore have special infrastructure and equipment storage requirements. All spaces in this 20,000-square-foot building are strategically located in relation to the centrally placed apparatus rig, the most important element in the house. Responding to the restricted site, functions are stacked: physical work areas and storage occupy the ground and basement levels; rest, study and dining are on the second level; and training and fitness spaces are on the mezzanine. The primary design elements of the building's east façade are oversized Fire Department of New York red apparatus doors, which express the building's identity and create an open, yet secure, street presence.

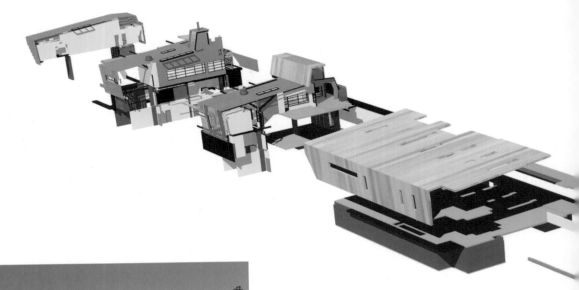

LEFT » Principal façade. BELOW,
LEFT » Apparatus bay. BELOW, TOP
RIGHT » Rear façade. BELOW, BOT-
TOM RIGHT » Corridor, level two.

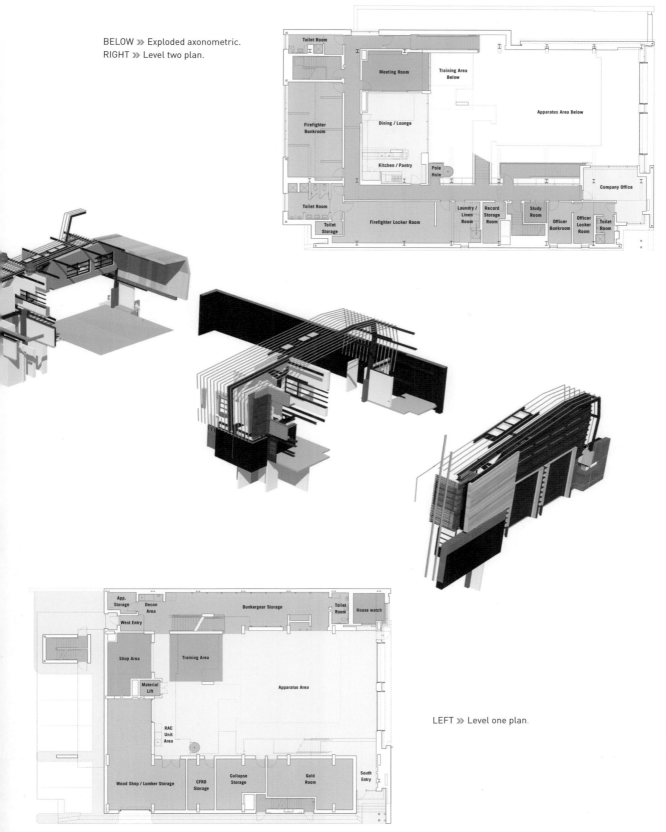

BELOW » Exploded axonometric.
RIGHT » Level two plan.

Toilet Room

Meeting Room

Training Area Below

Apparatus Area Below

Firefighter Bunkroom

Dining / Lounge

Kitchen / Pantry

Pole Hole

Company Office

Toilet Room

Toilet Storage

Firefighter Locker Room

Laundry / Linen Room

Record Storage Room

Study Room

Officer Bunkroom

Officer Locker Room

Toilet Room

App. Storage

Decon Area

Bunkergear Storage

Toilet Room

House watch

West Entry

Shop Area

Training Area

Material Lift

Apparatus Area

RAC Unit Area

Wood Shop / Lumber Storage

CFRD Storage

Collapse Storage

Gold Room

South Entry

LEFT » Level one plan.

►► ROCKAWAY EMS STATION + FIREHOUSE

> QUEENS, 303 Beach 49th Street
> BEYHAN KARAHAN & ASSOCIATES, ARCHITECTS
> Percent for Art: Jane Greengold
> Fire Department of New York, 2006

OPPOSITE ►► Exterior.
RIGHT ►► Exterior artwork
by artist Jane Greengold.

This new facility combined four service units of the Fire Department under one roof—Engine Company 265, Ladder Company 121, Battalion 47, and Emergency Medical Services (EMS) Station 47. The approximately 20,000-square-foot, two-story building houses 180 personnel. Offices, dormitories, EMS bunkrooms, kitchen, fitness and locker rooms wrap around the main apparatus room shared by firefighters and the EMS personnel.

The building partly consists of walls running parallel to the Rockaway Beach Boulevard and the nearby edge of the Atlantic Ocean. All the spaces are designed to receive daylight and to benefit from the natural ventilation of sea breezes to reduce the energy consumption of this 24-hour building.

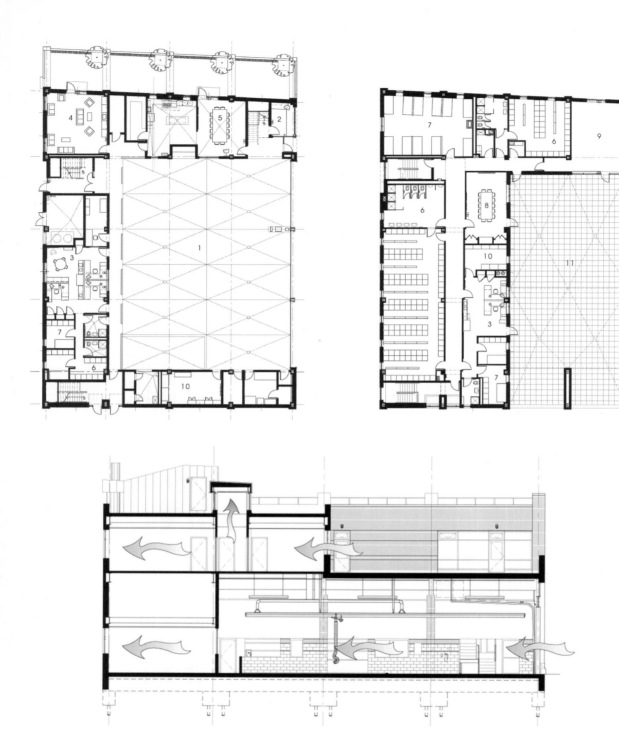

ABOVE » First floor plan (left) Second floor plan (right): 1. Apparatus, 2. House-Watch, 3. Office, 4. Lounge, 5. Dining area and kitchen, 6. Locker room, 7. Bunk room/Dormitory, 8. Training room, 9. Fitness area, 10. Storage, 11. Terrace.
RIGHT » Every space in the building receives daylight and is cross-ventilated with the breezes to function without dependence on artificial sources of power.

LEFT » Interior, stair.
TOP RIGHT » The staff
entrances to the building.
BOTTOM RIGHT » Interior stair.
BOTTOM LEFT » Exterior.

⟫ WOODHULL EMS STATION

⟩ BROOKLYN, 720 Flushing Avenue
⟩ BEYHAN KARAHAN & ASSOCIATES, ARCHITECTS
⟩ Fire Department of New York, 1999

OPPOSITE ⟫ Woodhull Station.
ABOVE ⟫ Harlem Station.

The Woodhull building is divided into three zone one is for office and administration, another for apparatus parking and decontamination, and the third is for mechanical services and storage. This separation allows the most economical use of energy by differentiating the distinct heating and cooling needs of each zone.

After the completion of the first building on the campus of the Woodhull Hospital in Brooklyn, four new buildings followed in Harlem, Bathgate, Kings County and Springfield Gardens. In each location, the public presence of the building was designed with sensitivity to its architectural context; sometimes to stand out and sometimes to blend in with the character of the surrounding neighborhoods.

In the process of locating sites for the new EMS buildings, a few existing structures were found. In these locations, a new adaptive reuse strategy was used to house similar proximities and program elements that were in the original program.

The Woodhull project received the Special Design Recognition Award by the Art Commission of the City of New York in 1999.

ABOVE » Springfield Station.
BELOW » King's County Station.
OPPOSITE » Prototype plans.

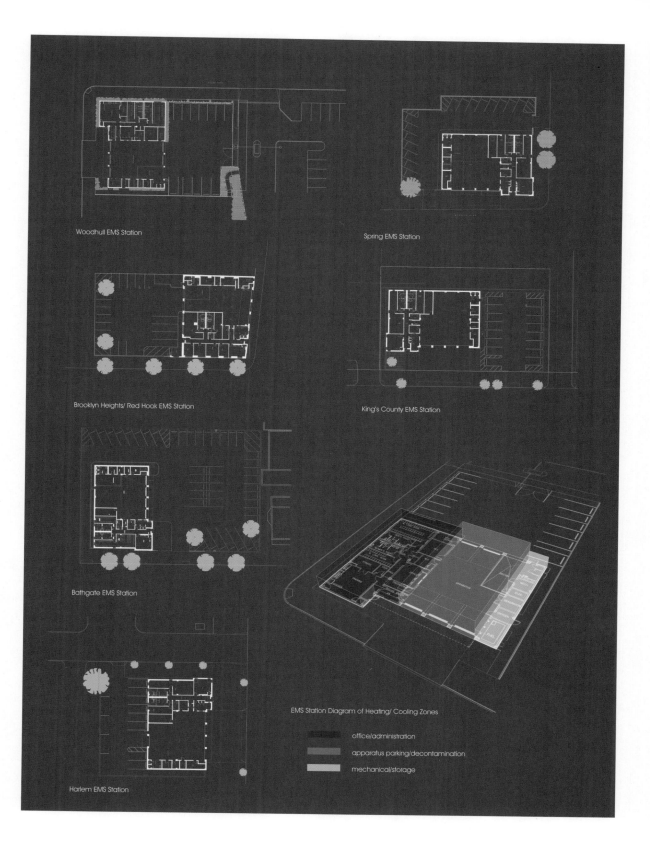

Woodhull EMS Station

Spring EMS Station

Brooklyn Heights/ Red Hook EMS Station

King's County EMS Station

Bathgate EMS Station

Harlem EMS Station

EMS Station Diagram of Heating/ Cooling Zones

office/administration

apparatus parking/decontamination

mechanical/storage

›› ZEREGA AVENUE EMS STATION

> THE BRONX, 501 Zerega Avenue
> SMITH-MILLER + HAWKINSON ARCHITECTS
> Fire Department of New York, 2014

This project's site was once an abandoned lot that was converted into a community garden. It shares the district with low-rise industrial and manufacturing warehouses, high-rise housing project towers, and the Bronx River. The new facility brings emergency services to the community and, by design, broadcasts an optimistic message. Its green roof, visible from the street and the high-rises alike, its translucent luminous polycarbonate skin transparent by day and beacon-like at night, and its welcoming cantilevered portico all portend a bright future for the neighborhood.

The green-roofed 13,500-square-foot building is designed to help mitigate the loss of the 28,350-square-foot site's existing garden. The project aligns itself with the City's vision of sustainable urban development. Sustainable features include reducing stormwater runoff through strategically located porous paving, storm and grey water reuse, planning and material strategies for natural ventilation and daylighting, use of recycled materials, and reduced energy use through efficient building systems and equipment.

OPPOSITE, LEFT ≫ Contruction photo of west façade. OPPOSITE, RIGHT ≫ Interior. LEFT ≫ Exterior. ABOVE ≫ Rendering of west façade.

Winter
SUN ANGLE

Summer

HEAT BUFFER

EVAPORATION

AIRFLOW MOVEMENT
DRIVE-THROUGH

OPPOSITE, TOP AND CENTER ⟩⟩ Elevation views of model. OPPOSITE, BOTTOM ⟩⟩ Natural ventilation diagram. LEFT ⟩⟩ Exterior. BELOW ⟩⟩ View to Bronx-Whitestone bridge.

INFRASTRUCTURE PROJECTS IN THE 5 BOROUGHS

>> **PEDESTRIAN RAMPS**

>> **SIDEWALKS**

>> **SEWER**

>> **WATER**

>> **STREET RECONSTRUCTION**

>> **STREET RESURFACING**

>> **INFRASTRUCTURE RESTORATION**

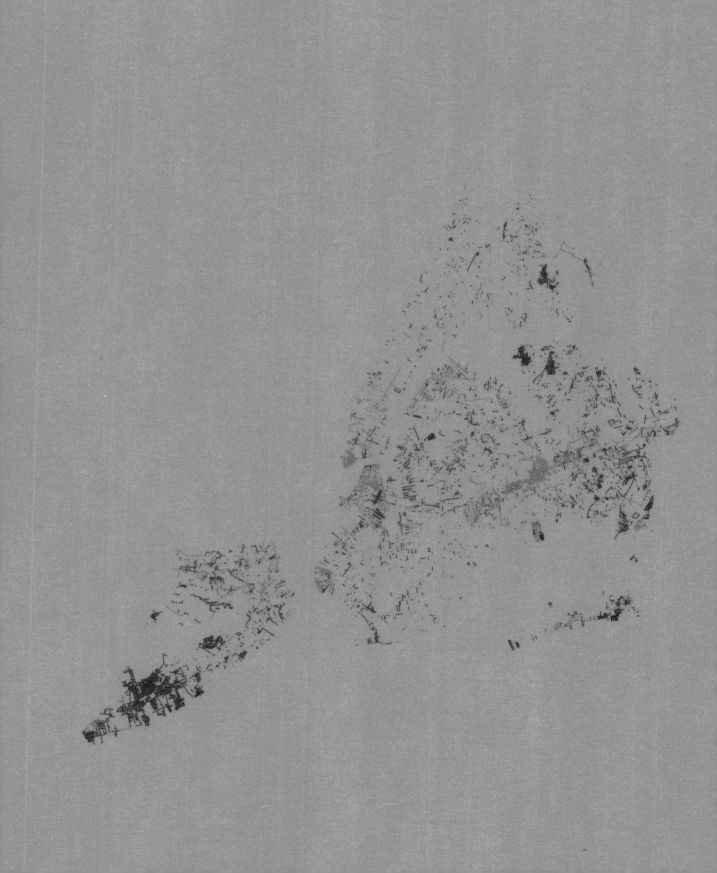

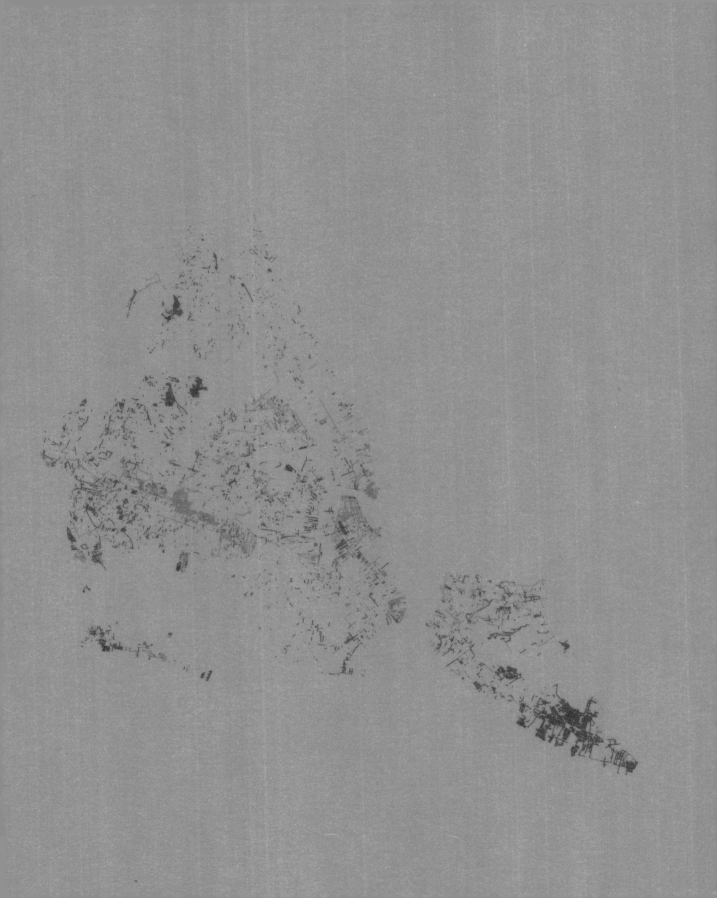

INFRA-STRUCTURE

» **WATER MAIN PROJECTS**

» **TRENCHLESS TECHNOLOGY**

» **STORMWATER MANAGEMENT**

» **INFRASTRUCTURE SUPPORT BUILDINGS**

While sophisticated museums, lively public plazas on reclaimed streets, and welcoming neighborhood libraries may make great impressions, it is likely that rarely seen infrastructure improvements may actually make a bigger difference in New Yorkers' daily lives.

Besides building an extensive network of streets, water mains, and storm and sanitary sewers, DDC builds and rehabilitates step streets (where there are steep grade changes), retaining walls, and community plazas. The agency has also repaired and restored historic streets, such as Stone Street and Houston Street, between the Bowery and West streets, in Manhattan, and Water Street in the DUMBO area of Brooklyn. Houston Street was modernized and landscaped, and a park was created at Bedford Triangle, while its water supply system was updated for the necessary link to City Water Tunnel No. 3. on the west side and for residents on the east. Historic High Bridge between Manhattan and the Bronx, which was built as part of the 19th century Croton Aqueduct, is being repaired, reinforced, and will reopen as a pedestrian bridge and living museum.

While DDC is building, it is also developing and using innovative and sustainable construction strategies. Trenchless technology keeps busy streets functioning while major work takes place underground. A trenchless slip lining method was used along Madison Avenue, in Manhattan, without signficantly disrupting traffic, commerce, or residents. The same technology is now being used under Lincoln Center and on 62nd Street between Amsterdam and Columbus avenues. Another type of trenchless method, microtunneling, was used on construction projects along the Belt Parkway in Queens, on Hamilton Parkway in Brooklyn, and on the South Shore of Staten Island. Even before the City experienced unprecedented flooding due to recent catastrophic storms, DDC and the Department of Environmental Protection (DEP) have been working on developing stormwater management systems.

Keeping New York City's infrastructure working requires specialized support buildings and facilities that provide for ongoing repair and maintenance of the City's water mains, sewers, roadways, and sidewalks. These buildings are critical to the operations of the DEP and the Department of Transportation (DOT). They include everything from the new Remsen Ave Yard for the DEP, where their vehicles are serviced, to the new Hamilton Avenue asphalt plant that DOT uses to produce asphalt with high recycled content for repairing potholes and resurfacing streets.

WATER MAIN PROJECTS ›› ›› ››

›› CITY WATER TUNNEL NO. 3 SHAFT CONNECTIONS + WATER MAIN INSTALLATIONS

> MANHATTAN, Grand Street, Hudson Street, Lafayette Street, Second Avenue, Eighth Avenue, West 30th Street, East 31st Street, West 48th Street (including Lincoln Center area), East 58th Street, East 59th Street, and East 60th Street

> Department of Environment Protection, (construction started in 2009 and is ongoing)

OPPOSITE AND FOLLOWING SPREAD ›› Hudson Street shaft connection.

The New York City water supply system provides approximately 1.2 billion gallons of drinking water daily to more than 8 million residents of New York City, as well as to approximately one million people living in nearby Westchester, Putnam, Ulster, and Orange counties. This water originates as far as 125 miles north and west of the City in three watersheds comprising 19 reservoirs and three controlled lakes, and covers a total area of almost 2,000 square miles.

The water flows through aqueducts to balancing reservoirs, and then to the City's two main water tunnels, then into the City's approximately 7,000 miles of water mains, which deliver water to the service lines of homes and buildings and eventually to individual faucets.

Until now, the two original tunnels—Nos. 1 and 2—have conveyed all of New York City's water. Both are located deep within the bedrock of the City and need to be closed for inspection and repairs. To facilitate this work, the City is constructing a new 60-mile long water tunnel—Tunnel No. 3. The City's Department of Environment Protection has completed construction of ten shafts to connect Tunnel No. 3, which is below the major bridges between the boroughs, to a new water main system that DDC is installing. These water mains (mostly 48 and 60 inches in diameter), located throughout the borough of Manhattan, will distribute drinking water consumed daily in New York City. The new water main work will also include installation of new sewers, drainage facilities, sidewalks, and roadways.

TRENCHLESS TECHNOLOGY ≫ ≫ ≫ ≫ ≫ ≫ ≫ ≫ ≫

> MANHATTAN, Madison Avenue from 41st Street to 78th Street
> BROOKLYN, Fort Hamilton Parkway
> Department of Environmental Protection, 2010

BELOW ≫ Madison Avenue, slip lining.

At the end of the Civil War, as New York City continued to expand, there was a need to increase the water supply for lower Manhattan, so a cast iron 48-inch water main was built under Madison Avenue from the Central Park reservoir to downtown. For more than a hundred years, this water main provided safe, clean water for New Yorkers. In more recent years, the water main began to show its age, so the City needed to lower its operating pressure to ensure its safe use.

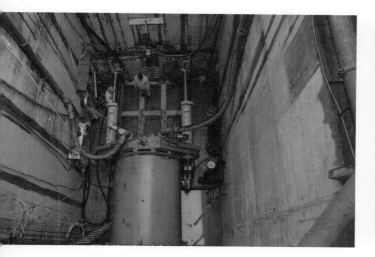

ABOVE » Fort Hamilton Parkway, pipe jacking.

To rehabilitate the aged pipes, the Department of Environmental Protection and DDC worked together to replace two miles of the water main. Recognizing the enormous disruption it would create if an open trench excavation method was used, DDC sought alternative methods to rehabilitate this main and chose pipe relining trenchless technology. Using this method, a polyethylene liner was folded into and pulled through the main from one small pit to others located at strategic points further down the main. This method eliminated the need for extensive trenching and avoided significant impact on local businesses and residential neighborhoods, as well as on traffic where four city bus routes are located. The pipe relining method also reduced delays from the impact of utility interference that are typically associated with large, open trench construction. Environmentally, it also reduced traffic congestion, pollution from trucking, and disposal of excess waste material.

Once completed, the project earned the world's record for the longest re-lining of a large diameter trunk water main. DDC is now looking to implement the same rehabilitation method to upgrade several other large diameter water mains, including those at the New York Botanical Garden in the Bronx.

DDC's Fort Hamilton Parkway project used a different type of trenchless technology, the pipe-jacking method, to alleviate severe flooding conditions and to improve water service in the Bay Ridge area of Brooklyn.

The pipe-jacking work replaced a century-old brick sewer pipe with a large, reinforced concrete pipe. During the pipe-jacking process, a tunneling machine slowly advances, removing only the amount of earth needed to incrementally advance the new pipe forward. The tunneling machine can be equipped with a wide variety of cutting heads that will allow the machine to pass through dry or saturated solids, sand, or rock. It is usually steered by an operator above a small jacking pit.

STORMWATER MANAGEMENT »»»»»»»

» BEST MANAGEMENT PRACTICES

> STATEN ISLAND BLUE BELT
> Department of Environmental Protection,
> BMP construction projects started in 1997 and are on-going

OPPOSITE, TOP LEFT, TOP RIGHT, BOTTOM » BMPs on Staten Island.

One of the most important environmental concepts implemented as part of the City's water system is the management of stormwater runoff using natural landscapes. These concepts are collectively called Best Management Practices (BPMs).

In much of New York City, stormwater runoff eventually enters the sanitary sewer system. When storms occur, this outflow can easily overwhelm the City's sewage systems causing combined sewer and rainwater ("CSOs") to overflow directly into the rivers and harbors. BPMs mitigate these extreme runoff conditions, thereby protecting the rivers and oceans around New York from the negative influences of stormwater runoff.

One of the largest and best examples of the use of BPMs is on Staten Island's Bluebelt, where drainage corridors that include streams, ponds, and marshes already exist. Using BMPs, DDC projects use natural enhancements, such as stilling basins, plantings, and swales, to slow down and retain the stormwater. Instead of entering into the already overworked stormwater runoff system, the extra water is held and filtered by rocks, sand, plants, and other natural devices, and then slowly released into the waterways. The Department of Environmental Protection, the City agency that initiated the BMP program, would like to reduce the stormwater flow by 10 percent in those areas where there is chronic overflow.

LEFT, BELOW LEFT,
BELOW RIGHT »
BMPs on Staten Island.

The Blue Belt has become an excellent example of a cost-effective storm-water management system for approximately one-third of Staten Island's land area. It avoids the construction of massive drainage culverts, which was standard practice in the past. It also has the additional benefit of providing open space and diverse habitats for native plants, land, aquatic animals, and migratory birds.

OPPOSITE TOP,
OPPOSITE BOTTOM »
BMPs on Staten Island.

INFRASTRUCTURE SUPPORT BUILDINGS »»»»»»

Continually updating New York City's infrastructure requires specialized buildings for materials and vehicle storage, as well as for their accompanying administrative services. These buildings are critical to the operations of the Department of Environmental Protection and the Department of Transportation and include everything from the new Remsen Avenue Yard for DEP, where its vehicles are serviced, to the new Hamilton Avenue Asphalt Plant that DOT uses to produce asphalt with high recycled content for repairing potholes and resurfacing highways.

» DELANCEY AND ESSEX MUNICIPAL PARKING GARAGE

> MANHATTAN, 107 Essex Street, Lower East Side
> MICHIELLI + WYETZNER ARCHITECTS
> Department of Transportation, 2014

OPPOSITE » Night perspective looking south. BELOW » The proposed façade for the Delancey + Essex Garage is a three dimensional surface of lines that is produced by offsetting two layers of composite cables.

This rehabilitation of the five-story, 40-year-old Municipal Parking Garage includes replacing the existing precast concrete panel façades facing Essex and Ludlow streets with a lightweight, naturally ventilated, visually dynamic façade that contributes to the rich texture of the neighborhood.

The proposed façade for the garage is composed of a three-dimensional surface of lines produced by offsetting two layers of composite cables. When the two layers, one planar and the other folded, are viewed together, moiré patterns are created when the pieces cross. The patterns seemingly move across the face of the building as the viewer's position changes whether they are walking or approaching by car. The patterns produced and the suggestion of movement are linked to the dynamic nature of moving vehicles occupying the structure.

The pattern of the cable design was inspired by the work of various abstract artists, such as Naum Gabo and Fred Sandback, who defined form and space simply with lines. The scheme to captures the dynamic quality of optical art from the

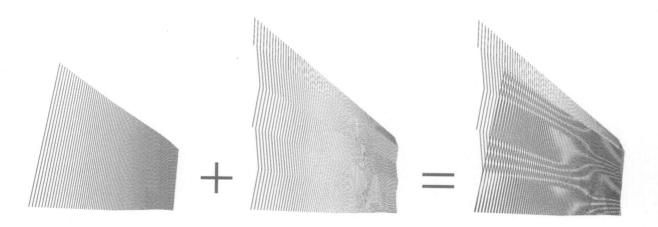

BELOW » Cable support details.

1960s, including Françoise Morellet's "Grillage" drawings, in which simple geometries were juxtaposed to create new, larger scale patterns.

The cable material itself is a standard Department of Transportation road barrier material, but here it is used in a new way—by turning its elements sideways and spanning vertically. The cables are positioned as if they were woven on a loom. This concept of weaving is loosely associated with the history of the Lower East Side and the garment industry that flourished there.

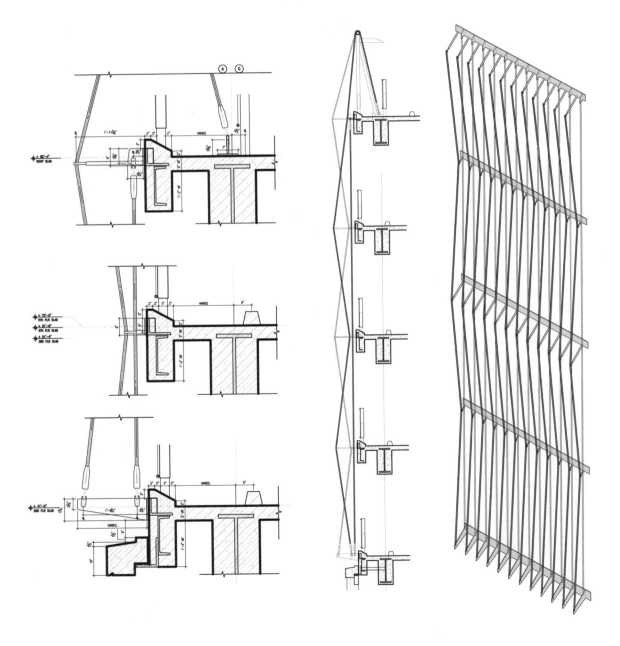

BELOW » Essex Street view.

The mid-block building has gated entrances on two streets. The ground floor office and restrooms are being renovated and 22 bicycle spaces will be added. The roof and elevators are being replaced and the supporting infrastructure upgraded.

A continuous edge of decorative lighting runs between the roof and the second level at the southern portion of the façade. The lighting grazes the cable screen and accentuates the geometry of the façade and, ultimately, the viewers' experience of it.

>> HARPER STREET YARD MAINTENANCE FACILITY

> QUEENS, 32-11 Harper Street
> nARCHITECTS
> Department of Transportation, 2009-2015

BELOW >> Diagram showing electrical connections to existing buildings. OPPOSITE >> View of electrical building entry and green roof.

As part of a renovation of the Department of Transportation's maintenance facility, nARCHITECTS designed a new electrical building and a monitoring booth that improves traffic patterns for a new diesel pump station. The new 500-square-foot electrical building will house panels and transformers for the DOT's asphalt plant. The building's appearance takes cues from the electrical symbol denoting a step up in power. Its green roof will be visible from a nearby highway. The booth's black and white tile cladding takes its cue from traffic signage; its façade literally indicates the flow of traffic. The project was honored with an Excellence in Design award by the Public Design Commission of the City of New York in 2011.

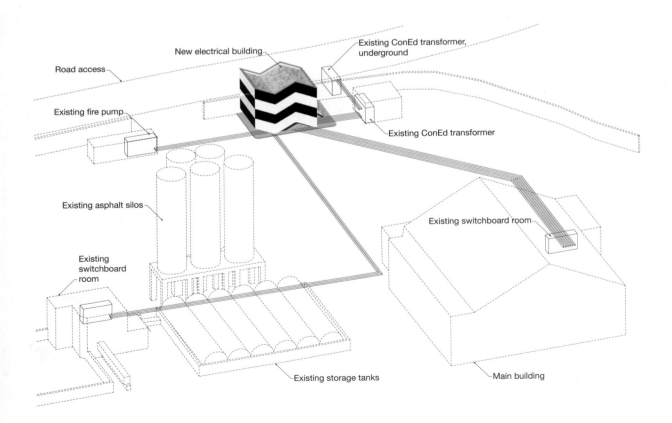

Road access

New electrical building

Existing ConEd transformer, underground

Existing fire pump

Existing ConEd transformer

Existing asphalt silos

Existing switchboard room

Existing switchboard room

Existing storage tanks

Main building

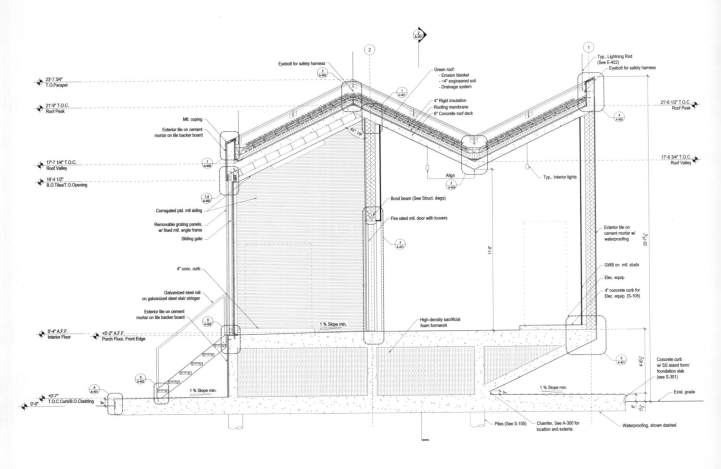

23'-7 3/4"
T.O.Parapet

21'-9" T.O.C.
Roof Peak

17'-7 1/4" T.O.C.
Roof Valley

16'-4 1/2"
B.O.Tiles/T.O.Opening

5'-4" A.F.F.
Interior Floor

+5'-2" A.F.F.
Porch Floor, Front Edge

+0'-7"
T.O.C.Curb/B.O.Cladding

0'-0"

21'-6 1/2" T.O.C.
Roof Peak

17'-6 3/4" T.O.C.
Roof Valley

Eyebolt for safety harness

Green roof:
- Erosion blanket
- ~4" engineered soil
- Drainage system

4" Rigid insulation
Roofing membrane
6" Concrete roof deck

Typ., Lightning Rod
(See E-402)
Eyebolt for safety harness

Mtl. coping

Exterior tile on cement
mortar on tile backer board

Align

Typ., Interior lights

Corrugated ptd. mtl siding

Bond beam (See Struct. dwgs)

Fire rated mtl. door with louvers

Exterior tile on
cement mortar w/
waterproofing

Removable grating panels,
w/ fixed mtl. angle frame

Sliding gate

GWB on mtl. studs

Elec. equip

4" conc. curb

4" concrete curb for
Elec. equip. (S-105)

Galvanized steel rail
on galvanized steel stair stringer

Exterior tile on cement
mortar on tile backer board

1 % Slope min.

High-density sacrificial
foam formwork

Concrete curb
w/ SS island form/
foundation slab
(see S-301)

Exist. grade

1 % Slope min.

1 % Slope min.

Piles (See S-105)

Chamfer, See A-300 for
location and extents

Waterproofing, shown dashed

ABOVE » Building section.
LEFT » View from site entry.
OPPOSITE, TOP » View of
east and north façades.
OPPOSITE, BOTTOM »
Diagram of electrical circuit.

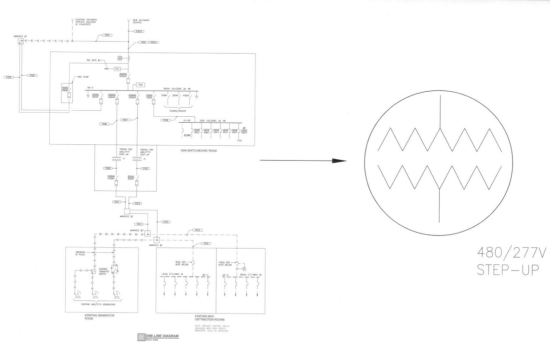

480/277V
STEP–UP

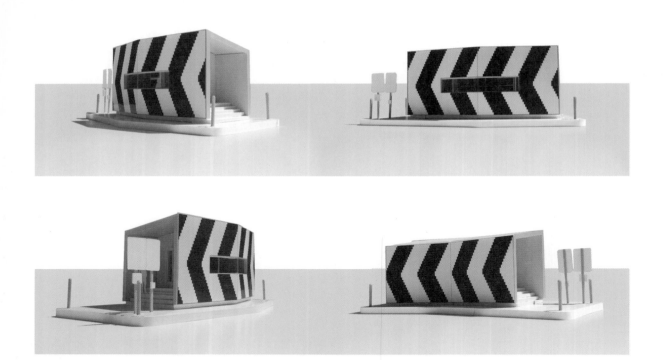

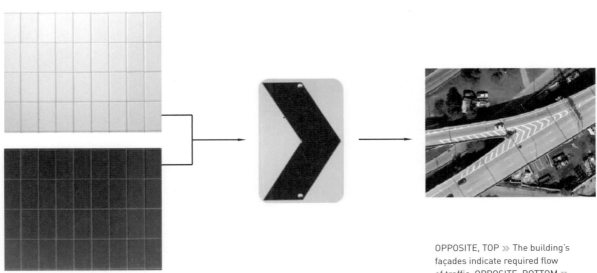

OPPOSITE, TOP » The building's façades indicate required flow of traffic. OPPOSITE, BOTTOM » View of building situated in asphalt landscape. ABOVE » Alternating light and dark bands of tile in the spirit of traffic symbols and road markings. RIGHT » Building elevations and diagram illustrating tile pattern.

» JEROME YARD

> THE BRONX, 3201 Jerome Avenue
> 1100 ARCHITECT
> Department of Environmental Protection, 2008

BELOW » Jerome Yard was intended to be a New York City Department of Design and Construction High Performance Pilot project, and as such was designed to exceed the sustainability requirements of Local Law 86 and target LEED Silver certification.

This 144,000-square-foot administrative and maintenance facility is located in the center of a dense Bronx neighborhood, which includes a landmarked brick Romanesque Revival pumping house and various other masonry buildings that do not meet the Department of Environmental Protection's needs. 1100 Architect completed a feasibility study and concept design for the yard in 2008. To optimize security, circulation, and sustainability on the site, the design preserves the existing landmark, proposes the demolition of ancillary structures, and adds a new facility to house offices, a garage, and maintenance services.

Designed to achieve LEED Silver certification, sustainable features include daylight harvesting, solar water heating, and rainwater capture and reuse. To maximize the efficiency of the site, offices will be centrally located opposite the main vehicular access road and the main truck garage is located to the south. Arranging the buildings in a compact manner allows for future expansion to the north while providing the most straightforward vehicular circulation possible. The faceted planes of the glass-enclosed office structure recall the triangular form of the pumping station's gable, presenting a contemporary yet site-sensitive counterpoint to the landmarked building. The column-free garage is wrapped with metal mesh façades and gates.

ABOVE » 1100 Architect's design approach to the Jerome Yard complex would greatly improve security and circulation on the site.
RIGHT » Site Plan.

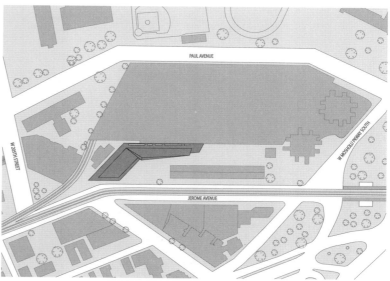

MANHATTAN COMMUNITY DISTRICTS 1/2/5 GARAGE AND SALT SHED

> MANHATTAN, 500 Washington Street, 297 West Street
> DATTNER ARCHITECTS with WXY Architecture + Urban Design
> Department of Sanitation, 2016

Overlooking the Hudson River at the corner of Spring and West streets, next to the Holland Tunnel vent shaft, this structure will house three district garages for the Department of Sanitation. The new 425,000-square-foot, multi-story building will accommodate more than 150 sanitation vehicles and personnel facilities for each district, as well as centralized fueling and repair facilities.

A double-skin façade wraps the curtain wall with perforated metal fins to vertically articulate the massing and limit sun exposure. The fins are operable for the occupied spaces. An extensive green roof softens views from neighboring buildings, protects the roof, and enhances stormwater retention and thermal performance. The garage is designed to achieve LEED Gold certification.

On the adjacent site, the Spring Street Salt Shed's solid, crystalline surface acts as a counterpoint to the diaphanous, scrim-like façade of the garage to the north. The cast-in-place concrete 6,300-square-foot structure tapers toward the bottom—creating more pedestrian space—and rises from a glazed moat that will be illuminated at night. Standing nearly 70 feet tall, the shed will house 4,000 tons of salt and create an iconic landmark at this important intersection.

ABOVE ›› West elevation. RIGHT ›› Rendering view from Hudson River Park of Manhattan Districts 1/2/5 Garage and Spring Street Salt Shed.

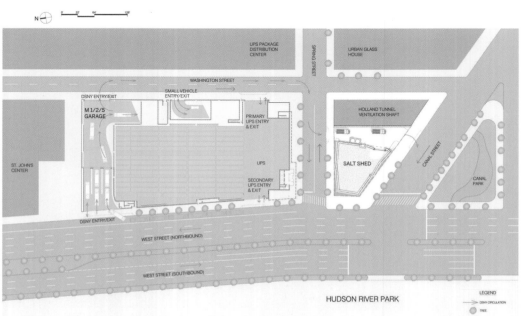

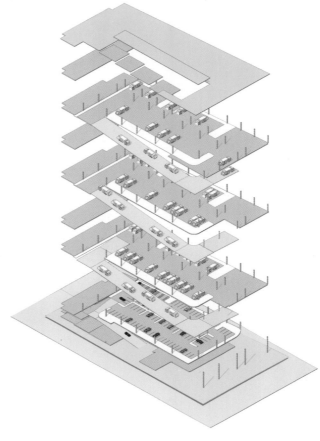

LEFT » Site plan. ABOVE » View
of garage from Hudson River Park.
OPPOSITE, TOP » Axon. OPPOSITE,
BOTTOM LEFT » Section through
personnel mezzanine levels.
OPPOSITE, BOTTOM RIGHT »
Section through garage level.

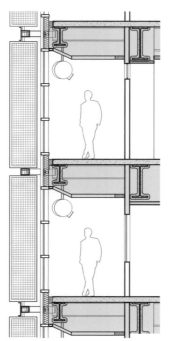

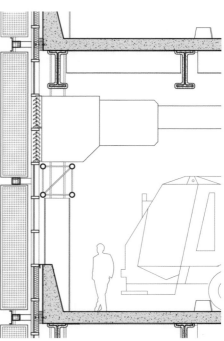

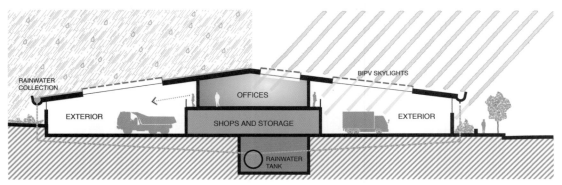

RAINWATER COLLECTION

BIPV SKYLIGHTS

OFFICES

EXTERIOR

SHOPS AND STORAGE

EXTERIOR

RAINWATER TANK

⟫ REMSEN YARD

> BROOKLYN, 855 Remsen Avenue
> KISS + CATHCART ARCHITECTS
> Department of Environmental Protection, 2012

OPPOSITE, TOP ⟫ Reclaimed brickwork and new landscape at main entrance. OPPOSITE, BOTTOM ⟫ Environmental response diagram. ABOVE ⟫ Plans, elevations, and section.

This 2.5-acre facility in Canarsie is a critical maintenance center for New York City's water supply and sewer systems. Although Remsen Yard is one of the Department of Environmental Protection's largest, it had been constructed piecemeal since the 1930s. Kiss + Cathcart reconfigured and optimized the layout, mandating high design standards and environmental sustainability in a building type that has often been treated only as utilitarian infrastructure. Most of the site was to remain a vehicular lot, with perimeter piles for material storage, but workshops and administrative offices were also to be rebuilt and enlarged.

While the agency had anticipated that most vehicle areas would be inside a heated garage, early workshops on program and sustainability produced a breakthrough idea—instead of completely enclosing the lots, they could be roofed for sun and rain protection but otherwise remain open.

The challenge was to figure out how this roof could provide light, ventilation, and rainwater collection. A standard skylight module, coordinated with the structural system, provides appropriate even light levels in all covered spaces. At the high end of each skylight strip, a custom-designed vent draws air out, so that vehicle exhaust does not build up under the roof. Monocrystalline photovoltaic cells in the skylights double as translucent glazing to minimize material use.

More than an acre in area, the productive roof collects up to one million gallons of rain and snow a year. Collected water, which passes through two first-flush drywells, is stored in a 20,000-gallon tank. It is then treated and dispensed for truck washing and materials misting for dust control.

The site was surrounded by a Works Progress Administration's-era brick wall in a striking vertical bond. The new design incorporates 400 feet of rehabilitated wall along Avenue D and reuses the brick mosaic for signage at the new entrance. Where Remsen Yard had appeared inaccessible behind a high wall, the new building is set 15 feet back from the original perimeter, behind a linear garden. Portions of the brick wall cut away to mark the new entrance and provide street-side seating. Low-maintenance native plantings establish a swale to filter runoff from the roof that is not diverted to the facility's catchment system. The ground surface of the swale is covered in a mix of stones and crushed recycled glass. This landscape strategy puts a green edge where the most people will experience it, discouraging graffiti by masking exposed walls with plantings.

Remsen was designed to be straightforward and economical. The oversailing roof is a clear and repetitive structural module, and its steel trusses and deck are left exposed as expressive elements. Conventional materials achieve unconventional effects of translucency and layering. Instead of costly metal screens, perforated corrugated sheet and chainlink mesh produce striking results inexpensively. Enclosed garages are simply fair-faced concrete block construction; offices are clad in yellow panels that complement the industrial finishes.

Remsen's administrative offices are on a mezzanine, above the noise and exhaust of the vehicle lots, with an overview of activities. This is important for security, since much of the equipment and material on site is valuable.

The efficient office layout left a block of unassigned space, which is now an exterior courtyard with recycled-resin picnic tables, artificial turf, and lightweight planters—an unexpected amenity for the staff.

BELOW ≫ Open courtyard at mezzanine level. ABOVE ≫ Mezzanine walkway with standard materials used to emphasize translucency and daylighting. OPPOSITE ≫ Stair to office mezzanine.

» SIMS SUNSET PARK MATERIALS RECYCLING FACILITY

> BROOKLYN, 30th Street Pier, South Brooklyn Marine Terminal
> SELLDORF ARCHITECTS
> Department of Sanitation, 2013

BELOW » View looking east of the tipping building (right) and the visitor center and administration building (left). OPPOSITE, LEFT » The tipping building's structural elements are expressed on the exterior allowing steel girders and lateral bracing to make a visual impact. OPPOSITE, RIGHT » Equipment inside the processing building sorts recyclables.

The Sunset Park Materials Recycling Facility is a center for processing for metal, glass, and plastic recyclables being undertaken by Sims Municipal Recycling and New York City. It will be the largest facility of its kind in the United States. The project is located on an 11-acre waterfront site in Sunset Park adjacent to a former manufacturing and shipping terminal built in the 19th century. The facility's design was influenced by the neighborhood's industrial history, as well as its programmatic use as a recycling center, which inspired reuse throughout.

The master plan devotes 36 percent of the site to newly created greenspace which remediates the brownfield land with native plantings and bioswales. Another critical aspect of the plan is the creation of distinct circulation systems, separating visitors from facility operations and a truck delivery route. The 125,000-square-foot facility includes a tipping building, where recyclables arrive by barge; processing and bale storage buildings; and a visitor center and administration building, where students and the public learn about recycling. In anticipation of rising sea levels, buildings sit 4 feet higher than specified by current requirements.

Working within the constraints of a pre-engineered building, one of the design challenges was to build a facility that would distinguish it from ordinary big box construction. In response, structural elements are inverted to appear on the exterior, causing the steel girders and lateral bracing to make a visual impact.

The facility will make a major environmental contribution to the City by delivering recyclables by barge—a strategy which minimizes the distance collection trucks must travel and eliminates 260,000 miles of annual vehicle travel from roadways. Other sustainable measures being implemented include the largest application of photovoltaics in New York City, a wind turbine that generates 25 percent of the facility's power, and bioswales for stormwater filtration. Recycled materials are used throughout: site fill is made from a composite of recycled glass, asphalt, and rock reclaimed from the Manhattan's Second Avenue subway construction; the metal buildings are 98% recycled U.S. steel; and visitor plazas are finished with recycled glass.

STATEN ISLAND FERRY TERMINAL + PETER MINUIT PLAZA

> MANHATTAN, 4 South Street and Whitehall Street
> FREDERIC SCHWARTZ ARCHITECTS
> Department of Transportation, 2005

Handling more than 21 million commuters and tourists each year, the 225,000-square-foot Staten Island Ferry Terminal is located at one of the most spectacular sites in the world at the tip of Manhattan. With the historic New York Harbor as foreground and the city skyline as background, the building's dramatic location, its symbolic role as a gateway to the city, and its function as a major intermodal transportation node demanded a strong civic presence. The terminal is a lively gathering space that hosts music, art installations, dance performances, and other cultural events. The 75-foot-high entry hall and surrounding glass curtain wall allow the downtown skyline that dramatically defines the site to be brought into the building, providing expansive space for the 70,000 commuters and tourists who pass through the terminal every day and look out on the harbor and the Statue of Liberty.

LEFT ≫ Upper entry level.
ABOVE ≫ Entrance.

This project introduced measures to reduce energy use by more than 40 percent, such as the largest and first major public installation in Manhattan of south-facing integrated photovoltaic spandrel and roof panels that provide five percent of the building's electrical load. Other sustainable strategies include passive ventilation for cooling, a radiant floor heating system, low-energy mechanical systems, alternative transportation, bicycle friendliness, water-

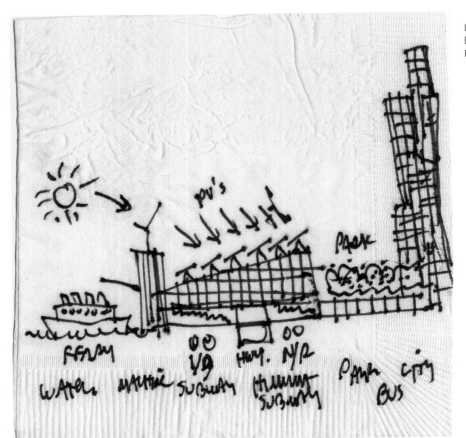

LEFT » Concept sketch
(by Frederic Schwartz).
BELOW » Building section.

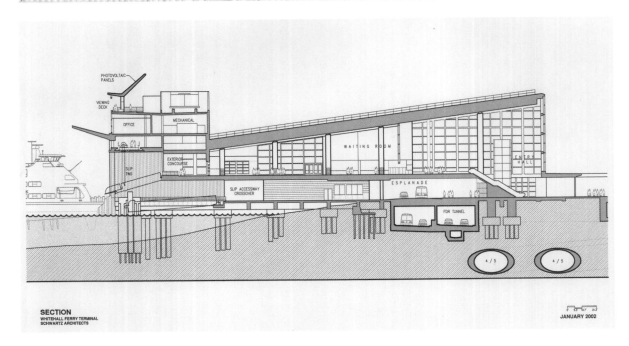

PHOTOVOLTAIC
PANELS

VIEWING
DECK

OFFICE   MECHANICAL

                                        WAITING ROOM   ENTRY
                                                               HALL

EXTERIOR
CONCOURSE

SLIP
TWO

                    SLIP ACCESSWAY   ESPLANADE
                    CROSSOVER

                                                        FDR TUNNEL

                                                    4 / 5   4 / 5

SECTION
WHITEHALL FERRY TERMINAL
SCHWARTZ ARCHITECTS

JANUARY 2002

ABOVE » Harborside façade.

efficient landscaping, use of local and low-emitting materials, thermal comfort, daylight, and access to views. The design involved the first reconfiguration of Lower Manhattan streets in more than 100 years and, by removing a parking lot, restored a tidal wetland and viewing corridor to the waterfront. This major intermodal transportation hub also incorporates a new 1.3-acre public plaza and a safer streetscape with dedicated bicycle, bus, and taxi lanes.

The design overcame some of the most difficult engineering and construction challenges of any public project in the city. Imagine taking down a 100-year-old building and simultaneously building a new terminal directly on top of three of the oldest and most fragile subway tunnels in the system, as well as an underground highway—while 70,000 people a day were passing through the construction site with uninterrupted ferry service—without a single incident.

>> SUNRISE YARD

> QUEENS, 88-20 Pitkin Avenue
> GRUZEN SAMTON ARCHITECTS (now part of IBI Group)
> Percent for Art: Samm Kunce
> Department of Transportation, 2010

Sunrise Yard is a high-performance home base for the carpenters, electricians, and plumbers who maintain and support all of the buildings run by the Department of Transportation. The 27,000 square-foot structure, located in a residential area, demonstrates that sustainable facilities are achievable using low-tech strategies.

A new building with an energy efficient and comfortable working environment was the primary project goal. The architect's analysis led to a three-zone building that met both functional and environmental objectives. One area is devoted to offices, a second to workshops, and the third to a stock and storage room. Their differing requirements for mechanical systems, daylighting, and finishes became the core of the design and green strategies.

Office and personnel support areas, which are fully occupied during normal working hours, face the street with a southern exposure shaded by mature trees. Diffused, north facing monitors prevent direct sun penetration into the workshops where dangerous machines are used. Daylight provides a uniform 50-foot candle or higher light level for most of the year. Radiant floor heating

LEFT >> Stock room.
ABOVE >> Exterior.

and natural ventilation, augmented when necessary with fans, condition the shops, where air conditioning is not required. The stock room is occupied minimally; and, therefore, less sensitive to sun penetration and more tolerant of temperature fluctuation. The folded roof form and articulated eave details filter light from above. A neighborhood scale is established by horizontal elements punctuated with a rhythm of vertical slots, clerestories, louvers. Materials include a standing seam metal roof and a masonry palette of warm brick and ground face block. As part of the City's Percent for Art Program, a 250-foot-long wall that links the site to its previous history. It was constructed from brick reclaimed from the site's former buildings. This project achieved LEED Platinum certification.

LEFT » Detail of art wall. OPPOSITE, TOP » Art wall featuring reclaimed brick. OPPOSITE, BOTTOM LEFT » Workshop. OPPOSITE, BOTTOM RIGHT » Model.

COMPANY PROFILES »

≫ 1100 ARCHITECT

1100 Architect is the New York- and Frankfurt-based architectural firm of principals David Piscuskas, FAIA, LEED AP and Juergen Riehm, FAIA, BDA. 1100 provides architectural design, programming, space analysis, interior design, and master planning services to public and private clients. The firm's domestic and international work spans a vast array of typologies, including educational and arts institutions, libraries, offices, residences, retail environments, and civic facilities.

1100 Architect is known for works of architecture that are timeless manifestations of place, at once distinctive and modern while always thoughtful about site, setting, and environment. Fundamental to this pursuit is the belief that building design is a progressive process informed by client aspirations, site, history, available resources, and time.

The firm believes that design can motivate and inspire users, and make an affirmative, lasting impact on individuals and communities alike. The studio avoids dogmatic strictures, instead favoring a careful consideration of light, material, and detail that is specific to the nature of each project. The end products are functional, beautiful, innovative, and sustainable spaces that elegantly integrate with their surroundings.

1100 Architect's unwavering dedication to design excellence and community service is supported by advanced thinking in sustainability and high-performance design. Based on its experience designing projects both within and outside of the U.S. Green Building Council's LEED requirements, its view is that good design and environmental sustainability are interconnected elements of a thoughtful, responsible project.

LEFT, TOP ≫ Main: East Side Lofts, Frankfurt, Germany. LEFT ≫ The New York Public Library, Battery Park City, New York, NY. ABOVE ≫ 1100 Architect's New York office.

⟫ AECOM

AECOM provides professional design, planning, and engineering services. Although globally renowned, the firm prides itself in regional practices that work locally and bring its distinguished resources to provide client-focused and place-focused solutions. AECOM is deeply rooted in the creation and transformation of public space; its design and planning services have enjoyed working on the restoration of Flatbush Avenue and Myrtle Avenue, and have played major roles in the City's investment for many streetscape and waterfront parks in various capacities.

As a global professional services firm, AECOM was built by design to provide tailored and integrated solutions to the complex challenges of built, natural, and social environments. The result of an evolution spanning more than 20 years, AECOM was first launched as an employee-owned company in 1990, growing to assimilate more than 30 of the world's leading design, engineering, and management services companies into a multi-disciplinary company that is now one of the largest and most respected providers of professional technical services in the world.

In the course of assembling the unique and flexible platform that they have today, AECOM listened carefully to the needs and requests of many of its clients. Informed by these perspectives, the firm has constructed a company capable of adapting to local client-centric requirements while accessing the collective wisdom and relevant experiences from its experience in global operations. AECOM has learned the value of transparency and collaboration with its clients, along with engaged participation and shared ownership of issues and outcomes as central tenets of successful business models.

A unique aspect of AECOM is the scope and nature of its global footprint. AECOM is a significant presence in many geographies, and those who benefit from its efforts are neighbors. In serving its worldwide clientele, AECOM focuses on solving problems and overcoming challenges while capturing the important aesthetics and functional qualities of each project. AECOM blends the knowledge and value of long experience with the culture and spirit of each place and client it serves.

» ANDREW BERMAN ARCHITECT

Andrew Berman Architect is focused on the realization of unique and finely executed buildings and spaces. The work of the studio capitalizes on the qualities of place and seeks opportunities in the desires and programmatic requirements of each of their clients. Informed by working within the constraints of the dense urban fabric of New York City, Andrew Berman Architect utilizes an economy of means to create dignified and spatially rich architecture. Natural light, carefully chosen views, and appropriate materials are the mediums through which we engage our work with its context and place.

Andrew Berman Architect works on a wide range of project types and scales for an equally wide range of clients; public, institutional, and private. Their interests and experiences allow to approach each project on its own unique terms through an intense engagement with user and site, while drawing on our varied experiences in design and construction. Andrew Berman is the lead designer on all commissions. ABA has a staff of ten architects who possess the range of skills and experiences required to support the design and execution of our commissions.

Since its founding in 1995 the practice has gained recognition through notable projects such as the Center for Architecture for the American Institute of Architects (2003,) Bellport Library (2008,) FDNY Engine Company 259 Firehouse (2009) and MoMA PS1 Entrance Building (2011). In 2010, ABA received the Emerging Voices Award given by The Architectural League of New York. Current public commissions through the New York City Department of Design and Construction Design Excellence Program include the New York Public Library Stapleton Branch, an addition and renovation for the SculptureCenter, gallery renovations for MoMA/PS1, and a new two stage theater facility for MCC Theater. Current private commissions include several artists' studios, residential lofts in downtown Manhattan, and a residence in Maine.

LEFT » MoMA PS1 Entrance Building.
ABOVE » Andrew Berman.

» ATELIER PAGNAMENTA TORRIANI

Atelier Pagnamenta Torriani is an architectural design studio established in 1992 by Anna Torriani and Lorenzo Pagnamenta.

Atelier's office is like a laboratory where architecture, art, new technology, materials, and ideas are researched, experimented with, and implemented.

Special consideration is given to passive technologies and sustainable materials. Passive technologies, such as the use of controlled natural light and low energy cooling, as well as sustainability measures like high efficiency lighting, utilizing recycled building components into the design and economy of means are constantly present in its projects.

Atelier interprets the history, culture, and typology; studies the context, the local materials and construction methods for each project to establish a true connection to each site and its surroundings.

The firm strongly believes in the benefits of an inspired environment that provides residents with both a sense of pride and a pleasant space to inhabit.

LEFT, TOP » A. E. Smith High School Library.
LEFT » Central Park East School Library.

>> BELMONT FREEMAN ARCHITECTS

Belmont Freeman Architects is an award-winning design firm that provides architectural services to institutional, civic, commercial, and residential clients. The firm enjoys a reputation for innovative design, highly personalized service, and efficient management of the most complex construction and renovation projects. Belmont Freeman Architects has received numerous awards for its work, which has been published widely in the international design press. Founded in 1986 and based in New York City, the firm has built work in North America, Europe, and Asia.

Belmont Freeman Architects offers full architectural services, from programming and schematic planning to computer visualization, construction administration, and interior design. BFA also provides structural, mechanical, electrical, IT & AV, civil, and landscape design through its experienced team of subconsultants.

The firm thrives on the analytical rigor required to bring order to complex functional, technical, and contextual problems, and the progressive design that their intelligent synthesis can yield. Belmont Freeman Architects is pleased to avoid over-specialization in its practice, and welcomes the opportunities for cross fertilization that the firm's varied project types afford.

On every job it is Belmont Freeman Architects' approach to assemble a team of architects, designers, and consulting engineers, and to have that one group of individuals see a project through from site assessment and schematic design to working drawings and construction. Only in this way can it guarantee the level of consistency, continuity, client contact, and staff commitment that it considers essential in producing the highest-quality architecture. BFA is not a large office, so constant communication between the principal, senior management, and staff is the norm and the key to the firm's efficient operation.

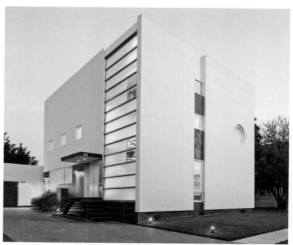

RIGHT, TOP >> Zilkha Gallery.
RIGHT >> Kowalewski Residence.

≫ BEYHAN KARAHAN & ASSOCIATES, ARCHITECTS

Beyhan Karahan & Associates, Architects was founded in 1997. As the founder and principal of the firm, Beyhan Karahan takes the leading role and responsibility for the firm's projects.

Ms. Karahan is a practicing architect and teacher. She is a Professor of Architecture at the New York Institute of Technology School of Architecture and Design. She is also a member of AIA, US Green Building Council and served on the Architecture Planning and Design panel for the New York State Council on the Arts. Prior to BKAA, Ms. Karahan was a founding partner of Karahan/Schwarting Architecture Company between 1984-1997. Since the early '80s she has enthusiastically embraced the importance of the architect's role in the public realm and completed numerous projects ranging from urban spaces, parks, and public buildings in the City of New York. Ms. Karahan has a Master of Architecture degree from Columbia University Graduate School of Architecture Planning and Preservation (1977) and a Bachelor of Science Degree in Mathematics from SUNY at Stony Brook and Middle East Technical University Ankara, Turkey (1974).

Beyond the public experience, Beyhan Karahan has completed significant academic projects, and a large number of high-end residential works mostly in the New York metropolitan area.

The firm received the 2008 AIA New York State Award of Excellence for large residential projects, AIA New York Chapter Housing Design Award in 2005, Preservation League of New York State Award for Excellence in Historic Preservation in 2002, and Special Recognition in Design Award from the Art Commission of the City of New York in 1998. The firm's work has been exhibited at several galleries, and published in the USA and Europe.

ABOVE ≫ Beyhan Karahan &
Associates, Architects' offices.
RIGHT ≫ Chocolate Factory courtyard.

>> BKSK ARCHITECTS

Founded in 1985, BKSK Architects is a New York City-based firm specializing in design that is socially, contextually, and ecologically engaged. The firm's diverse range of work includes award-winning cultural, civic, educational, liturgical, and residential projects. Individual projects designed by the firm have received more than 40 design awards, including a 2008 AIA National Housing Award for a new multi-family development; a 2008 AIA Committee on the Environment (COTE) Award for a LEED Platinum-certified visitor center; and two Palladio Awards for traditional residential architecture.

BKSK is directed by six partners: Joan Krevlin, George Schieferdecker, Harry Kendall, Stephen Byrns, Julie Nelson, and Todd Poisson. The firm's character is based on a longstanding and robust exchange of ideas and information between partners. Echoing that, BKSK's interaction with clients and consultants involves a consensus-driven process that yields a sense of shared authorship. As a result, the firm's design work explores the relationship between institutional mission, form, and place. The result has been a series of buildings and spaces that are embraced by the community.

The firm has been at the forefront of the sustainable architecture movement. Notably, BKSK was responsible for the design of the first civic building in NYC to earn a LEED Platinum certification and has addressed a flood-prone City agency headquarters site with innovative water management strategies. At both sites, natural forces become elements of design, and the building reveals itself as integral to the ecology of the site. In so doing, the architecture enhances one's awareness of the environment, with an emphasis on the qualitative experiences that create a connection to the natural world.

ABOVE, TOP >> BKSK Architects' offices.
ABOVE, BOTTOM >> Queens Botanical Garden.

» CAPLES JEFFERSON ARCHITECTS

CAPLES JEFFERSON ARCHITECTS is an award-winning New York City-based architecture firm that was founded in 1987 by Everardo Jefferson and Sara Caples. With a commitment to community, sustainability, and cultural enrichment, the practice has built significant projects such as the Queens Theatre in the Park and the Weeksville Heritage Center. CJA offers master planning, urban design, research, and programming, architecture and interior design services. The firm has completed more than 100 projects for civic, corporate, educational, cultural, and private clients in the United States and abroad. In 2012, the firm was honored as AIA's New York State Firm of the Year.

ABOVE » Marcus Garvey Community Center, Aerial view.
RIGHT » Sara Caples & Everardo Jefferson.

EVERARDO JEFFERSON, AIA, has made significant contributions in New York and throughout the U.S., many of which are included in national exhibitions of contemporary architecture. His design for the new Weeksville Heritage Center was well-received by the City's arts commission, the Brooklyn community, and national audiences. The Weeksville design process demanded both a resonant exploration of African architectural form and a sensitive reading of the African-American experience. Jefferson has been published widely and received multiple awards from NOMA and the AIA, including a National Honor. He was selected as an Emerging Voice of the Architectural League.

SARA CAPLES, AIA, has spent her career creating positive civic anchors in the public realm—buildings that broaden the cultural frame of modern architecture through a joyous use of form, movement, light, and color. Caples has shared her knowledge as a lecturer and teacher of young architects in universities, in the office, and at the AIA, both in New York and throughout the country and abroad. Using her collaborative design process as a springboard, Sara Caples continues to share her enthusiasm for creating work that responds to deep needs with conceptually enriched, programmatically anchored, carefully crafted assemblages of space, light, and color.

» CHRISTOFF:FINIO ARCHITECTURE

Christoff:Finio Architecture (C:FA) is a New York-based architecture and design studio with a wide range of interests that arise from its ongoing collaborations with forward-thinking clients and consultants.

As the practice grows, so do opportunities to ask what architecture can do. Every project represents some important discovery for the firm, or brings a repeating inquiry to light.

The firm's concern lies with the people who engage with its work, and how form, technology, craft, and material affect their lives. C:FA is interested in how architecture performs. How it shows people where they are—in place and in time—and how it helps them thrive.

Ideas drive C:FA's work. Ideas about making. Christoff:Finio is most committed to the time and attention it takes to create architecture; to manifest ideas in physical form with precision and clarity, elegance and restraint.

The firm is committed to making buildings and environments that bring meaning to place. It wants to make physical and cultural connections in its work as a way to help shape the public and personal space of memory. It takes great joy in exploring a contemporary language of architecture rooted in material expression and intellectual rigor.

Led by partners Taryn Christoff and Martin Finio, the projects of the eight-person studio are unified by their response to context, culture, and performance goals. Through an energetic and interactive process from conception to completion, C:FA approaches each project with a sense of invention and innovation. Designs are calibrated to perform optimally at all scales, from new buildings, to furniture, to collaborations with artists.

ABOVE » Carriage house, Manhattan.
RIGHT » Exterior.

» DATTNER ARCHITECTS

Dattner Architects delivers excellence in civic architecture—improving and sustaining communities and the urban environment through the firm's designs. Their portfolio includes master planning and buildings for public agencies, not-for-profit groups and corporate clients, educational and cultural institutions; historic preservation and adaptive reuse; and interior design. Dattner Architects' work aims at the realization of their clients' highest aspirations while respecting shared social responsibility and building within available resources. They believe that each individual project is linked to a larger context; they explore those connections in all their work.

The firm has a long-standing commitment to sustainable design that combines passive low-tech solutions with more complex active systems, analysis and controls. Each new commission is an opportunity to push beyond the conventional standards for sus-

tainability, innovating high-performance approaches that work with the building program, the site, and the budget. Dattner Architects is a signatory to the AIA 2030 Commitment to achieve benchmark energy and greenhouse gas reductions.

Dattner Architects has earned a strong reputation as a firm that can handle complex projects. With a staff of 80, a hands-on approach characterizes the practice and allows large and small projects to receive a consistently high quality of service, design, and technical rigor.

The firm has received more than 100 design awards. Notable recognition includes a GSA Design Award, the New York City Green Building Award from the US Environmental Protection Agency, a Medal of Honor and a Citation for Design Excellence from the New York State American Institute of Architects, and several Awards from the Public Design Commission of the City of New York.

» DEAN/WOLF ARCHITECTS

New York City-based Dean/Wolf Architects have been praised for their uncanny ability to turn architectural constraints into powerful generators of form. Since founding their firm in 1991, architects Kathryn Dean and Charles Wolf have completed residential and institutional projects at a variety of scales. These projects are distinguished by a highly thought-provoking manipulation of light and space. The firm's award-winning projects are precisely crafted wonders made from sensual materials such as concrete, steel, wood, and glass. Dean/Wolf activates these highly resonant materials with deliberately focused light in order to dissolve boundaries of interior and exterior space. For Dean/Wolf, this requires not only the consideration of physical space, but also a psychological engagement between the client's mind and the space they inhabit.

Driven by design excellence, Kathryn Dean, Charles Wolf and their associate partner Christopher Kroner lead a dynamic combination of architects and designers. This team expertly perceives the inherent power of place to inform their design process. Capitalizing upon the latent potentials of every unique site and program, the firm is renowned for envisioning and

realizing dramatically new patterns of use. Incorporating the latest technological advances, the office commits itself to architectural research realized through construction. To that goal, the partners are committed to both teaching and professional practice, having all held professorships at prestigious universities across the country while maintaining the Manhattan office. In addition to leading designs at the office, Kathryn Dean has served as the Director of Graduate Programs and is currently the JoAnne Stolaroff Cotsen Professor of Architecture at Washington University in St. Louis.

The award-winning career of the office is consistently published internationally in publications such as *Architectural Record*, *Architectural Review*, and *GA*, and has garnered numerous design distinctions. The work has received multiple AIA honor award citations, notably for Spiral House (1998), Urban Interface Loft (1998), Operable Boundary Townhouse Garden (2007), Implied Rotation Townhouse (2011) and Inverted Warehouse/Townhouse (2011). Restless Response, Queens Hospital Emergency Medical Station 50 was awarded a Society of American Registered Architects Design Award (2006) and the Art Commission of the City of New York Excellence in Design Award (2007). More recently, a renovated townhouse with a CNC fabricated staircase received a R+D award from Architect Magazine (2011) and the design for "Ephemeral Edge," a single family residence currently under construction, was awarded a *Progressive Architecture* citation by *Architect Magazine* (2012).

LEFT » Dean/Wolf Architects staff.

≫ ENNEAD ARCHITECTS

Ennead Architects is recognized internationally for architectural excellence. Projects have been published extensively and have received numerous awards for design excellence, including national, state, and local AIA awards. The firm's portfolio is diverse in typology, scale and location and includes new construction, renovation and expansion, historic preservation, interior design, and master planning. Clients are principally cultural, educational, scientific, and governmental institutions.

Having evolved from Polshek Partnership, Ennead Architects was launched in June 2010, culminating a transition in organizational structure and design leadership begun more than 30 years before. The new name recognizes the collaborative and innovative culture of our studio, fueled by the intelligence, energy, resourcefulness, and creativity of our staff. Eleven partners share responsibility for the vision and operation of the studio: Joseph Fleischer, Timothy Hartung, Duncan Hazard, Guy Maxwell, Kevin McClurkan, Richard Olcott, Susan Rodriguez, Tomas Rossant, Todd Schliemann, Don Weinreich, and Thomas Wong.

The firm makes buildings whose designs authentically express the progressive missions of their cultural, educational, scientific, and governmental institutions and are responsive to their specific environmental conditions. They demonstrate technical and artistic excellence and significantly contribute both to the cultural life of their communities and to the enhancement of their precincts. Ennead Architect's collaborative process is rooted in extensive research involving the analysis of context, program, public image, emerging technologies, and a commitment to sustainable solutions.

LEFT ≫ William J. Clinton Presidential Center and Park. BOTTOM, LEFT ≫ Frank Sinatra School of the Arts. BOTTOM, RIGHT ≫ American Museum of Natural History, Rose Center for Earth and Space.

>> FREDERIC SCHWARTZ ARCHITECTS [FSA]

LEFT >> World Trade Center Master Plan, Manhattan.

Founded in 1985, Frederic Schwartz Architects (FSA) is an internationally recognized award-winning design firm with a wealth of experience working on major architectural and planning projects in New York City, the United States, India, China, and Africa. Its work encompasses all types and sizes, and is noted for bold ideas and innovation supported by expertise in sustainable design. FSA's design excellence has been recognized with 28 American Institute of Architects awards and 17 winning designs in major national and international competitions.

FSA's work is global and local: our clients include major cities (New York, Singapore, Shanghai, San Diego), countries (USA, India, Germany, France, Kuwait, Ghana), and companies (Nike, Deutsch, Knoll, MTV). As winners of invited international design competitions, FSA recently completed three new major airports for India (Chennai, Goa and Vadodara), where the scope includes master planning and architectural design. With projects ranging from housing to airport terminals, master plans to mixed-use developments, the success of the firm's projects lies in its ability to produce inspiring designs on schedule and within budget.

Principal Frederic Schwartz was credited by *The New York Times* with changing the course of post-9/11 planning in New York City and profiled as "The Man Who Dared the City to THINK Again." The firm's subsequent work (as founding principal of the THINK team) for the Lower Manhattan Development Corporation resulted in a finalist master plan for 10 million square feet of transportation, retail, and cultural facilities at the World Trade Center site.

FSA thrives on the talent of Senior Associates Henry Rollmann and Douglas Romines, and Associates Jessica Jamroz, Helge Fuhrmann and Tza-Ping Leng. Frederic Schwartz, FAIA, has received many awards for public work, including the AIA New York City Chapter's Harry B. Rutkins Award for "realizing the value of superior design as a means to achieve social equity for clients in the public realm...with built work that has consistently demonstrated advocacy of design excellence and creatively intelligent design solutions to serve all people."

>> THE GALANTE ARCHITECTURE STUDIO (TGAS)

LEFT >> Ted Galante.

The Galante Architecture Studio (TGAS) is a practice of architecture whose focus is based on exploring design issues through the act of making.

The Studio was awarded contracts for the Falmouth Recreation Center and The Ashby Public Library, in Massachusetts. Both of these projects started with explorations into physical possibility leading to larger issues of planning, program arrangement, and financing capabilities.

TGAS's work is carried out in both digital and physical form. The studio occupies two floors in the Harvard Square area of Cambridge, Massachusetts. The upper floor is digital, dry work. The lower floor houses an ever evolving workshop. Prototypes are made downstairs, then brought upstairs for extrapolation into larger computer models to study their implication. In turn, physical models are made based on computer models, which lead to refined prototypes.

The firm has been honored with awards starting in 1998 with the Architectural League of New York's Young Architect's award, and adding others along the way. It has been published in *Architecture*, *Dwell*, *Architectural Record*, and books like *Materials for Design*, by Victoria Ballard Bell. Many of TGAS clients are larger agencies, (Amtrak, City of Boston, City of New York, Harvard University).

» GARRISON ARCHITECTS

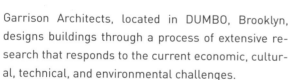

LEFT » U.S. Border Patrol Station, Murietta, California. BELOW » U.S. Consulate Residence, Apia, Samoa.

Garrison Architects, located in DUMBO, Brooklyn, designs buildings through a process of extensive research that responds to the current economic, cultural, technical, and environmental challenges.

The firm integrates this critical approach with a highly refined modernist aesthetic. This has enabled Garrison Architects to collaborate with an extensive group of designers, engineers, and manufacturers to create truly innovative work in industrialized building process and sustainable design.

Garrison Architects was founded in 1991 as a mid-sized firm with highly personalized service. The firm has an extremely wide range of experience with projects that have included urban design and planning, interior design, product design, feasibility analysis, modular structures, and LEED certification services. The firm utilizes a collaborative design approach with the goal of integrating building form and materials with passive environmental technologies. This allows the dramatic reduction of energy consumption as it increases the usable life of buildings.

» GRIMSHAW ARCHITECTS

Grimshaw was founded by Sir Nicholas Grimshaw in 1980. The practice became a Partnership in 2007 and operates worldwide with offices in New York, London, Melbourne, Sydney, and Doha.

Grimshaw's international portfolio covers all major sectors, and has been honored with more than 150 international design awards including the prestigious Lubetkin Prize.

The practice is dedicated to the deepest level of involvement in the design of its buildings to deliver projects that meet the highest possible standards of excellence. The company's work is characterized by strong conceptual legibility, innovation, and a rigorous approach to detailing, all underpinned by the principles of humane, enduring, and sustainable design.

The firm's work responds to the needs and resources of the contemporary world. The buildings produced come from a detailed understanding of the functions they must fulfill, the conditions they have to provide, and the materials from which they are constructed. This understanding is directly translated into form and detail.

Grimshaw's ultimate goal is to design buildings and environments that work, inspire people, and transform communities. Through careful evaluation of relevant opportunities, inspired ideas will drive a good design to something that is extraordinary, challenging, and completely unique. Everything it produces from buildings and masterplans to industrial design is

characterized by its legibility. Designs are innovative; they often surprise but are always precisely tuned to the requirements of the client.

With each project the firm learns more about creating forms and places, serving processes and people, and minimizing energy use in providing comfortable and healthy environments. Grimshaw is constantly developing new components, exploring new ways of using materials, and developing innovative environmental responses. Its objective is to search for optimal solutions to create a built environment that uses the planet's resources carefully. The results are functional, economic, and elegant.

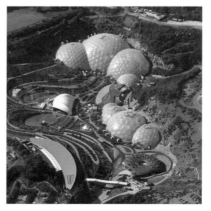

TOP » The Experimental Media and Performing Arts Center is a nexus of technological and artistic innovation and optimised performance space, where the intersection of science and the arts is explored through sound, movement and light. RIGHT » The second phase of the Eden Project's development refers to the 'biomes', a sequence of eight inter-linked geodesic transparent domes threading around 2.2 hectares of the site, encapsulating vast humid tropic and warm temperate regions.

>> GRUZEN SAMTON ARCHITECTS (JOINED IBI GROUP)

In May 2009, Gruzen Samton joined IBI Group, a multi-disciplinary consulting firm offering services in four core disciplines: urban land, building facilities, transportation networks, and systems technology. IBI Group was formed in 1974 as a partnership and currently employs more than 2,400 persons in more than 60 offices across North America, Europe, the Middle East, and Asia. The firm offers comprehensive professional services to meet the challenges of the 21st century.

The firm has an award winning portfolio of planning and design both new construction and renovation for a wide variety of needs in several market sectors including arts and cultural facilities, government and civic institutions, office buildings and corporate interiors, residential (market rate, affordable & senior housing), schools and universities, transportation facilities, urban and master planning. The scope of these projects has ranged from small renovation to new construction. IBI Group has long recognized the value of integrating the four core disciplines to ensure a holistic approach toward creating innovative and responsive solutions for its clients in both the public and private sectors. The collaborative nature of the practice allows the firm to effectively address the complexities inherent in the development of sustainable environments. IBI Group works to positively shape the cities of the future.

Collaboration is the key to its success. IBI Group's offices work together as global "virtual studios," utilizing a variety of collaborative technologies including video conferencing, intranet portals, and computer networks, enabling the efficient communication among team members regardless of their physical location. This system enables the firm to commit the best and most appropriate staff to each project and utilize all resources around the clock and around the world. IBI Group is an ISO 9001:2000 registered company and has firmly established quality management mechanisms built into the daily regimen for all technical discipline deliverables and management processes.

LEFT, TOP >> Cornell University, Human Ecology Building. The photographer is Paul Warchol.
LEFT >> Port Imperial Ferry Terminal.

≫ KISS + CATHCART

ABOVE ≫ Solar 2 Environmental
Center at Stuyvesant Cove Park.
RIGHT ≫ Stillwell Avenue
MTA Terminus.

Kiss + Cathcart is a versatile and progressive architectural practice that has completed a wide range of projects to high standards of design, economy, and ecological soundness. Its work explores the potential of sustainable methods and technologies to satisfy the perennial needs of use, value, and comfort.

Since its founding in 1983, the practice has successfully pursued this approach across a spectrum of project types, from major civic infrastructure to high-technology manufacturing facilities to schools, shops, and homes. Kiss + Cathcart's practice has pioneered construction technologies that are both environmentally and financially responsible: building integrated photovoltaics (BIPV), structural insulated panels (SIPS), and building integrated agriculture.

Skilled at identifying the most promising potentials of a project and getting the best value out of any budget, challenging or generous, its practice has been consistently recognized with international awards, invited lectures, and research grants, and its work has been featured in publications such as *Architectural Record*, the *New York Times*, *Wired*, and *Dwell Magazine*.

>> LEESER ARCHITECTURE

Since 1989, as principal of his own firm—LEESER Architecture— architect Thomas LEESER has achieved worldwide recognition for his influential, innovative designs. His interest in challenging the conventional notions of architecture with the use of new technologies and radical design, integrated within the contemporary cultural, social, and technological context produces rich architectural spaces, new programmatic relationships, and beautifully simple organizations.

As the winner of numerous awards including the internationally acclaimed 2013 Red Dot Design Award and New York City's 2011 and 2010 Public Design Commission Award, LEESER Architecture is internationally sought after for its reputation of creating innovative, cutting-edge architectural design solutions.

The 3 Legged Dog Art & Technology Center in New York City, which houses the production and viewing of cutting edge, large scale, multimedia performance and art, represents "a more organic way of making the arts part of rebuilding downtown" (*The New York Times*).

Current projects in construction that showcase their design capabilities are Brooklyn's new arts and education center, BAM (Brooklyn Academy of Music) Cultural District, a 2.7 million-square-foot mixed use neighborhood positioned to be Asia's leading retail and entertainment hub in Thailand and a 100,000+ square-foot tri-climatic biosphere for the Royal Family in Abu Dhabi, UAE.

Named "the finest recent American example of radical design" by the Wall Street Journal, LEESER Architecture's design for the Museum of Moving Image is yet another example of their ability to produce iconic architectural designs.

The success of LEESER's projects is the result of a positive and well structured collaboration between client, design team, and consultant team. They partner closely with their clients to identify the unique opportunities of their project, enabling them to develop a deep understanding of their design and programmatic challenges and to propose solutions that are specific to their needs.

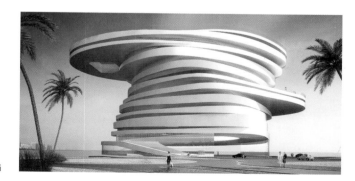

ABOVE >> Thomas Leeser and
the LEESER Architecture team.
RIGHT >> The Helix Hotel, Abu Dhabi

⟫ MARBLE FAIRBANKS

Marble Fairbanks is an architecture, design, and research office founded in 1990 by Scott Marble and Karen Fairbanks. The firm is committed to highly innovative design through research and analysis of the core issues surrounding each project. Building on the combined experience of completed work and ongoing research, Marble Fairbanks approaches every project as unique and searches for original solutions. The firm's continuing connection to academia inspires a creative and highly collaborative working environment where theory and practice are informed by each other.

Marble Fairbanks' most recent work has focused on cultural and institutional projects for public and private clients including the New York Public Library, Queens Library, the Museum of Modern Art, Princeton University, Hunter College, The New School, New York University, and Columbia University. The research-based practice is at the forefront of discussions concerning digital technology, integrated design processes, and education.

Marble Fairbanks is the recipient of numerous local, national, and international design awards. The firm was awarded an AIA Honor Award in Architecture for the Toni Stabile Student Center, their tenth AIA Award from the New York Chapter. They were commissioned by MoMA to design a speculative project for the exhibition *Home Delivery: Fabricating the Modern Dwelling*. Scott Marble and Karen Fairbanks were the Michael Owen Jones Memorial Lecturers at the University of Virginia and the Charles and Ray Eames Lecturers at the University of Michigan. Their book, *Marble Fairbanks: Bootstrapping*, was published on the occasion of that lecture. The work of Marble Fairbanks is published internationally and has been exhibited in galleries and museums around the world including the Architectural Association in London, the Nara Prefectural Museum of Art in Japan, and the Museum of Modern Art in New York where their drawings are part of the museum's permanent collection.

>> MARPILLERO POLLAK ARCHITECTS

Marpillero Pollak Architects' multidisciplinary design practice, rooted in the strengths and sensibilities of its partners, spans architecture, landscape, and urban design, enabling it to mine the rich and often unseen potentials of a project and site. Its award-winning projects in the United States and elsewhere receive acclaim for the skill with which they redefine their contexts at multiple scales, not only realizing innovative and technically robust design solutions, but also enriching a project's productive impact on its surroundings.

Sandro Marpillero and Linda Pollak are licensed professionals, with experience producing projects for institutional, residential, and commercial clients. They have worked together since 1991, first as associates, then as partners in the firm MPArchitects. In his 20 years of professional experience in the USA and Europe, Sandro Marpillero has focused extensively on the relationship between architecture, urbanism, and art. Linda Pollak contributes professional and academic experience with issues of landscape in the city, and for the architectural quality of relationships between indoor and outdoor spaces.

For MPA, design is a way to take things that exist in the world and intensively revalue them through invention and design innovation. Closely examining what is, the firm derives meaning and expresses identity through reciprocity: inside and outside, architecture and landscape, existing and new. Engaging everyday materials, site conditions, and light in new relationships, it generates strong iconic images that establish the character of a place while providing flexibility to accommodate growth and change.

MPA designs and implements transformative environments, which catalyze social, economic, and ecological sustainability while maximizing the value of existing conditions. It takes an integrative approach to sustainability, shaping healthy, active places whose innovative energy, stormwater, and maintenance practices contribute to the life of the project.

ABOVE >> Linda Pollak (left) and Sandro Marpillero (right). RIGHT >> MPA projects overview.

≫ MICHIELLI + WYETZNER ARCHITECTS

FAR LEFT ≫ Frank Michielli.
LEFT ≫ Michael Wyetzner.

Michielli + Wyetzner Architects is a full-service design firm founded by architects who have created award-winning contemporary architecture for institutional and corporate clients across the United States and abroad. Its projects are distinguished by a clarity of form, elegance of execution, and innovative use of materials. The thoroughness of the firm's design approach has resulted in well-integrated solutions to often-complex facility requirements.

Founded in 2004, Michielli + Wyetzner joins the enthusiasm and high-energy of a start-up with the discipline and expediency of a seasoned practitioner. With the combined experience of almost 50 years, the firm is knowledgeable in a wide variety of building types and is responsive, efficient, creative, and resourceful. Years of experience following projects through to completion of construction has refined its design sensibility, so that building sustainability, longevity, constructability, and operating costs are considerations as ingrained to its design process as aesthetics. The firm brings value to the projects it designs by delving deep to solve its clients' problems and then appropriately detailing and documenting the results. The result is compelling architecture with the flexibility and craftsmanship to serve clients for years to come.

The Michielli + Wyetzner design methodology approaches each project on its own terms. It begins with an analysis of the owner's requirements and site to find those unique qualities that will define an organizing concept for their building. With this process, it goes beyond mere problem solving and deals with the experiential and tactile dimensions of architecture and resolve functional, formal, and symbolic aspects as a coherent whole.

The firm's aim is to develop simple and natural solutions that are seemingly self-evident and inevitable. This is achieved by a high level of synthesis that smoothly integrates all components and results in forms that are a distillation of the several purposes they serve. Space, structure, skin, and building systems are interdependent and tightly integrated. The firm assembles highly collaborative teams to solve problems, with consultants and specialists contributing right from the start. Like a natural organism, the result is functional and expressive.

›› nARCHITECTS

nARCHITECTS is an emerging internationally recognized practice founded by Eric Bunge, AIA, and Mimi Hoang, AIA, in 1999. The Brooklyn-based firm brings an open-ended and playful approach to design and collaboration, joining conceptual clarity with technical innovation in the further elaboration of their projects. Complex client identities, layered sites, and phasing requirements are unpacked and reframed as straightforward design opportunities. Their approach to context is nuanced and agile—sensitive to opportunities and irreverent to clichés.

The firm approaches environmental questions as both technical and social issues. As an overriding goal, nARCHITECTS aims for simple designs that produce a richness and flexibility of experience, with an economy of conceptual and material means.

Ongoing work includes the design of the Wyckoff House Museum in Brooklyn, recipient of an AIANY Design Merit Award; Ellicott Park at Buffalo Niagara Medical Campus; Pierscape at Chicago's Navy Pier, a competition-winning project led by James Corner Field Operations; and MY MICRO NY, the winning entry for the groundbreaking adAPT NYC competition to design a micro-unit building in Manhattan.

The firm's recent work has focused on a wide range of scales from buildings and interiors to public space design. Recent examples include the ABC Dbayeh Department Store in Beirut, Lebanon; Switch Building in Manhattan, recipient of an AIA Building Type Award; the bamboo MoMA PS1 Canopy, recipient of an AIA Design Honor Award; Forest Pavilion in Taiwan, recipient of an Architect Annual Design Award; and New Aqueous City, their proposal for a future New York resilient to storm surges and sea level rise, as part of the MoMA Rising Currents exhibition. nARCHITECTS is currently retained by Design Excellence programs of both the NYC Department of Parks and Recreation and the NYC Department of Design and Construction.

ABOVE, LEFT ›› Eric Bunge.
ABOVE, RIGHT ›› Mimi Hoang.
FAR LEFT ›› Joe-Kesrouani
front night view. LEFT ››
Swith building front facade

⟫ PERKINS + WILL

Since 1935, Perkins+Will has created innovative and award-winning designs for the world's most forward-thinking clients. Its teams consist of architects, interior designers, urban designers, landscape architects, consultants, and branded environment experts who approach design from all scales and perspectives. The global staff of 1,500 professionals, including more than 1,000 LEED-a Accredited professionals, bring together high design, functional performance, and social responsibility to effectively advance client goals through engaged, accessible, and collaborative processes.

Inspired by the programs within, Perkins+Will teams design from the inside out. By combining a deeply humanistic approach with results-driven pragmatism, the firm continually creates dynamic spaces for people. Every project is an opportunity to reimagine how space can be used to foster stronger ties between communities, the built environment, and nature. Sustainable design and the use of healthy building materials are fundamental to the approach of every project. The results are transformative designs, which help students learn better, patients heal faster, business teams perform stronger, and city dwellers have more meaningful daily experiences.

Perkins+Will's New York office is one of the first U.S. offices established by the firm, and it has a long history of leadership in design, practice, and environmental stewardship in the Northeast region and beyond. The multiple-practice office is renowned for its strengths in the design and execution of major architecture, interiors, and planning projects, including branded environments. A broad range of clients have worked with Perkins+Will New York, from such market sectors as corporate/commercial, civic, healthcare, higher education, K-12, and science/technology. Perkins+Will New York also functions as the center of the firm's innovative strategic workplace planning practice.

Everyone at Perkins+Will, both in the New York office and beyond, upholds the belief that design has the power to create positive long-term environmental, economic, and social change, and to set new paradigms for the future.

≫ PKSB ARCHITECTS

PKSB Architects is recognized as an award-winning full-service firm with a long history of completing projects of every scale and scope. Celebrating more than 40 years in practice, PKSB has been creating architecture and interior spaces with an ever-expanding range – including academic, preservation, institutional, residential, hospitality, public housing, infrastructure, public art, civic memorials, and houses of worship. PKSB's efforts have been rewarded with numerous design awards, including the prestigious P/A Award and AIA honor awards on the local, state, and national levels, most recently with the AIA 2010 Institute Honor Award for Architecture.

PKSB is a firm of diversely skilled architects and designers flourishing under the guidance of the three principals: Sherida Paulsen, William Fellows and Tim Witzig. A longstanding commitment to architectural excellence in support of humanist values provides the continuity of expression that distinguishes our work.

Based in New York City, their perspective extends beyond the geographic boundaries of our practice. They continue to evolve without losing sight of their

commitment to modern design that serves the needs of their clients and the community. Their reliance on direct principal involvement consistently achieves the highest quality of design. They continue to draw strength from the original studio approach to architectural practice. Each project is the responsibility of a team that includes the Principal-in-Charge, the Project Architect, and staff members who work together in an atmosphere of collaboration and exploration. PKSB moves forward to embrace the increasingly powerful confluence of art, architecture, and technology.

ABOVE ≫ Principals at PKSB. FAR LEFT ≫ Triple Bridge Gateway, New York, NY. LEFT ≫ Father Duffy Square, New York, NY.

>> PRENDERGAST LAUREL ARCHITECTS

The firm of Prendergast Laurel Architects (until 2001, David W. Prendergast, Architects) has devoted its practice to public design. Working in New York City for more than three decades, the firm has completed a wide variety of projects, including museums, libraries, schools, offices, firehouses, medical centers, restaurants, theaters, private residences, transportation structures, and recreation centers. Their work responds to the dynamism and diversity of this great city with carefully crafted spaces that contribute to the public realm. Historic buildings have been repurposed with keen attention given to preserving significant details while seamlessly merging program and form.

The firm believes that architecture is a public art, with the potential to support and enhance the life of the community, whether the project is a shared space such as a library or a school, or a private structure within the metropolis. PLA also understands that architecture is a collaborative art and that there are many contributors to a great project. PLA strives to mobilize the expertise of each project's diverse team including client, contractor, engineers, and community representatives.

The firm has a long history working with many of New York's public agencies including the New York City Department of Design & Construction, Department of Parks & Recreation, School Construction Authority, City University of New York, Fire Department of New York and Economic Development Corporation. The firm's clients in the not-for-profit realm include the New York Public Library, the Queens Borough Public Library, the Lighthouse (NY Association for the Blind), Community Healthcare Network, NYU Medical Center, and the PS1 Contemporary Art Center.

The firm's projects have appeared in professional and general interest publications, including Architectural Record, Interior Design, and The New York Times. The Sedgwick Branch Library appeared on the cover of the June 1995 issue of Architectural Record. Books that feature the firm's work include Robert A. M. Stern's *New York 2000: Architecture and Urbanism from the Bicentennial to the Millennium*, the *AIA Guide to New York City*, and *New York – A Guide to Recent Architecture*.

The firm's projects have been recognized for design distinction by the New York City Design Commission and the American Institute of Architects.

>> RAFAEL VIÑOLY ARCHITECTS

Rafael Viñoly Architects was founded in New York in 1983, and has since become known internationally for its architectural and planning projects around the globe. The firm maintains headquarters in New York and branch offices in London and Abu Dhabi, in addition to project offices in the United States, South America, Europe, and the Middle East.

The unusually diverse work the firm has completed includes award-winning courthouses, museums, performing arts centers, convention centers, athletic facilities, banks, hotels, hospitals, laboratories, recreational venues, residential complexes, and commercial, industrial, and educational facilities. Projects range in scale from laboratory casework to large urban commercial and institutional master plans. The firm has also completed several projects involving the restoration and expansion of buildings of significant historical and architectural value.

Guided by the design leadership of principal Rafael Viñoly, the firm is managed by Vice President Jay Bargmann, who also administers projects jointly with each of the firm's partners and project directors—many of whom have been with the firm for two decades or more, and share the advanced, centralized resources of the firm, as well as a high level of commitment and a rich database of knowledge. This structure guarantees consistency and high standards of design and documentation and enables the firm to maintain its longstanding record of successfully completed fast-track design/build projects, as well as conventionally scheduled and organized assignments worldwide.

The practice's atelier design intelligence coupled with the capabilities of a large, multidisciplinary firm produces appropriate, creative responses to program requirements. Intensive research and informed evaluation lead to a variety of design and technical alternatives. These innovations and refinements often result in buildings that function measurably beyond client expectations.

LEFT >> Rafael Viñoly
Architects' offices.
ABOVE >> Rafael Viñoly.

✇ RICE + LIPKA ARCHITECTS

ABOVE ≫ Lyn Rice (left) and Astrid Lipka (right). Architects' offices.
LEFT ≫ Rice + Lipka Architects' offices.

Rice+Lipka Architects is an innovative, New York City-based architectural platform for a range of building, planning, art, exhibition, and cultural research projects. The award-winning practice is widely recognized for its ability to engage the public with contemporary built works that emerge from fresh programmatic and formal speculations, and to integrate new construction techniques and materials.

The practice has developed an iterative design approach that takes pleasure in teasing out the unexpected potential of projects by inventively embracing their practical constraints. Principal Lyn Rice was a design principal-in-charge and architect-of-record for one of the world's large contemporary art museums, Dia:Beacon, and with Astrid Lipka has led design work for the Museum of Contemporary Art Detroit, the Shei-

la C. Johnson Design Center (New York), Ordos 100: Villa 007 (China), as well as multiple projects for the New York Public Library (New York).

Since its founding in 2004, the firm has been awarded nine American Institute of Architects Design Awards, the Architectural Review Future Projects Award (2013), NYC Public Design Commission Award (2012), the International Architecture Award (by the European Centre for Architecture Art & Design/Chicago Athenaeum, 2009), and the New York Municipal Art Society Masterwork Award (2008) among others. RLA's work has been widely published, internationally exhibited, and Rice was selected as one of the Architectural League of New York's Emerging Voices in 2002 and named part of the 2003 Design Vanguard by Architectural Record.

>> SAGE + COOMBE ARCHITECTS

Sage + Coombe Architects is dedicated to elevating the quality of public architecture and civic life. Where challenging budgets, schedules, and a multiplicity of voices often govern the design process, the use of green strategies, innovative materials, and the unexpected are at the core of its design practice and built work.

The firm's clients include the Department of Design and Construction, Department of Parks and Recreation, Noguchi Museum, the Bronx River Art Center, the FDNY, the NYC Economic Development Corporation, the Greater Newark Conservancy, the New York Public Library and a range of charter and independent schools and institutions of higher education. For the Mayor's Office, the Parks Department, and the Department of Design and Construction, Sage + Coombe was asked to respond to the damage of Hurricane Sandy and design the restoration of the beaches in the Rockaways.

The Public Design Commission of the City of New York honored Sage and Coombe for its public projects with a record three design awards in 2010: the Bronx River Art Center, the Ocean Breeze Track and Fieldhouse and the Marine 9 Firehouse. In 2012, the Commission again honored the firm with a design award for a series of structures in the southern extension of Riverside Park. From the AIA, the Bronx River Art Center project received an AIA Design Award.

LEFT >> Firm interior.
BELOW >> Sage + Coombe Architects' offices.

⟫ SELLDORF ARCHITECTS

Selldorf Architects has acquired an international reputation for work that is sensitive to context and program, thoughtful in execution, and timeless. Established by Annabelle Selldorf in 1988, the firm has worked on public and private projects that range from museums and libraries to a recycling facility; and at scales from the construction of new buildings to the restoration of historic interiors and exhibition design.

Clients include cultural institutions and universities such as the Neue Galerie New York, the Sterling and Francine Clark Art Institute, Brown University, and New York University's Institute for the Study of the Ancient World. In addition, the firm has designed galleries for Hauser & Wirth, Gladstone Gallery, Michael Werner, and Acquavella Galleries among others. Other recent work includes several condominiums in New York City; the first LEED certified commercial art gallery for David Zwirner; and *Le Stanze del Vetro*, a new museum dedicated to modern and contemporary glass in Venice.

Annabelle Selldorf, FAIA, is the principal of Selldorf Architects. Born and raised in Germany, she received a Bachelor of Architecture degree from Pratt Institute and a Master of Architecture degree from Syracuse University in Florence, Italy. Ms. Selldorf is a Fellow of the American Institute of Architects, President of the Board of the Architectural League of New York, and serves on the Board of the Chinati Foundation.

ABOVE ⟫ Annabelle Selldorf.
RIGHT ⟫ Selldorf Architects' offices.

>> SEN ARCHITECTS LLP

Sen Architects, founded in 1986, is an award-winning Architectural and Interior Design firm, dedicated to providing excellent services to all clients, whether individuals, corporations, communities or governmental agencies. Planning, design, and construction experience is combined with the best outside skills in other areas. The firm offers a complete range of architectural and planning services including: historic restoration, rehabilitation, and reuse; commercial, residential, and interior design for new and existing structures; interior design and space planning.

Since its inception in 1986, Sen Architects has successfully completed a wide variety of projects.

Its understanding of the complete developmental process, including real estate, regulatory requirement, construction management, marketing, and building operations result in cost-effective implementation of projects. The work of Sen Architects is not limited to any style or dogma. The firm's work is known for its excellent design, and deep commitment to the particulars of the space and user. It understands the physical and psychological requirements of the program, absorbs the subtleties of the space and climate, the character of the corporations and institutions and reflects it in the design. The firm is committed to an environmentally conscious approach and has completed several LEED certified projects. The firm is also passionate about preservation and adaptive reuse, which it sees as a sustainable approach to design. Sen Architects has received numerous awards for its commitment to design excellence, and the firm's work has been published in numerous journals.

Recent awards include the NYC Art Commission award for Design Excellence for the New Kensington Branch Library, Society of American Registered Architects award, and an award from the NYC Landmarks Preservation Commission for the Grand Central Terminal Revitalization Project. Sen Architects has their headquarters in New York City. A branch office is located in the Hudson Valley in Salt Point, New York.

ABOVE, LEFT >> Robin Sen.
ABOVE, RIGHT >> Rashmi Sen.
RIGHT >> Exterior.

≫ SKIDMORE, OWINGS & MERRILL LLP

Founded in 1936, Skidmore, Owings & Merrill LLP (SOM) is one of the leading architecture, interior architecture, urban design and planning, and engineering firms in the world. The firm's sophistication in building technology applications and commitment to design quality has resulted in a portfolio that features some of the most important architectural accomplishments of the 20th and 21st centuries.

Since SOM's beginnings, the firm's work has ranged from the architectural design and engineering of individual buildings to the master planning and design of entire communities. The firm's long-standing integration of urban design, master planning, architecture, engineering, and interior design has resulted in more than 15,000 projects located in more than 50 countries.

SOM is responsible for the design and construction of several of the world's tallest buildings, including the Burj Khalifa in Dubai – the tallest building in the world – and the 109-story Sears Tower in Chicago and One World Trade Center in New York City – the two tallest buildings in North America. Recent and current projects range from super tall commercial towers; to government work; to education projects to health and science projects; to transportation projects; and master planning projects.

SOM has received more than 1,600 design awards, including two Firm of the Year awards from the American Institute of Architects. The firm maintains offices in New York, Chicago, San Francisco, Los Angeles, Dulles, Washington, London, Hong Kong, Shanghai, Mumbai, Qatar, and Abu Dhabi.

ABOVE ≫ US Census Bureau Headquarters, Suitland, Maryland. FAR LEFT ≫ 510 Fifth Avenue Renovation and Adaptive Reuse, New York City. LEFT ≫ 7 World Trade Center, New York City.

» SLADE ARCHITECTURE

ABOVE » James Slade (left) and Hayes Slade (right). RIGHT » Slade Architecture's offices.

Slade Architecture, founded in 2002, seeks to focus on architecture and design across different scales and program types. Its design approach is unique for each project but framed by a continued exploration of primary architectural concerns.

As architects and designers, Slade operates with intrinsic architectural interests: the relationship between the body and space, movement, scale, time, perception, materiality and its intersection with form. These form the basis of their continued architectural exploration.

Layered on this foundation, is an inventive investigation of the specific project context. Broad definition of the project context considers any conditions affecting a specific project: program, sustainability, budget, operation, culture, site, technology, image/branding, etc. Working at the intersection of these considerations, Slade creates designs that are simultaneously functional and innovative.

Slade has completed a diverse range of international and domestic projects and their work has been recognized internationally with more than 200 publications, exhibits, and awards. Slade has been recognized with Progressive Architecture Awards, several AIA NY Awards, an Award for Design Excellence in Public Architecture by the New York City Public Design Commission, a national AIA Small Project Award, several Best of the Year Awards from Interior Design Magazine, and multiple multiple Store-of-the-Year awards. Slade Architecture was also one of the Architectural League of New York's "2010 Emerging Voices."

Slade's work has been exhibited in the Venice Biennale, the National Building Museum, the Museum of Modern Art, The German Architecture Museum, and many other galleries and institutions in Europe, Asia, and the United States.

≫ SMITH-MILLER + HAWKINSON ARCHITECTS LLP

Smith-Miller + Hawkinson Architects LLP (SM+H) is a New York City-based design studio in architecture, urban design, installations and exhibitions, objects and products. Across the United States and abroad, SM+H has designed public and private projects including museums, parks, transportation terminals, performing arts spaces, private residences, government facilities, a series of museum exhibitions and installations, as well as furniture and objects.

The studio's work derives inspiration from an ongoing investigation into contemporary culture, its history, and its complex changing relationship to society and contemporary ideas. The work process is transformative in the way it reinterprets basic programs and negotiates traditional craft with vanguard techniques. The office is a laboratory for speculation and making, for investigation and practice: two strands that are woven together in all of the projects from the initial concept to their final realization.

Recent awards include a 2012 New York State AIA Award for the Dillon and a 2010 U.S. General Services Administration award for the Massena Land Port of Entry. The studio has also won the AIA New York Chapter Medal of Honor, The National Academy of Design Canon Prize for The New York Public Library Project, and The Arnold W. Brunner Memorial Prize in Architecture from the American Academy of Arts and Letters for Excellence in Art and Architecture.

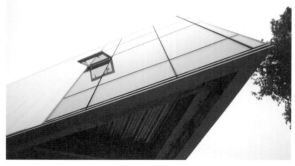

ABOVE, LEFT ≫ Champlain LPOE. ABOVE, RIGHT ≫ Zerega Avenue EMS Station. RIGHT ≫ Ohio State University Veterinarian Hospital (addition/renovation).

>> SNØHETTA

Snøhetta values human interaction. All of the studio's work strives to enhance a sense of place, identity, and relationship to others and the physical spaces people inhabit, whether natural or human-made. Art museums, reindeer observatories, and dollhouses get the same care and attention to purpose. Trends are often blithely ignored and essence is hotly pursued.

For more than 20 years, Snøhetta has designed some of the world's most notable public and cultural projects. Snøhetta kick-started its career in 1989 with the competition-winning entry for the new library of Alexandria, Egypt. This was later followed by the commission for the Norwegian National Opera in Oslo and the National September 11th Memorial Museum Pavilion at the World Trade Center in New York City. Since its inception, the practice has maintained its original trans-disciplinary approach, integrating architectural, landscape, and interior design in all of its projects.

Snøhetta is currently working on a number of civic and cultural projects internationally including the expansion of the San Francisco Museum of Modern Art in California, the King Abdulaziz Center for World Culture in Saudi Arabia, the Isabel Bader Centre for the Performing Arts at Queens University in Kingston, Ontario, the Far Rockaway Public Library, the Westchester Branch Public Library, and the redevelopment of Times Square all located in New York City.

Among its many recognitions, Snøhetta has received the World Architecture Award for both the Bibliotheca Alexandrina and the Norwegian National Opera and Ballet, as well as the Aga Kahn Prize for Architecture for Alexandria Library. Since its completion in 2008, the Norwegian National Opera and Ballet has also garnered the Mies van der Rohe - European Union Prize for Architecture and the EDRA (Environmental Design Research Association) Great Places Award, as well as the European Prize for Urban Public Space, The International Architecture Award, and The Global Award for Sustainable Architecture in 2010.

ABOVE >> Design Charette at Snøhetta's New York office.
RIGHT >> Norwegian National Opera and Ballet, Oslo, Norway.

>> STANTEC

Stantec has led and collaborated on the transformation of many beloved parks, plazas, streetscapes, and transportation corridors throughout New York City—building communities by drawing neighbors together in enhanced public spaces. As New Yorkers, Stantec designers' understanding of their city informs the firm's vision, allowing them to bring technical expertise and creativity to each of their projects.

Stantec is especially proud of its success on Manhattan's west side as it led the design of West Street's vibrant signature boulevard and bikeway, truly a landmark complete street exemplifying City residents'

passion and need for active living, pedestrian prioritization, and waterfront access. Some of the firm's other achievements include the reconstruction of the Historic Japanese Hill and Pond Garden at the Brooklyn Botanic Garden, Central Park's Great Lawn, Midtown's Columbus Circle, and the popular Herald and Greeley Squares.

The firm is a seasoned interdisciplinary practice, with a skill-set that was critical in its delivery of design and project management services for the Yankee Upland Parks Development including the new award-winning, 13-acre community recreation space on the grounds of the former Yankee Stadium. Stantec's design of this new park, in collaboration with its client and the community, now enriches the lives and well-being of thousands of residents in the Bronx.

Since 1954, Stantec has focused on a balanced and integrated engineering, landscape architecture, and architecture practice through teamwork, creative thinking, and careful analysis. The firm is a globally recognized and top-ranked design firm with deep roots in New York City. Its experience ranges from the City's built and naturalized waterfront, its vibrant streets and structures, and the infrastructure that sustains them, to the civic spaces that bring local communities together. In all that it does, Stantec aims to enhance the built environment and the communities that define New York City.

LEFT, TOP >> Columbus Circle, Manhattan.
LEFT >> West Side bikeway and walkway, Manhattan.

>> STEPHEN YABLON ARCHITECT

Stephen Yablon Architect is dedicated to creating architecture that is transformative: enabling organizations, communities, and individuals to flourish in today's world. SYA's approach is focused on design that engenders a connection to the broader contemporary culture and the unique communities, identities, and places of their clients. The firm is known for a poetic, open, and light-filled architecture that is carefully crafted, responsive to context, and focused on spaces that encourage social interaction.

SYA's projects include institutional and commercial facilities, for a wide range of clients, including the City of New York, Columbia University, City University of New York, Planned Parenthood of NYC, the United Nations International School, SONY, and residential projects for individuals. Some of the firm's most notable work has contributed to creating more sustainable and healthy communities, including groundbreaking community centers and free public health clinics.

Stephen Yablon Architect has been widely recognized for design excellence demonstrated by the firm's numerous awards, publications, and exhibits, and invited lectures. The firm's Betances Community Center for NYCHA has been awarded six national and local design awards and exhibited extensively including AIANY's *FitNation* in 2013. SYA won the Grand Prize for the international competition for the Boston Harbor Islands National Park Visitors Pavilion and the firm's innovative approach for creating more resilient coastal barrier island communities was selected as one of the winners of MoMA/PS1's *Rockaway Call for Ideas*. Earlier, the office was recognized as an important emerging design firm in *Interior Design* magazine and AIANY's exhibit and publication, *New York Next: Faces of the Future*.

TOP LEFT >> Betances Community Center, Bronx, NY.
BOTTOM LEFT >> Guest Pavilion, Sullivan's Island, South Carolina.
LEFT >> Stephen Yablon.

≫ STEVEN HOLL ARCHITECTS

Steven Holl Architects is a 40-person innovative architecture and urban design office working globally as one office from two locations; New York City and Beijing. Steven Holl leads the office with senior partner Chris McVoy, and junior parner Noah Yaffe. Steven Holl Architects is internationally honored with architecture's most prestigious awards, publications, and exhibitions for excellence in design. Steven Holl Architects has realized architectural works nationally and overseas, with extensive experience in campus and educational facilities, the arts (including museum, gallery, and exhibition design), and residential work. Other projects include retail design, office design, public utilities, and master planning.

With each project, Steven Holl Architects explores new ways to integrate an organizing idea with the programmatic and functional essence of a building. Rather than imposing a style upon different sites and climates, or pursued irrespective of program, the unique character of a program and a site becomes the starting point for an architectural idea. While anchoring each work in its specific site and circumstance, the firm endeavors to obtain a deeper beginning in the experience of time, space, light, and materials. The phenomena of the space of a room, the sunlight entering through a window, and the color and reflection of materials on a wall and floor all have integral relationships. Following this approach, Steven Holl Architects is recognized for the ability to shape space and light with great contextual sensitivity and to utilize the unique qualities of each project to create a concept-driven design. Steven Holl Architects has been recognized with architecture's most prestigious awards and prizes.

Steven Holl is a tenured faculty member at Columbia University where he has taught since 1981, and has received many honors and awards, from the 2012 AIA Gold Medal to being named an Honorary Fellow of the Royal Institute of British Architects.

LEFT ≫ Steven Holl Architects' studio.
ABOVE, LEFT ≫ Steven Holl.
ABOVE, RIGHT ≫ Chris McVoy.

» THOMAS BALSLEY ASSOCIATES

RIGHT » Riverside Park South.

Thomas Balsley Associates is an award-winning design firm providing landscape architecture, site planning, and urban design services throughout the United States and abroad. Over 35 years of experience have produced projects of virtually every size and type ranging from master plans to small urban spaces and from feasibility planning studies to completed institutional, academic, and cultural landscapes, parks, and waterfronts.

The firm's well-earned international reputation is built on a refreshing approach to design and planning in which creativity and innovation are informed by the realities of site and stakeholder input as well as budgets and schedules.

Much of the firm's work entails collaborative relationships with the country's finest architects and designers. The firm's commitment to urban landscape design excellence extends beyond the traditional role of landscape architects as designers or technicians. The result is an impressive portfolio of notable projects. In New York City alone, Thomas Balsley Associates has designed more than 100 public spaces including awarding winning projects such as Capitol Plaza, Riverside Park South, Chelsea Waterside Park, Peggy Rockefeller Plaza and Gantry Plaza State Park. In an unexpected gesture of recognition for Mr. Balsley's contribution to New York City's public realm, a park he designed on 57th Street was renamed Balsley Park.

Every year brings international recognition in the form of awards and citations from professional and civic organizations, including the American Society of Landscape Architects, the American Institute of Architects, Environmental Design Research Association, the Institute for Urban Design and the Waterfront Center. Thomas Balsley Associates' work regularly appears in national and international publications and media. Spacemaker Press devoted a monograph to Thomas Balsley's work, entitled *Thomas Balsley: The Urban Landscape*.

>> THOMAS PHIFER AND PARTNERS

Thomas Phifer approaches modernism from a humanistic standpoint, connecting the built environment to the natural world with a heightened sense of openness and community spirit that is based on a collaborative, interdisciplinary process.

Thomas Phifer's buildings have been repeatedly honored by the American Institute of Architects, including seven AIA National Honor Awards and twelve AIA New York Honor Awards. In 2011, the North Carolina Museum of Art won a National Honor Award from the AIA and, in 2010, the Raymond and Susan Brochstein Pavilion also won a National Honor Award. The international competition-winning design for the City Lights light fixture for New York City won a Research and Development Award from Architect magazine in 2009, and in 2008 the Salt Point House won an American Architecture Award from the Chicago Atheneum. His projects have been published and exhibited extensively in the United States and overseas.

In 2004, Thomas Phifer was awarded the Medal of Honor, the highest award given to an individual or firm, from the New York Chapter of the AIA. In 1995, he received the prestigious Rome Prize from the American Academy in Rome, and, in 2011, he was elected an Academician of the National Academy of Design. In 2013, he received the Arts and Letters Award in Architecture from the American Academy of Arts and Letters. He is a Fellow of the American Institute of Architects and is serving as a Peer for the General Services Administration. He received his Bachelor of Architecture in 1975 and his Master of Architecture in 1977, both from Clemson University.

>> OVI OFFICE

Office for Visual Interaction (OVI) has created some of the world's most inventive lighting design, illuminating prominent architectural works. OVI has pioneered lighting design solutions which are an integrated, natural extension of the architectural design language, and not 'applied'. OVI's lighting design is tailored to complement each project's unique design and optimizes the use of state-of-art technology. Sustainability is an entwined part of our work approach and lighting logic - optimizing design opportunities going beyond energy-efficient luminaires and light sources and providing smart, innovative designs that inherently save energy.

From contemporary classics and historic structures to the most extreme avant-guard works, OVI's designs have been recognized with the most prestigious awards worldwide.

>> URS CORPORATION

URS Corporation is a leading provider of engineering, construction, and technical services for public agencies and private sector companies around the world. The company offers a full range of program management; planning, design, and engineering; systems engineering and technical assistance; construction and construction management; operations and maintenance; and decommissioning and closure services. As a fully integrated organization, URS has the capabilities to support the full project life cycle.

URS is committed to business practices, operations, and projects that improve economic, environmental, and societal outcomes. It has a long and successful history of providing engineering and construction management services to New York City and State agencies and has worked continuously for the New York City Department of Design and Construction since its founding in 1996. Its commitment to the revitalization of the City's streetsscapes and plazas includes design for the 9th Avenue/Gansevoort area in the Meatpacking District, Pershing Square West at Grand Central Terminal, Forsyth Street Plaza in Chinatown, and the Harriet Tubman Memorial in Harlem.

In the New York area, URS provides all of the services required to design, build, expand, and modernize transportation and water resources infrastructure, as well as many types of facilities, such as schools, courthouses, and other public buildings. The firm's expertise in the infrastructure sector encompasses highways, bridges, and tunnels; airports; rail and transit systems; ports and harbors; water supply, storage, and distribution systems; wastewater treatment systems; and security.

W is an interdisciplinary woman-owned studio that builds on links between architecture and landscape architecture to create spaces that engage both nature and urbanism. W is organized around the commitment of principal Barbara Wilks to quality design and active participation in all levels of the firm's projects. With more than 35 years of experience, she believes that effective leadership on complex projects requires vision, a collaborative and talented team, effective communication, and persistent commitment to finding solutions to project goals and aspirations. The staff of 15 is organized in a flexible studio manner and includes experienced project managers, urban designers, landscape architects and LEED-accredited professionals, who engage in each project through its successful completion.

W works closely with the team to achieve consensus on an authentic and delightful design that combines strong conceptual ideas with environmental concerns. Projects are often complex involving multiple constituencies with differing points of view, on challenging sites with sensitive environmental conditions and infrastructure. W's creative outlook on what exists maximizes the value of what is there and turns constraints into opportunities to expand project possibilities. W is committed to thorough collaboration across traditional design boundaries, bringing together a team of specialists tailored to the needs of each project. Those might include artists, lighting designers, ecologists, engineers, and economists. Research into the history of the place and the processes that have shaped it, coupled with analysis of opportunities and constraints enables creative solutions that align finance, policy, sustainability, and design.

W's work seeks to engage its visitors. A synthesis of landscape and architectural design facilitates the transition between regional planning, urban infrastructure, public spaces, individual buildings, and private landscapes. Projects range in scale from private homes to educational campuses to entire urban neighborhoods. W's designs have received top national design awards in landscape architecture and urban and regional design in the 10 years since the firm's founding, and have been published in many books and periodicals around the world.

LEFT, TOP » Fog.
LEFT » Exterior.

>> WORKac

WORKac is a 40-person, New York City-based firm known for architecture and urban planning projects that engage issues of culture and the environment with vision and pragmatism. Since the founding of WORKac in 2003, principals Dan Wood and Amale Andraos have achieved international acclaim for projects that reinvent the relationships between the City and nature, the future of working and living, and between historic structures and new interventions. From initial concepts to construction details, each project is studied and tested to produce project-specific solutions.

Recent projects include the design of a new cultural center on the historic New Holland Island in Saint Petersburg, Russia, an extension for the Blaffer Art Museum at the University of Houston, a branch library for Kew Gardens Hills in Queens, and the first Edible Schoolyard New York City with chef Alice Waters. WORKac was awarded first place in the international competition for the redesign of Hua Qiang Bei Road, Shenzhen's busiest shopping street. The firm was recently a finalist in the competition to design the Washington Monument Grounds and Sylvan Theater in Washington, DC and is currently designing the new Conference Center in Libreville, Gabon that will host the 2014 Summit of the African Union: the building will attain LEED Gold certification.

In 2010, WORKac was the recipient of a New York Public Design Commission of the City of New York award and nominated for the Chernikhov Prize.

LEFT >> Dan Wood (left) and Amale Andraos (right). BELOW >> WORKac's office.

In 2009, WORKac was honored at the White House as a Finalist for a National Design Award and in 2008, the firm was selected for the Architectural League's Emerging Voices series and identified by *Icon Magazine* as one of the 25 most-influential new architecture firms in the world. WORKac is also the recipient of five AIA Merit Awards and a MASterwork Award for best Historic Restoration from the Municipal Arts Society.

>> WXY ARCHITECTURE AND URBAN DESIGN

WXY is an award-winning, studio-based multidisciplinary practice focusing on innovative approaches to public space, structures, and cities. Celebrated for its focus on community and urban design and for their agility with incorporating new technologies and green design, WXY excels in complex urban challenges, education and civic buildings, parks and waterfront developments, and other projects ranging from furniture designs to city master plans.

Claire Weisz is founding principal of the New York-based practice, working alongside partners Mark Yoes, Layng Pew, and Adam Lubinsky. WXY's integrated design process involves clients and stakeholders, to coordinate and solve complex design problems,

yielding solutions as noteworthy for their intimacy and detail as for their civic dignity and amenity.

The broad capabilities of WXY are evinced by a wide variety of planning, consulting, and design challenges, many of which are in the public interest. The firm's work ranges from building and industrial design to large-scale urban waterfront planning and consulting on school assignment policies and renewable energy infrastructure.

The firm's work has been widely published and exhibited, including in the leading major design media and at the German Center for Architecture DAZ in Berlin and the Center for Architecture in New York. Since receiving the Young Architects Award in 1993, the firm has won numerous AIA and ASLA design awards and was featured as a 2006 Design Innovator by Chrysler/House Beautiful. WXY was one of The Architectural League of New York's *New York Designs* awardees in 2006 and again in 2009. Recent honors include the Emerging Voices designation in 2011.

The recently published book, *New York Dozen*, authored by influential architecture writer and academic Michael J. Crosbie, Ph.D., includes WXY as one of "New York's most celebrated living architects, the latest new-generation practitioners." The firm is certified as a women-owned business enterprise.

LEFT, TOP >> Xinjin Bridge.
LEFT >> Far Rockaway Pavilion.

SPONSORS

▸▸ TECTONIC ENGINEERING & SURVEYING CONSULTANTS P.C.

Practical Solutions, Exceptional Service

Founded in 1986, Tectonic Engineering & Surveying Consultants P.C. has emerged as one of the leading, privately-owned, engineering firms in New York offering geotechnical, environmental, structural and civil engineering; surveying; construction management, construction inspection, special inspections, and materials testing services across the chief market sectors of Transportation, Land Planning, Water Resources and Wireless Telecommunications/Energy. Tectonic provides design and construction support services that enable our clients to succeed across a wide range of goals– regardless of size, scope or complexity.

TECTONIC's corporate office in Mountainville, New York is located in the heart of the Hudson Valley region with branch offices in Newburgh and Latham, New York. Regional offices are located in Long Island City, New York; Rocky Hill, Connecticut; Saddle Brook, New Jersey; Richmond, Virginia; Tempe, Arizona; Albuquerque, New Mexico; and Boca Raton, Florida.

TECTONIC is one of the few professional engineering firms maintaining two state-of-the-art materials testing laboratories in Long Island City (NYC) and Newburgh, New York. Our laboratories are accredited by the International Accreditation Service (IAS) as required by the NYC Department of Buildings to perform Special Inspections; and licensed by the NYC Department of Buildings. We are an AASHTO Accredited Laboratory for Quality Systems; Hot Mix Asphalt, Soil; Aggregate; Sprayed Fire-Resistive Material; Portland Cement

Concrete; and Masonry. Tectonic participates in the Cement and Concrete Reference Laboratory (CCRL) proficiency sample and on-site inspection program. Our L.I.C. laboratory is also a member of NVLAP.

TECTONIC is comprised of a growing staff of 483 professionals across disciplines including 60 Professional Engineers and over 200 construction inspectors certified by the National Institute for Certification in Engineering Technologies (NICET) Levels I to IV, the American Concrete Institute (ACI), the International Code Council (ICC) and the American Welding Society (AWS).

The firm has knowledge and experience in the areas of infrastructure, institutional, industrial, commercial and residential construction to ensure that for any given project, the most talented, dedicated, and cost conscious staff will be available.

Throughout the delivery of our services, Tectonic focuses on Value, Technical Feasibility, Constructability, Timeliness, and Safety.

The firm delivers a project that meets and exceeds their Clients' expectations by engaging stakeholders fully from the early planning stages right through to operation and close-out.

TECTONIC commits its resources to provide one point of accountability to reduce risks and project costs and at the same time provide a level of responsiveness that engenders our Clients' confidence and trust in our ability.

⟫ TISHMAN CONSTRUCTION, AN AECOM COMPANY

Tishman Construction, an AECOM company, provides a wide range of construction and construction-related services for projects of varying scope, budget, schedule and complexity. Known for successfully managing iconic projects, Tishman is responsible for the construction of more than 450 million square feet of space, incorporating facilities of every size and type, including arts and culture, commercial, convention centers, education, gaming, government, healthcare, hospitality, residential, retail, sports and leisure, technology and transportation.

More than a century of achievement comes from longstanding relationships with clients and design professionals. We value these relationships and con-

sider them to be a cornerstone of our success. Our goal is to help each of our clients realize their vision by managing the complexity inherent in construction projects and becoming a key part of the project team.

Tishman is currently managing construction for the 1,776-foot-high One World Trade Center, the Public Safety Answering Center (PSAC) II and the Javits Convention Center expansion and renovation in New York; the new headquarters for the U.S. Department of Homeland Security in Washington, D.C.; and the new Anaheim Regional Transportation Intermodal Center for high-speed trains in California. For more information, visit www.tishmanconstruction.com.

≫ WEIDLINGER ASSOCIATES, INC.

Weidlinger Associates is a renowned structural engineering firm specializing in buildings, bridges, infrastructure, applied science, security, and investigations. With a staff of more than 300, the firm has seven U.S. offices and an office in the United Kingdom. Since its establishment in 1949, Weidlinger has received awards for technical excellence, creative design, and scientific achievement on several hundred projects. An American Institute of Architects Honor Award cited Weidlinger for being at the "leading edge of structural design for more than thirty years."

Weidlinger has produced buildings and other structures of every type and size for public agencies, private developers, institutions, corporations, and contractors. The firm has pioneered the economic design of high-rise, long-span, tensegrity, and other special structures, as well as in seismic and blast analysis and protective design—innovation is always coupled with a concern for cost-effectiveness and constructability.

The firm's structural and civil engineers, who specialize in bridges and infrastructure, have designed and rehabilitated numerous bridges, highways, transit and railroad facilities, tunnels, and waterfront structures. They also perform planning and feasibility studies, make emergency and in-depth inspections, develop rehabilitation procedures, and supervise construction. Staff members have contributed to the profession in the form of original design and construction methods for long-span bridges, concrete segmental bridges, cut-and-cover and soft-ground tunnels, urban highways, and cofferdams.

The Applied Science Staff engages in research, development, and testing for U.S. government agencies and private industry. Projects range widely within the fields of applied mechanics, applied mathematics, materials science, and computational methods. The results translate directly into practical design methods and computer software development. Applied Science Staff collaborates with others throughout the firm on the security aspects of all types of projects.

The goals of Weidlinger's hazard mitigation services are to save lives, prevent injury, protect property, and protect the environment. Hazard mitigation projects draw on staff expertise in seismic studies, wind engineering, risk analysis, and applied science. Like security concerns, hazard mitigation is an integral part of a broad range of projects, particularly those in geographic areas subject to extreme natural conditions. Related to hazard mitigation is Weidlinger's investigations practice, which provides seismic evaluation, field investigation and failure analysis, expert testimony and legal support services, risk analysis, and wind engineering services to the design, real estate, investment, legal, and insurance communities.